RED RUBBER

THE STORY OF THE RUBBER SLAVE
TRADE FLOURISHING ON THE
CONGO IN THE YEAR OF GRACE 1906

BY

E. D. MOREL

WITH AN INTRODUCTION BY

SIR HARRY H. JOHNSTON, G. C. M. G., K. C. B.

AND TWO MAPS

NEGRO UNIVERSITIES PRESS
NEW YORK

DT
655
M6.
1969

Originally published in 1906
by The Nassau Print, New York

Reprinted 1969 by
Negro Universities Press
A DIVISION OF GREENWOOD PUBLISHING CORP.
NEW YORK

SBN 8371-1161-7

"The standard of emancipation is now unfurled.
Let all the enemies of the persecuted blacks tremble.
I will be as harsh as truth and as uncompromising as justice.
I am in earnest ;
I will not equivocate ;
I will not excuse ;
I will not retreat a single inch ;
And I will be heard.
Posterity will bear testimony that I was right."

WILLIAM LLOYD GARRISON.

v

INTRODUCTORY CHAPTER

By Sir Harry Johnston

In June, 1905, I took the chair, very unwillingly, at an important meeting held by the Congo Reform Association, which was intended to bring before the British public the need for a drastic reform in the Government of the Congo Free State. My "unwillingness" was due at that time partly to a belief that the King of the Belgians (not having then received the full report of his Committee of Inquiry) was still loath to believe in the results of his commercial policy, and in the effect produced on the natives of the Congo by the methods which his officials adopted to produce a revenue. Also I entered the arena of strife with great reluctance because I realised that our own past Colonial history and that of other European nations in Africa was very far from being stainless, and, on the other hand, I had known Belgians on the Congo (and had seen them at work) whose efforts to introduce stable and civilised government were altogether praiseworthy. I was unwilling to join in any movement which might be directed against Belgium or Belgian enterprise, and only accepted the disagreeable position of Chairman at this meeting because I was perhaps the only survivor of the band of Congo explorers who, between 1879 and 1884 had visited the interior Congo regions, and had seen them when they were utterly un-influenced by the white man, and before and after they had been threatened with Arab domination. My attitude at the meeting in question was that of one desiring to find a way out of a difficult position for a Sovereign whose name was

vii

Introductory

still associated in my memory with some of the best intentions ever expressed on paper regarding Africa.

Not long afterwards, the report of the King-Sovereign's Commission was issued. Whether the report was published exactly as sent in by the Commissioners is open to question. But taking it in the form in which it received the *imprimatur* of King Leopold himself, it was a sufficient justification of the accusations levelled at the Congo Free State by Mr. Morel, by various British missionaries and travellers, and by Swedes, Frenchmen, and Italians. But in one's desire to judge as charitably as possible a man who might have been misled, one saw that a logical corollary to the publication of this report would be an attempt made by King Leopold to sweep away a system which has been one of the most shocking—one of the few shocking—results of white intervention in Negro Africa. A year has passed since the publication of this report, and creditable testimony tends rather to show that the evils complained of in Congo territories have been intensified, while the direct utterances of the King of the Belgians on the subject of his work on the Congo are deplorable in their sardonic indifference to the real condition of the natives of the great African dominion which Europe entrusted to his charge.

So far as I am aware, if Mr. Morel had consulted his own interests he would never have undertaken, and he certainly would not have maintained, his long crusade against the work of the Congo Free State. Neither was it to the interest of the English Baptist missionaries to put before the world the damning evidence they have supplied on the evils of Congo Free State government. In the early stages of their mission (I can speak as an eye-witness), they afforded the infant Congo State the most whole-hearted support. When I first visited the western regions of the Congo it was in the days of dawning Imperialism, when most young Britishers abroad could conceive of no better fate for an undeveloped country than to come under the British flag. The outcome of Stanley's work seemed to *me* clear ; it should be eventually the Britannicising of much of the Congo Basin, perhaps in friendly agreement and partition of interests with France and Portugal. But Stanley himself was working really

Introductory

towards the creation of a larger Liberia, and the Secretary of his Committee, the Belgian Colonel Strauch, like his compatriot, Colonel Wauvermans, was eagerly in favour of this " international " solution of the question.   With them again sided the Baptist missionaries Comber, Grenfell, and Bentley, who anticipated troubles and bloodshed arising from any attempt on the part of Great Britain to subdue the vast and unknown regions of the Congo, not even then clearly threatened by Arabs.   They indeed resented the coming of the French or of the Portuguese.   A larger Liberia, devised on more practical lines, was the ideal which they believed the King of the Belgians was pursuing as a pure philanthropist.   It was known that the King, by shrewd investments in the Suez Canal shares and in other directions, had made—by most respectable methods—a considerable fortune. He had also spoken publicly of devoting the money that had belonged to his dead son to some noble purpose in the world.   He had, in fact, attempted the regeneration of Negro Africa by a kind of International Board before Stanley's discovery of the Congo.   One of his agents— Captain Storms—had reached Tanganyika, and had effected wonders in arming the natives against the Arab slave-traders. The work of Storms had been most generously appreciated by the missionaries of the London Missionary Society on Tanganyika, and news of it had just reached their colleagues of different denominations who were at work on the Congo. In short, every one who was any one in the missionary world, or in that section of London society devoted to philanthropic ideals (such as the Baroness Burdett-Coutts, the present Earl Grey, Cardinal Manning, Sir Harry Verney, Sir William Mackinnon) decried any attempt on the part of Great Britain to import base commercial ambitions into the political settlement of Equatorial Africa, and hailed King Leopold as the man who would gradually raise the millions of Central African Negroes to a condition of peaceable self-government, free, on the one hand, from the curse of the Arab, and, on the other, from the alcoholising European.

These men of the Baptist Missions of America and Great Britain so frequently ranged themselves on the side of the Congo Free State in its early days that it must have cost

Introductory

them much to testify in later times against that form of government.

I wished on the occasion of the public meeting already referred to, and I wish again in these few introductory words, to testify to the good work which has been done by Belgians in the Congo Free State, and to dissociate the country of Belgium from the odium with which her Monarch is now regarded by educated people in Europe, Africa, and America. The names of *Nilis, Vangèle, Orban, Coquilhat, Hanssens, Meura, Storms* (and many others with whom I was not personally acquainted) should be recorded as those of men who attempted to do great things for the Congo people, and on whose records there has been no stain. If there have been bad Belgians on the Congo, there have been bad Englishmen, ruthless Frenchmen, pitiless Swedes, cruel Danes, unscrupulous Italians. Belgium has only to bear the brunt of the movement which is now threatening the existence of the Congo Free State, in its present form, because the Sovereign of that mis-governed State is also King of the Belgians. Many of us have felt, and still feel, that when the King's autocratic rule as Sovereign over this African dominion had been proved to be such an appalling blot on the history of European intervention in Africa as to be no longer tolerated, that the individual sacrifices made by Belgium and by the Belgian people should be recognised by the handing over of the Congo Free State to Belgium as a Belgian Protectorate, a region which Belgium might endeavour to administer as England, Germany, and Portugal administer Eastern Africa ; and France, England, and Portugal deal with Western Africa. The creation of a huge independent African State in the basin of the Congo is felt to be an impossibility in the *present* state of Negro development in those regions. To divide this vast country between the colonial dominions of the limitrophe Powers might be productive of jealousy and other embarrassments. Belgium, we thought, fully deserved a share of the undeveloped surface of the earth as an outlet for her energies : "let her then" (said many) "take over the Congo and govern it as a Constitutional Monarchy does govern a foreign dominion."

Introductory

But it would seem as though Belgium were unable to take up the burden, either because her public men and institutions are too much under the control of the present Sovereign, or because she is not rich enough in men or money to undertake such a mighty task. If this is the case, then there would seem to be no escape from the present deadlock : an International Conference should once more be summoned to meet at Berlin, the Hague, or Paris, and the Congo State must be remodelled by its original creators.

Whatever its fate may be, let us hope that it will not be an International enterprise ! There is as yet no International Conscience, though such a thing is beginning to come into existence. The state of what is now the Anglo-Egyptian Sudan under the nominal rule of the Khedives between 1850 and 1882 was somewhat analogous to the present condition of the Congo Free State. Though the Khedive was titular lord, the agents he employed to conquer and administer the basin of the Nile were of many nationalities, and their doings did not appeal singly to the conscience of any one state. Some of Gordon's most trusted lieutenants relate in their reports of military action against the Arab slave-traders and their native following, or against the independent native sultans of the Bahr-al-Ghazal, how their cannibal levies (from regions which have subsequently furnished troops to the King of the Belgians) found their commissariat in the bodies of the slain. Many of the Congo horrors were anticipated under the rule of British, Italian, American, French, German, Greek, and Turkish officials in the pay of the Egyptian Khedive.

In like manner there has been no national conscience to appeal to, other perhaps than that of Belgium (indirectly concerned), in the government of the Congo Free State. Crimes and mistakes have been committed by the French in their adjoining territories. Some episodes in the early history of the Uganda Protectorate, in the creation of Rhodesia, in Sierra Leone, in Ashanti, have been written up in the world's ledger against Great Britain. Germany has had to reveal, face, and erase many a scandal in the Cameroons, in South-West and in East Africa. Portugal

Introductory

is now confronted with serious charges against her administration of Inner Angola. But in all these instances there is
the conscience of a nation to appeal to; the country at
fault is one governed by constitutional methods, and the
voice of the people when once they are acquainted with the
wrongdoing attributable to their fellow-countrymen insists
on amendment. But in the case of the Congo Free State,
there is only one conscience to appeal to, that of King
Leopold, a conscience which seems indurated against
evidence, against shame, against the terror of an immortality
of bad renown.

I am still anxious that this question should be treated
without hysterics. Let me say, therefore, for the consolation of any who may be wringing their hands over the
present condition of the Congo Free State, that the Congo
Basin was not a region of ideal happiness and peace for the
Negro before the white man or the Arab broke in upon the
life of the Stone Age, burst upon primitive peoples who had
lost all contact with the Caucasian for two thousand years.

Before 1879 the Congo Basin west of the longitude of
Stanley Pool was a region fairly well populated by Negroes
in a very low state of civilisation. Some, like the Pygmies,
had not left the hunter stage. Others were agriculturists
and fishermen, keeping few domestic animals, and cultivating but few plants. They were not so much subject as
at the present day to the ravages of epidemics like smallpox
and sleeping sickness, because each cluster of villages, each
small tribe of a few thousand people, was usually at war
with the rest of the world, and communications between
one congeries of settlements and another were uncertain
and interrupted. It was, in fact, a region of isolated tribes
and communities, almost the whole of which, except in the
south, were confirmed cannibals. In the northern half of
the Congo Free State incessant wars and slave raids took
place, not with a view to supplying labour, but with the
intention of obtaining wives, and, above all, victims for the
cannibal feasts.

In the southern half of the Congo Basin the slave-trade
was in full swing, had been for one or two centuries,
prompted chiefly by the British, Portuguese, and

Introductory

Americans. Portuguese half-castes ranged right across the Congo Basin from Angola to Tanganyika, and to the borders of what is now Rhodesia. Through their supplies of guns and powder one tribe conquered another, and empires were built up containing a degree of civilisation approaching that of modern Uganda. Cannibalism may have been wiped out by this rise in civilisation, but a slave-trade for the supply of labour in distant countries took its place as an incentive to constant wars. An advance in religious ideas accentuated cruelties connected with fetish practices and a belief in sorcery. Then, of course, many of the people lost their lives from the attacks of lions, leopards, elephants, hippopotamuses, and crocodiles.

No ; the condition of man in the Congo Basin was very far from a state of happiness before the Arab penetrated these regions from the East Coast and the European from the West. The Arabs did much to suppress cannibalism and to introduce a far higher standard of comfort, and many important articles of food. But they carried the ravages of the slave-trade further and further, depopulating a district before they settled it anew with their domestic slaves.

The King of the Belgians stood forward as the champion of what was best in European civilisation, and all that was to regenerate this vast region of potential wealth : too thickly inhabited by a vigorous race to be regarded as a No Man's Land, and yet devoid of any indigenous government which could establish law and order. It is no excuse for the evil doings of the Congo Free State that the Congo Basin was a land of much misery before King Leopold took it in hand.

Neither is it any palliative to point to the mistakes which the principal countries of Europe have made in their attempt to better the African's condition on his own continent. Most of the countries of Western and Central Europe embarked on African enterprises with no protestations of high philanthropy. They wanted an outlet for their manufactures, a colony for their superfluous population, or a field for national aggrandisement. I do not hesitate to say that the *general* results of their work, even

Introductory

if it was undertaken from no high motive, have, on the whole, produced regions of greater happiness, denser population, and a higher standard of human life than could be ascribed to those portions of Africa prior to European control.

But the genesis of the Congo Free State was vastly different from the general standpoint of the European partition of Africa. To judge of this one has only to read the speeches and letters of the King of the Belgians himself between the years 1875 and 1894. Over and over again he declared that his one object in entering on this African enterprise was *disinterested*. At the outside he only desired to get back his out-of-pocket expenses. If ever there was a portion of Africa in which a ruler's private profits from State monopolies were precluded by an honourable adhesion to first principles, it was the Congo Free State.

A few words as to the logic of my own position as a critic of King Leopold's rule on the Congo. I have been reminded in some of the publications issued by the Congo Government that I have instituted a Hut Tax in regions entrusted to my administration ; that I have created Crown Lands which have become the property of the Government ; that as an agent of that Government I have sold and leased portions of African soil to European traders ; that I have favoured, or at any rate have not condemned the assumption by an African State of control over natural sources of wealth ; that I have advocated measures which have installed the European as the master—for the time being— over the uncivilised Negro or the semi-civilised Somali, Arab, or Berber.

All these charges may be true without the admission constituting any sort of apology for the results of twenty-one years of King Leopold's government in the Congo Free State. As regards the Negro or any other backward race, I am not a sentimentalist. I have no pity in retrospect for the sufferings of the Celtic and Iberian inhabitants of Great Britain during their conquest by the Romans, I do not regret the Norman remodelling of England. These movements have done much to make the United Kingdom one of the foremost amongst the civilised free nations. The greater part of Africa has got to submit to a similar discipline. There are many tribes of Negroes at the present day who are leading lives not much superior in intellectual advancement to those of brutes ; *but there is not an existing race of men in Africa that is not emphatically human and capable of improvement.* Yet I do not think that they are to be improved by European tutors without *some* effort on their own part. They should contribute reasonably, and with due regard to the happiness of their own lives, to the public resources of their country. Taxation which is not oppressive must be imposed. If the adult native cannot pay his contribution in money he can furnish it in labour. But the assessment of his contribution to the income of his own country must be strictly proportionate to his means ; in other words, to that share of happiness and enjoyment of life to which he is entitled like any other human being. The Crown Lands, the control of which is assumed by the British Government, or by the Government of any civilised state in Africa, are—or should be—administered first and foremost in the interest of the community in which they are situated. For example, revenue derived from the Crown Lands in British Central Africa or in Uganda goes to meet the cost of the administration of those countries and the maintenance of law and order therein, of the construction of public works, the prevention of disease, the improvement of communications, the advancement of education. The utmost gain to *us* that is derived from this administration of state monopolies is the easing of the pocket of the British taxpayer. Even if (which is not the case) the administration of these public lands gradually re-paid to the British taxpayer the moneys he has invested in founding these new Protectorates, I should not think the principle an unjust one ; since a good deal of the work done by England, France, Italy, Portugal, and Germany in Africa has been purely philanthropic. Money and valuable lives have been spent in putting down devastating wars amongst the natives or in repelling cruel invaders like the Arabs or the Tawareq, Abyssinians, or Fulas. A fairly safe and happy existence has been

Introductory

guaranteed to the natives of the soil, and it is only fair that by degrees the resources of these countries should provide the means for the upkeep of a civilised government which more and more is tending to become the native government of those countries. Where the land is absolutely waste land, without indigenous human inhabitants, I have counted it no sin that such a wilderness should be allotted to foreign settlers of our own or of any other race seeking a home beyond the seas. But I do count it a sin to oust one race to put another in its place, unless and until any such race has shown itself the foe of humanity in general.

But the Crown Lands, the public forests, the natural resources of the Congo Free State instead of being administered as a national fund for the maintenance and improvement of that State, and the promotion of the welfare of its inhabitants, are actually diverted to the private profit of King Leopold and some of his associates. *It is this that is the inherently false principle in the scheme of the Congo Free State.* The public revenues collected from these regions are not publicly accounted for.

The danger in this state of affairs lies in the ferment of hatred which is being created against the white race in general by the agents of the King of the Belgians in the minds of the Congo Negroes. The Negro has a remarkably keen sense of justice. He recognises in British Central Africa, in East Africa, in Nigeria, in South Africa, in Togoland, Dahome, the Gold Coast, Sierra Leone, and Senegambia, that, on the whole, though the White Men ruling in those regions have made some mistakes and committed some crimes, have been guilty of some injustice, yet that the state of affairs they have brought into existence as regards the Black Man is one infinitely superior to that which proceeded the arrival of the White Man as a temporary ruler. Therefore, though there may be a rising here or a partial tumult there the mass of the people increase and multiply with content, and acquiesce in our tutelary position. Were it otherwise, any attempt at combination on their part would soon overwhelm us and extinguish our rule. Why, in the majority of cases, the

Introductory

very soldiers with whom we keep them in subjection are of
their own race. But unless some stop can be put to the
misgovernment of the Congo regions I venture to warn
those who are interested in African politics that a movement is already begun and is spreading fast, which will
unite the Negroes against the White race, a movement
which will prematurely stamp out the beginnings of the
new civilisation we are trying to implant, and against which
movement except so far as the actual coast-line is concerned
the resources of men and money which Europe can put into
the field will be powerless.

H. H. JOHNSTON.

PREFACE TO SECOND EDITION

In concluding the Preface to the first edition of this volume I asked, " Will the British Public, which in the ultimate resort has compelled exposure of a crime unparalleled in the annals of the world, compel the cessation of that crime ? "

Nothing which has taken place since is of a nature to induce me to alter that question, which dominates the situation. The Belgian Parliamentary debate is not over as I write these lines, and it may possibly reserve some surprises for us. But I doubt it. The Cabinet—that is the King—will triumph probably, even though the majority may be very small. And what is the policy of the King ? It was laid down by M. de Smet de Naeyer on the opening day of the discussion. The Belgian Government may begin the discussion during the present session, of the Annexation Bill which M. de Smet de Naeyer deposited in the Government pigeon holes in 1901 ! The Government will take into consideration the question of discussing details as to transfer with the Congo State ; but it will only do so when it thinks the time has come for that preliminary negotiation ! Precisely. We are where we were before —if the Debate closes on those lines ; with this exception, that British diplomacy will have received yet another rebuff at the hands of the Sovereign of the Congo State, who has declared (*vide* p. 171) that in regard to annexation he has " nothing to say at present."

The Debate threatens to close with an unending vista of procrastination, and, meanwhile, as the *Times*—which has been doing a real service to the cause of the helpless Congo natives by the very full reports of its Continental correspondents, and by its able leaders—says, the " part of regular mystification played upon the Belgian people and upon Europe " continues.

After a careful perusal of the many reviews which have appeared on this book, I see no reason to modify one line of what it contains—notably in regard to the last chapter in which I sketch out the action which Great Britain is able to adopt.

One or two papers appear in doubt as to the practical value of establishing Consular Courts. The alarm expressed at the suggestion by the henchmen in Parliament and in the Press of the Sovereign of the Congo State, should induce them to alter their views. Above all things this is what the Sovereign of the Congo State dreads and fears. " Caveant consules " ! It is the one decisive step— synonymous with a firm declaration of policy of the kind below mentioned—which will break the back of the atrocious system he has introduced on the Congo. And he knows it well.

Far from being a mere " irritant " as it has been somewhere said, consular jurisdiction would be the first plank in the constructive policy of the future which is absolutely required by the circumstances of the case. As I have said in this volume, other signatory Powers to the Act of the West African Conference of Berlin possess the same right, and were we to accompany our exercises of it with the clear intimation that we should rejoice if other Powers did

Preface to Second Edition

likewise, what could other Powers say by way of protest ? The Treaty, moreover, which confers upon us this right is a Treaty of our own with King Leopold : no other Power is concerned in it.

For the rest I can only repeat here what I have stated in this book. Until some Power (or Powers) insists upon the integral application in the Congo of the fundamental principles of the Berlin Conference, principles *which obtain everywhere* in the African tropics except, by a strange irony, in that vast portion of them to which the Act applies, the horrors of the Congo will continue on an ever-increasing scale, whether under the Congo, or under the Belgian flag. The Congo native, like the native of every part of the African tropics, must be protected in his rights in land, property, and labour. All those rights have been swept away from him by the most colossal act of spoliation ever imagined by mortal man. *The right of trading freely in the produce of his soil, and in the fruits of his labour must be restored to him.* What is trade ? Surely it is the most elementary function of humanity ? We are all traders in one form or another. It is the right to dispose of one's labour. It is the recognition of the possession of property. It is the essential basis of economics. It is the common link which unites all the branches of the human family. To remove from a primitive community the right to trade is to strangle for ever the economic development of that community, to reduce it to perpetual sterility, or to enslave it.

But King Leopold has done this. He has done so juridically, by claiming that a "State" (which he calls his enterprise) is empowered to appropriate the entire *merchantable products* of the land in which the citizens of that "State" dwell ; and, in practice, by appropriating the entire *labour* of the country, for the juridical claim is worthless without its practical accompaniment. In this manner

Preface to Second Edition

he has destroyed the normal or commercial relationship between the European and the negro throughout the Congo valley ; he has reduced juridically, the millions of natives inhabiting it from possessors of merchantable products, and from ownership over their own labour, to tenants upon *his* property ; he has reduced them, in practice, wherever he has been able to enforce his claim, to things—mere things ; chattels of his own ; articles of potential value for himself, his partners, and his heirs. And in so doing he has enslaved the whole population, for what motive power remains with which to acquire the products of the Congo except compulsion, since the commercial relationship has been eliminated with the claim to prior possession over those products ? And how can compulsion be exercised in the African tropics, save by arming one black man and stationing him with a loaded rifle in his hand over his unarmed brother ? Of this conception one of the most experienced of West African legislators and administrators has said, and said truly, that it "requires a soldier behind every producer."

I repeat again and yet again that until the Congo native is reinstalled in the right enjoyed by all black men under European over-lordship in Tropical Africa outside the Congo Basin, to buy and sell with the European, which necessitates the restoration of his rights of land tenure, and the disposal of his labour, there will be no change in his lot.

Surely, if this great truth is burned into the brains and hearts of our countrymen, we can afford to disregard the taunt of working for material ends, and the taunt of interested motives launched at us by the subsidised organs of the Leopoldian Press Bureau ?

"British interests" in this connection mean nothing more than the right provided under the Berlin Conference for the subjects of Britain, as for the subjects of the fourteen contracting Powers—neither more nor less—of commercial

xxii

intercourse with the natives of the Congo. If that commercial intercourse is re-established between the natives and Europeans of every nationality, Americans and Asiatics—and, if you like, South Sea Islanders—the inhabitant of the Congo ceases to be a slave in his own home, and becomes once more a man with a man's rights ; because, with its re-establishment, the inhabitant of the Congo enters once more into his own, is once more owner of his land, of its produce (which he alone can gather), and of his labour.

What the British Government will do I do not know. As to what ought to be done, I have no doubt whatever. The Government should proclaim before all the world its unshakable determination to repudiate absolutely and entirely these claims to the land, the produce of the soil, and the labour of the Congo native set up by King Leopold. It should decline before the world to even discuss any pretensions founded upon such impossible and utterly immoral claims. It should declare them to be a negation of the most vulgar conceptions of civilised and uncivilised usage ; opposed to all the legitimate interests of commercial nations ; and a violation of the Berlin Act. It should declare its unalterable determination not to recognise these claims, in practice, when the legitimate interests of British subjects white or black in the Congo, or in the territories adjacent to it, are affected by them. And, coupled with these declarations, it should provide, in the shape of an increased Consular staff, furnished with powers of jurisdiction and with independent means of conveyance, the machinery whereby its declarations can, in practice, be rendered effective.

In so doing, it would have a united nation at its back.

And what is the Power which could or would oppose us in this matter ? There is not one which could do so without repudiating the signatures of its own representatives to the Act of Berlin! There is not one which could advance the shadow of a moral right, or a material interest, against such a policy. The legitimate material interests of all the commercial and industrial communities in the world would be served by such action on our part—including that of Belgium. The fear of foreign complications is a bogey, which would only become a substance if England developed territorial ambitions, and it may be safely said that not one solitary human being in this country entertains such an idea.

At the conclusion of Sir Harry Johnston's introductory note to this volume, that eminent authority has given a clear and definite warning to the governing statesmen of the world as to the consequences which will ensue if the present system remains in force on the Congo. It may be specially recommended to those among us who are inclined to falter and hang back at the slightest signs of international friction accompanying positive action on the part of England; those of us who are essentially men of peace—and all honour to such. I venture to remind those men that the continuance of the present system is synonymous with the carrying of desolating war throughout the Congo Basin.

In conclusion, I would also venture to utter a note of warning. At the present moment this huge evil is comparatively easy to deal with. The longer action is delayed the greater the perils of eventual interference. And interference *must* come. It is utterly impossible that matters can remain as they are. By bold, courageous, straightforward action now the evil can be cauterised. If action is long delayed what is to-day an African question may to-morrow become a European question as well.

Let our governing statesmen be well assured of this. There is in the atmosphere of England at this moment a

Preface to Second Edition

singular determination to liberate, with God's help, the natives of the Congo from their unspeakable bondage, and to save Europe the shame of tolerating, by consent, the revival, under worse forms, of the African Slave Trade. It is a force to reckon with. It is a force which finds expression in these words of the Bishop of Southwark, words noble and true :—

"On the attitude and action of this country in reference to the Congo will depend in a great degree England's own moral future."

The statesman who comprehended this feeling of determination, based not upon unreasoning sentimentalism, but upon a sober realisation of responsibilities historically incurred, upon the clearest common sense and the soundest political wisdom, would create for himself in the annals of this country, an immortality—to paraphrase Sir Harry Johnston —of good renown.

Next March marks the centenary of the passage through both Houses of Parliament of the Total Abolition of Slavery Bill. The statesman who introduced that Bill into the House of Commons was Lord Howick, first Earl Grey, and Sir Edward Grey is that nobleman's collateral descendant.

E. D. MOREL.

HAWARDEN, *December* 1, 1906.

PS.—*Dec.* 8. As the Belgian Debate proceeds, we observe a perpetual insistence upon the King's "sovereign rights" over the Congo. The nature of those "sovereign rights" is strictly defined and limited by International Treaties. The interpretations he has since placed upon them are the very negation of those definitions and limitations. (See p. 167.)

AUTHOR'S PREFACE

—◦◇◦—

THIS book is written with the object of putting into the hands of the British public, at a cost which places it within the reach of many, a brief and up-to-date narrative of the Congo tragedy, avoiding side issues, and dealing with the main features of the story.

Much of it will be new to all save those who have followed the Congo question as students, and even as regards the latter it is hoped that the cumulative force of recent revelations here presented in their natural sequence may lead to an even clearer perception of the problem.

A crisis in this history has arrived.

The Report of the Commission of Inquiry, wrung from King Leopold by the pressure of British public opinion, Professor Cattier's volume, and the five days' debate on these two publications which took place last February in the Belgian House of Representatives,[1] have removed the last doubts which remained as to the accuracy of the charges publicly brought against the personal, uncontrolled, and unfettered management of the Congo territories by King Leopold.

Contention as to facts has disappeared. The controversial stage has, in that respect, gone for ever.

The truth, in all its international dangers, its greed, its

---

[1] Translated by E. D. Morel. Published by the Congo Reform Association, price 1s.

disordered ambitions, above everything in its horror, stands out naked.

Will the British Public, which in the ultimate resort has compelled exposure of a crime unparalleled in the annal of the world, compel the cessation of that crime?

It has the driving force to do so if it will.

E. D. MOREL.

Hawarden, *October*, 1906.

CONTENTS

MAPS

———◆———

xxxi

ISEKANSU

Mutilated by Sentries for Shortage in Rubber

MAP
Showing Revenue Divisions
Of The
"Congo Free State"

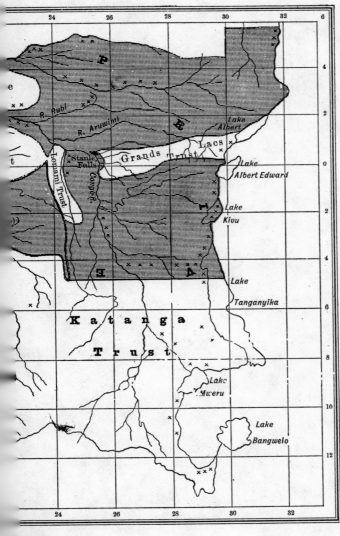

d not accounted for in any way whatsoever.

om he controls. This is the so-called "Concessionnaire" area.

eived.

THE HISTORY

I

FROM BEHIND THE VEIL

Arcana imperii

"How came England to be mixed up in this Congo business?"

"How did King Leopold come to hold the position he now does?"

"How is it that all this oppression and atrocity has only begun to be realised within a comparatively recent period by the general public?"

Those are three questions which are constantly being asked us. Detailed answers to the first two are to be found in one or two publications. They will be re-stated here. The answer to the third question is a more difficult and a somewhat delicate one to handle, but as a great deal of misconception exists on the subject, misconception which has done harm to the cause of the Congo natives here at home, and especially abroad, it seems advisable to deal with it frankly and at once, not from the standpoint of the critic, but from that of the recorder of facts.

People who suppose that the atrocities of King Leopold's African enterprise are a relatively new phase in the history of that enterprise are mistaken; but the mistake is natural. Those atrocities have been recorded in one unbroken stream since 1892, and even earlier, but they have not, in the main, been publicly accessible until recently. Slowly have they emerged into the light, some are still coming out, others continue to be hidden. Nothing even approximating to the whole truth *will ever be known.* The reasons for this are various.

Parliamentary apathy, comprehensible from the absence of informatiou.—Sir Charles Dilke, who, as every one knows, takes a deep interest in the welfare of the African races, brought the general treatment of those races, and especially the Congo races, before Parliament in April, 1897.[1] He suggested an International Conference, and was supported by Mr. Sydney Buxton, Sir George Baden-Powell, and Mr. John Dillon. From then to the great debate in May, 1903—a space of six years—I cannot find that the Congo was mentioned in Parliament, otherwise than by some chance and rare question and answer.

The attitude of the British Government.—In that interval the British Government received a number of reports from British officials and officers in, or adjacent to, the Congo, both as regards the general treatment of the natives of the country, and as regards the treatment of British coloured subjects employed in different capacities on the Congo. So numerous were the latter reports that a year previous to Sir Charles Dilke's early initiative, Mr. Chamberlain, replying to Mr. J. A. Pease, stated in the House that he had prohibited the recruiting of labourers by King Leopold's agents in the British West African Colonies. The nature of the reports may be gauged from Mr. Chamberlain's own words : " Complaints have been received of these British subjects having been employed without their consent as soldiers, and of their having been cruelly flogged and in some cases shot." I have been told, and I believe the statement is true, that Mr. Chamberlain, as a consequence of the frequency and nature of these reports, did his utmost to induce the Cabinet, but without success, to assume the rights of extra-territoriality on the Congo secured to Great Britain under the Convention with King Leopold of 1884. In its Note to the Powers of August 8, 1903—arising out of the resolution passed by Parliament in the May debate—the Government referred

---

[1] He played a prominent part in the later debates of 1903, 1904, 1905, and 1906, and has a complete mastery of the subject.

to both classes of reports. The Note says : "Moreover information which has reached His Majesty's Government from British officers in territory adjacent to that of the State tends to show that, notwithstanding the obligations accepted under Article II. of the Berlin Act, no attempt at any administration of the natives is made, and that officers of the Government do not apparently concern themselves with such work, but devote all their energy to the collection of revenue. The natives are left entirely to themselves, so far as any assistance in their government[1] or in their affairs are concerned. The Congo stations are shunned, the only natives seen being soldiers, prisoners, and men who are brought in to work. The neighbourhood of stations which are known to have been populous a few years ago is now uninhabited, and emigration on a large scale takes place to the territory of neighbouring states, the natives usually averring that they are driven away from their homes by the tyranny and exaction of the soldiers." In connection with British coloured subjects the Note, after referring to the " disadvantage " under which " His Majesty's Government have further laboured," owing to the fact that " British interests have not justified the main-tenance of a large Consular Staff in the Congo territories," goes on to state that a Consul " of wide African experience " (Mr. Casement) was appointed to " reside permanently in the State," but that " his time had been principally occupied in the investigation of complaints preferred by British sub-jects," and that he had not been able, therefore, to travel in the interior for the purpose of studying the general con-dition of the natives of the country. Mr. Casement's advices, the Note proceeds, disclosed, in connection with these complaints, " examples of grave maladministration and ill-treatment," occurring " in the immediate vicinity of Boma, the seat of the Central Staff."

The whole of these official reports were suppressed lock, stock, and barrel, and they have never been made public, although Mr. Alfred Emmott pressed for their production

[1] That is to say, assistance in their own internal administration. —*Vide* Section iv., pt. iii.

in the Parliamentary debate of 1904.[1] The British Government contented itself with making private representations to King Leopold through H.M. Minister in Brussels, the farcical "Commission for the protection of the natives," and sundry bogus "judicial reforms" coupled with an intensified period of oppression, being the sole results.

The Silence of the Missionary Societies.—As will be shown in Section II of this volume, there had been accumulating in the decade 1892–1902 in some of the Protestant mission stations of the Upper Congo, records of a comprehensive and appalling character. Enough information was available to have stormed every religious platform in this country. The Home Executives of the Missionary Societies took no public action, however, and for many years one Congo missionary, and one only, dared to confront, with the righteous indignation of a spirit stung to passionate anger by the fearful evidence of his own eyes, King Leopold's agents in Africa, and King Leopold himself in Europe. He was a Swede. His name was Sjoblöm, and he stands out an apostolic figure of those earlier days. His pendant of later times in energy and determination is John Harris (and Mrs. Harris), of whose courage in Africa and self-sacrifice in Europe it would be impossible to speak too highly. Two other missionaries followed in his footsteps, a Virginian and an Irish-American. With those three exceptions no missionary appears to have given expression to his experiences in a form available to the general public, until October, 1903, when Mr. J. H. Weeks, with whom I had come in touch through a mutual friend, sent me the first of his powerful communications. A number complained locally to the officials, and did, and have always done, all they could do for the natives. The Home Executives, or some of them, made private representations to King Leopold. So far as the Roman Catholic missions are concerned, neither the Home Executives nor the missionaries on the field made any public statement until this year, after

---

[1] I should say here that Mr. Alfred Emmott and Mr. Herbert Samuel have rendered the greatest services to the cause of the Congo natives. Humanity owes them a debt of gratitude.

the publication of the Report of the Commission of Inquiry. We know now that some of the Roman Catholic missionaries, like some of their Protestant brethren, complained locally to the officials. The Home Executives may have made representations to the king.[1] From the end of 1903 when the testimony of British and American missionaries became continuous, detailed, and insistent, the organs of the Roman Catholic Missions—and the Roman Catholic religious press, generally—attacked the former with great bitterness. This attitude was dictated by the Vatican direct, doubtless under the influence of King Leopold's assurances that the British movement disguised an attack upon the Roman Catholic Church, a legend which the king's agents were particularly active in propagating throughout the Roman Catholic world in the United States.[2] This attitude was maintained until the appearance of the Report of the Commission, when it underwent a complete change, at least as regards the Belgian religious orders and organs. I have said that this is not a criticism but a statement of fact, and I pass no opinion on the silence thus observed either in defence or stricture, contenting my-

---

[1] That great pressure was brought to bear upon the Roman Catholic Missionaries to keep silence is not, I think, doubtful. Speaking in the Belgian House in March last, M. Colfs, a Catholic Member of Parliament, said : " Our missionaries are expected to keep silence. As the *Bien Public* has so well put it optimistic statements are alone tolerated from them. There is, therefore, a gag. The gag is only placed in the mouths of Belgian missionaries, and it was to ensure this result that the Congo State urged the Vatican to agree that Catholic evangelisation on the Congo should be confined exclusively to Belgium." This utterance is the more notable since M. Colfs was the spokesman in the debate of the religious missions.

[2] When in the fall of 1904 I visited the United States with the dual mission of addressing the International Peace Conference at Boston on the Congo question, and presenting a Memorial to President Roosevelt signed by a number of public bodies and influential public men (which mission I carried out) I found myself—greatly to my astonishment—opposed by Cardinal Gibbons, head of the Roman Catholic Church in that country. The open correspondence which passed between his Eminence and myself is published in the official organ of the Congo Reform Association for November, 1904.

self with the remark that—as in the case of the British Government [1]—it delayed by many years the manifestation of the truth.

King Leopold's Active Opponents.—Until the Parliamentary debate of May, 1903, found all political parties so impressed with unofficial testimony and exposition, as to be united in demanding from the British Government a definite invitation to the powers for the convocation of an International Conference, the *active* opponents of the existing *régime* on the Congo were to all intents and purposes the Aborigines Protection Society and myself. Who says Aborigines Protection Society says Mr. H. R. Fox Bourne. So that there were only two men really to reckon with. When Mr. Fox Bourne, under the auspices of his Society, organised a public meeting—as at the Mansion House in 1902, and to hear the American missionary, Morrison, in 1903—he could always count upon Sir Charles Dilke (whose pen was not inactive in the cause) and other distinguished members of the Society. But the persistent hammering at the public, without which no movement can hope to make headway, and indispensable individual proselytising—this was left almost entirely to Mr. Fox Bourne and myself; Mr. Fox Bourne a long way ahead in point of time, for I only came on the scene in 1899 or 1900, while he, tired of making representations to King Leopold, had approached the British Government in the name of his Society as far back as 1896. Mutually convinced of one another's integrity of purpose, but working on wholly independent and slightly different lines,[2] we were terribly handicapped. The name of

---

[1] The Italian Government also possesses an enormous number of reports from its officers in the Congo army, but they are of more recent date. The German, French, Danish, and Swedish Governments also possess reports.

[2] Mr. Fox Bourne emphasising more particularly perhaps the atrocious nature of the deeds committed, while my endeavour from the first was to show that given certain premises—the repudiation of native rights in land and in the produce of the soil, and the destruction of trade as the basic factor in relationship between the European and the native in tropical Africa, of which this repudiation was the logical accompaniment—those deeds must *of necessity* take place.

From Behind the Veil

Fox Bourne is synonymous with unselfish devotion on behalf of subject races which cannot protect themselves, but I shall not, I feel sure, be causing offence if I submit that the Aborigines Protection Society is not a public body in the enjoyment of very wide popular support. It is respected by a number, and disliked probably by a much larger number. As for myself, I was known only in a restricted circle, through occasional signed articles on African questions which I used at that time to contribute to the Pall Mall Gazette chiefly. The odds were, therefore, severe. We had against us a King who was a multi-millionaire, with a then misguided nation at his back and all that this implies, and a Government at home which did not want to be bothered, whose policy had been a policy of silence. It was perfectly natural for the public to approach the terrible charges launched at the Congo State with a scepticism, proof against all but the most overwhelming demonstration. That scepticism had to be overcome and that demonstration made step by step, by slow, laborious, and painful degrees, while the forces at work to stop it grew in activity and unscrupulousness with its progression. The marvel is that headway was made at all. That success attended these efforts is owing in the main to the British Press, for whose support I have been personally indebted beyond words, especially when the campaign of charges, innuendo, and vilification against myself was set on foot by King Leopold's Press Bureau, and editorial offices were flooded with the most extraordinary fabrications concerning a humble and unknown individual, dragged by the force of circumstances into a notoriety which was anything but welcome.[1]

Consul Casement's famous report published early in 1904,

---

[1] I was the head of, or the agent of, "a syndicate of rubber merchants," jealous because the rubber from the Congo went to Antwerp instead of Liverpool: the tool of the British Government which masked territorial ambition behind my agitation ; a vulgar adventurer with a shady past seeking notoriety ; the possessor of large sums of money wherewith I bribed witnesses to manufacture stories of atrocity ; an unsuccessful black-mailer, etc., etc.

and the mass of missionary evidence which was then coming to hand suggested to my mind the formation of an association which should concentrate its energies upon one direct and simple issue—that of thrusting the Congo question to the front rank among international problems in urgent need of solution—and which could on those lines not only combine all individual effort, but appeal to a wide public on a platform divorced from politics, creed, or even nationality. This association came into being [1] with Earl Beauchamp as its first president, in April, 1904.

This plain and unvarnished recapitulation of events will, I venture to hope, suffice, with the summarised evidence in Section II., to clear up some points which have remained obscure to the majority.

---

[1] Mr. Alfred Emmott, Mr. John Holt, Dr. Guinness (Head of the Congo Balolo Mission), and two other personal friends gave me their early and invaluable assistance.

WHAT BRITAIN DID

"As to the question of the natives, the whole anti-slavery world had been swindled by the administration of the Congo Free State."—*Right Hon. Sir Charles W. Dilke, Bart., M.P., Sept.,* 1903.

I NOW propose to deal as briefly as the subject permits with the two first questions placed at the head of the last chapter.

In the sixties and seventies of the last century Central Africa, which had been a closed book to the world, became the scene of notable exploring feats which excited in the highest degree the scientific, commercial and political interest of the Western Powers. To the scientist in geographical and ethnological research an immense field for activity loomed upon the horizon. To the commercial nations was suddenly revealed enormous possibilities in the creation of new markets, and that revelation was accompanied by a desire, especially among the Protectionist Powers, to acquire as much of the African Eldorado as possible as an outlet for their own manufactures.

This desire led to what has been termed "the scramble for Africa." England, France, and Portugal were owners of African territory already : Germany and Italy became attracted by the African magnet, and so did King Leopold II. constitutional monarch of Belgium, which since 1831 had become a separate kingdom, owing primarily to the action of Great Britain, who led the way in recognising the series of events resulting in the secession of the Southern Provinces of the Netherlands from Holland.

Red Rubber

King Leopold's imperialist tendencies were at that time regarded without approval by the Belgian people.

Of all the exploring feats which had caused the Western world to focus its gaze upon Central Africa, Stanley's discovery of the Congo was the most sensational, and in that direction King Leopold bent his steps. He formed a Company styled the "International African Association" and sent several investigating expeditions at his own expense into the Congo region, mostly commanded by Englishmen and Germans, taking particular care to assure the world that his intentions were purely scientific and severely disinterested.

France despatched de Brazza to the Congo region on a political mission of a definite character, and Portugal revived her historical claims to the territory lying behind her possession of Angola.

King Leopold's plans were not nearly so altruistic as he professed, and fearing that they would be checkmated either by France or by Portugal, he appealed privately to England for support.[1]

What was the position of the King's "International African Association" at that period? It was a private enterprise anxious to secure international sympathies and calling itself "international" to that end, whose Managing-Director was nursing political and other ambitions. From the standpoint of international law it had no *status* whatever.

While conducting "a long private correspondence with Lord Granville,"[2] working American opinion through Mr. Henry Sanford, United States Minister at Brussels, and canvassing by various means the different European Courts, King Leopold was, meanwhile, posing before the world as the self-appointed philanthropist and saviour of the African race. He proposed to convert his Association into a "State" with "freedom" as its watchword, thus providing a neutral field for the legitimate activity of all commercial nations, whence rivalry should be *de facto* excluded, and

---

[1] "Life of Earl Granville." By Lord FitzMaurice. 1906.
[2] Ibid.

where the native would benefit by the blessings of even-handed justice, and good government. He repudiated with scorn the very notion of pursuing material ends, either for himself, or for Belgium (which, in point of fact, continued to view these schemes on the part of her Monarch with distaste and apprehension).

So admirably did the King play his cards that public opinion was captivated.

The King captured the British Chambers of Commerce by declaring that if the British commercial community supported his proposals, the Congo trade would be free to all the world, and would be exempt from such irritating restrictions as, for instance, characterise Portuguese fiscal policy. The Chambers "plumped" for King Leopold.

He captured the Protestant Missionary Societies of England and the United States by his fervid philanthropic protestations, and his promise to give every conceivable support to their propaganda. The Protestant Missionary Societies "plumped" for King Leopold.

He captured the Aborigines Protection Society, of which he became a member, and the philanthropic world of Great Britain—entire.

What was the attitude of the British Government?

Sir Robert Morier had some years before submitted a scheme to Lord Beaconsfield to place the Congo River under some form of international control on the model of the Danube Navigation Commission.[1] According to this scheme Great Britain was to recognise the claims of Portugal northwards from Ambriz to the southern bank of the Congo, while the northern bank was to become British.[2] Lord Beaconsfield did not favour it, and when (in 1875) Consul Lieutenant Cameron issued a proclamation on his own initiative taking possession of the basin of the Congo, his action was repudiated by Lord Carnarvon. Portugal, whose explorers had discovered the Lower Congo in the fifteenth century, which had spent large sums in the coastal regions north and south of the river, was the only

---

[1] "Life of Earl Granville." By Lord FitzMaurice. 1906.
[2] Ibid.

Red Rubber

Power which, historically speaking, could lay claim to
political rights in the Congo basin. She was our old ally,
and she was pressing ardently for British support. The
British Cabinet entertained the greatest objection to the
placing of protectionist France—with her hostile tariffs
directed at British trade—in control of the mighty Congo
basin, and Lord Granville did not believe in King Leopold.
Hence a friendly ear was turned to the Portuguese proposals. Mr. Gladstone wrote to Lord Granville (December,
1883): "I should be disposed to yield to the Portuguese
proposal, *still with the intention of appropriating no exclusive
advantage.*" [1]

Those proposals were that Great Britain should recognise
the sovereignty of Portugal on both banks of the river up
to a certain limit inland, and to draw an interior line which,
without expressly limiting Portuguese sovereignty for ever
in those regions, would put an end to the indefinite extension of her ancient claims ; leaving the interior to be
dealt with by conventions from time to time. It was
proposed to declare the river open to the trade of the
world, and to place it under an Anglo-Portuguese Navigation Commission, to which the accession of the Great
Powers would be welcome.[2]

The proposals were accepted, clauses were introduced
protecting international trade against exaggerated tariffs,
protecting religious teaching of whatever denomination,
and the rights of the native chiefs of the Coast who had
concluded treaties with British Consuls and merchants : and
the Treaty was signed.

But King Leopold had not been playing to the gallery
for nothing. The Treaty was denounced by the British
Chambers of Commerce and by the British philanthropic
world. The British Government was accused of be-
traying national interests. The Portuguese Government
was accused by its subjects of a similar crime. France,
encouraged by the clamour in England, fanned into stronger
flame by Stanley's impassioned diatribes, took up an attitude

---

[1] "Life of Earl Granville." By Lord FitzMaurice. 1906.
[2] Ibid.

14

of resolute hostility, and Bismarck, who in a fit of spleen had flung himself into competition with England on the Dark Continent, and who desired on the other hand to keep French eyes from the Rhenish frontier, was only too glad to kill two birds with one stone by administering a sly kick at the Anglo-Portuguese instrument.

France was now, seemingly, the mistress of the situation, and Central Africa ran the risk—so thought the British Government—of becoming a French preserve whence foreign trade would be barred. This Great Britain wished to prevent. King Leopold quickly realised the danger from his point of view, and Stanley, acting on his behalf, renewed the advances previously made to Lord Granville.

The only course left open to the British Government was to support the King's enterprise, but mistrusting the scheme and foreseeing its dangers, Lord Granville determined "to bind down the new State by conditions as stringent as those in the defunct Anglo-Portuguese Treaty, to secure freedom of trade and the protection of the natives." [1]

Bismarck's proposal for an International Conference on West African affairs was assented to.

[1] "Life of Earl Granville." By Lord FitzMaurice. 1906.

III

THE INTERNATIONAL AFRICAN
ASSOCIATION

" Recognition was accorded not to the Congo State, but to an
association professing an international character, and proclaiming
before the world as the object of its being not the accumulation
of rubber at an infinite cost of human life and suffering, but the
protection and civilisation of the natives of Africa."—LORD
PERCY, 1904.

ON October 21, 1884, Stanley, on behalf of King Leopold,
communicated to the British public a manifesto on behalf of
the "International African Association."

It is a long document. In it the Association states that
its "sole object" is to "enable commerce to follow the
Association's advance into inner equatorial Africa," and
announces that the sympathy and recognition of the
Government of the United States have been secured on
these grounds. Throughout the Congo "States" over
which the Association will exercise supervision the European merchant may "freely enter into commercial
negotiation with the natives"; "absolute freedom of
trade is ensured." The Association proposes to govern
these native "States" on the Congo "on the principles
of law recognised by civilised nations," and upon "philanthropic principles." Its aim is to "civilise Africa by
encouragement given to legitimate trade." The Congo
region is therein said to abound "in produce of various
kinds now lost to the world," but which, "thanks to
trade," "will enter into circulation." The natives of the
Congo "States" will be enriched thereby because, thanks

16

to European commercial activities which the Association's policy, by granting to them encouragement and protection, intends to promote, they will receive European merchandise in exchange for the produce of their country. "Thanks to trade" . . . "the counterpart of its value"—that is, the value of the produce collected by the natives—"will return to Africa, for which it will prove a source of prosperity." So anxious is the Association that nothing shall be allowed to restrict in any way whatsoever the development of trading relations between the white man and the natives on the Congo, that it will not even impose customs dues on European merchandise entering the country, believing such to be restrictive, a doctrine which "is also that of Richard Cobden and John Bright."[1] The document concludes with the assurance that "the Association will never part with any of its possessions without stipulating that the buyer shall maintain the absolute freedom of trade and the complete individual liberty which it has established."

On December 15, 1884, "Declarations" were exchanged between the British Government and the Association. The declaration of the Association opens as follows :—

"The International Association of the Congo, founded by His Majesty the King of the Belgians for the purpose of promoting the civilisation and commerce of Africa and for other humane and benevolent purposes, hereby declares . . ." The declaration thereupon sets forth that by treaties with certain native rulers, "legitimate Sovereigns," it has established and is establishing "free States" in the Congo region, whose administration by virtue of these treaties "is vested in the Association"; that foreigners will be guaranteed in the "free exercise of their religion, the rights of naviga- tion, commerce, and industry, and the right of buying, selling," &c. ; that everything possible will be done "to prevent the slave trade and suppress slavery."

The declaration of the British Government is laconic, and to the point :—

"The Government of Her Britannic Majesty declare their sympathy with, and approval of, the humane and benevolent

---

[1] This was specially for Manchester consumption.

17

purposes of the Association, and hereby recognise the flag of the Association, and of the free States under its administration, as the flag of a friendly Government."

On the same date a Convention was signed between the British Government and the Association. It consists of ten Articles, of which the most important are the second, fifth, and tenth, which read respectively as follows :—

Article II.—" British subjects shall have at all times the right of sojourning and of establishing themselves within the territories which are or shall be under the government of the said Association. They shall enjoy the same protection which is accorded to the subjects or citizens of the most favoured nation in all matters which regard their persons, their property, the free exercise of their religion, and the rights of navigation, commerce, and industry. Especially they shall have the right of buying, of selling, or letting and of hiring lands and buildings, mines, and forests, situated within the said territories, and of founding houses of commerce, and of carrying on commerce and a coasting trade under the British flag."

Article V.—" Every British Consul or Consular officer within the said territories who shall be thereunto duly authorised by Her Britannic Majesty's Government, may hold a Consular Court for the district assigned to him, and shall exercise sole and exclusive jurisdiction, both civil and criminal, over the persons and property of British subjects within the same, in accordance with British law."

Article X.—" In case of the Association being desirous to cede any portion of the territory now or hereafter under its government, it shall not cede it otherwise than as subject to all the engagements contracted by the Association under this Convention. Those engagements, and the rights thereby accorded to British subjects, shall continue to be in vigour after every cession made to any new occupant of any portion of the said territory."

The great " West African Conference " opened its sittings " in the name of Almighty God " at Berlin on November 25, 1884. It closed them on February 26, 1885. Fourteen Powers were represented. Count Bismarck began his opening speech with these words :—

" In convoking this Conference, the Imperial Government has been guided by the conviction that all the Governments invited share the desire of civilising the natives of Africa by opening the interior of that Continent to trade."

He defined the programme of the Conference as limited

"to the freedom of trade in the Basin of the Congo and its mouth."

Sir Edward Malet, the British representative who spoke immediately afterwards, read a long address, in the course of which he said :—

"I cannot forget that the natives are not represented among us, and that the decisions of the Conference will, nevertheless, have an extreme importance for them. The principle which will command the sympathy and support of Her Majesty's Government will be that of the advancement of legitimate commerce, with security for the equality of treatment of all nations, and for the well-being of the native races."

Throughout the discussion which took place before the final drafting and signature of the Act, we find the British delegate constantly making suggestions on behalf of the natives, in regard to their freedom in commercial matters, in regard to slavery and the slave-trade, in regard to the importation of alcoholic liquor.

A perusal of these discussions shows that in accordance with the inaugural statement of the President, all the delegates were at one in considering the *freedom of the natives to trade as the primary guarantee of their collective and individual liberty, their principal safeguard against oppression and injustice.* Baron Lambermont, the senior Belgian delegate, opined that this freedom in commercial transactions would prove in itself to be an impediment "to the temptation of imposing abusive taxes"; Baron de Courcel, the senior French delegate, was emphatic as to the need of guarding against the fundamental vice of sixteenth-century colonisation, which looked upon native peoples in the light of suppliers of revenue for a European metropolis. Count Launay, the delegate for Italy, was anxious to secure that freedom of trade should be protected from interference not for a specified period of years, but for all time. Herr Woermann—the great West African shipowner and merchant of Hamburg—one of the experts consulted by the Conference, explained the nature of West African trade, *e.g.*, the barter of forest or agricultural produce by the native owners and gatherers of such, for imported European merchandise. A special committee was appointed by the Conference to prepare a report on the subject, and this

Red Rubber

report, signed by the delegates of Belgium and France, was submitted to the Conference and adopted. All monopolies, or exclusive privileges in matters of trade, were prohibited : the words "monopoly" and "privilege" were analysed etymologically. In short, every conceivable precaution was taken to ensure Lord Granville's determination that "freedom of trade and the protection of the natives" should be secured throughout the Congo valley.

The last sitting of the Conference but one, on February 23, was noteworthy. The president opened it by reading out to the assembled delegates the contents of a letter communicated to him by the representative of King Leopold, in which the writer—Colonel Strauch—after notifying to the President in the name of the King of the Belgians that the International Association had concluded separate conventions with the delegates of all the Powers represented at the Conference save one, went on to say :—

"The meetings and deliberations of the distinguished Assembly sitting at Berlin under your high presidency, have materially contributed to hasten this happy result. The Conference to which it is my duty to render homage, would, I venture to hope, consider the accession of a Power whose exclusive mission is to introduce civilisation and trade into the centre of Africa, as a further pledge of the fruits which its important labour must produce."

Then ensued a pathetic scene ; the delegates, figuratively speaking, fell upon each other's necks and wept with emotion. "The new State," declared Baron de Courcel (France), "has been dedicated to the exercise of every liberty." Sir Edward Malet (England) followed with a panegyric of King Leopold.

"The whole world," exclaimed Count Launay (Italy), "can but testify to its sympathy and its encouragement for this civilising and humanitarian work which honours the nineteenth century, and from which the general interests of humanity benefit and will continue increasingly to benefit."

The Count of Banomar (Spain) shared the views of Count Launay as to the "humane and civilising work of His Majesty the King of the Belgians," and likewise M. de Vind (Denmark), and the representative of Sweden and

Norway. M. Sanford (America) rendered "homage to this great civilising work." Count van der Straeten-Ponthoz (Belgium) was grateful. He added :—

"The Belgian Government and nation will adhere, therefore, with gratitude to the labours of this High Assembly, and *thanks to which the existence of the new State is henceforth assured*, while principles have been laid down from which the general interests of humanity will profit."

The general Act of this West African Conference as agreed to, provides (Article I.) that :—

"The trade of all nations shall enjoy complete freedom."

Article V.—"No Power which exercises or shall exercise sovereign rights in the above-mentioned regions shall be allowed to grant therein a monopoly or favour of any kind in matters of trade. Foreigners without distinction shall enjoy protection of their persons and property, as well as the right of acquiring and transferring movable and immovable possessions ; and national rights and treatment in the exercise of their professions."

Article VI.—"All the Powers exercising sovereign rights or influence in the aforesaid territories bind themselves to watch over the preservation of the native tribes, and to care for the improvement of the condition of their moral and material well-being, and to help in suppressing slavery, and especially the Slave Trade. They shall, without distinction of creed or nation, protect and favour all religious, scientific, or charitable institutions, and undertakings created and organised for the above ends, or which aim at instructing the natives and bringing home to them the blessings of civilisation.

"Christian missionaries, scientists, and explorers, with their followers, property and collections, shall likewise be the objects of especial protection.

" Freedom of conscience and religious toleration are expressly guaranteed to the natives, no less than to subjects and foreigners. The free and public exercise of all forms of Divine worship, and the right to build edifices for religious purposes, and to organise religious missions belonging to all creeds, shall not be limited or fettered in any way whatsoever."

Articles XIII. to XXV. deal with the navigation of the Congo, of which more anon.

On August 1, 1885, King Leopold notified the Signatory Powers that the International Association would be henceforth known as the " Congo Free State," and himself as Sovereign of that "State."

Let us summarise these facts :

I. Sir Robert Morier proposes to Lord Beaconsfield that " the *régime* of the Congo should form a leading chapter in a large settlement of African affairs." [1]   One feature of this scheme is that the river " be placed under some form of international control." Lord Beaconsfield rejects the idea and Lord Carnarvon repudiates Consul Cameron's proclamation taking possession of the Congo basin in the name of Great Britain.

II. Stanley's discoveries of the mighty fluvial system of the Congo, bend all eyes towards Central Africa.

III. The King of the Belgians founds an International Association ostensibly to promote " civilisation and trade " in Central Africa.

IV. France and Portugal take alarm and put forward political claims in that direction.

V. King Leopold fearing for his enterprise which has already begun to assume a political and—we may presume by subsequent events—financial complexion, appeals to the British Government privately for support.

VI. Portugal appeals to Great Britain likewise. She proposes that the River Congo shall be thrown open to the trade of the whole world, that the river itself shall be placed under an Anglo-Portuguese River Commission to which the successive adhesion of the other Powers would be welcome.

VII. King Leopold's scheme is not trusted by the British Government, which favours the Portuguese proposal, and Mr. Gladstone recommends agreement while making it clear that England has no intention of securing any exclusive advantage for herself.

VIII. King Leopold is, meanwhile, making desperate efforts to capture British public opinion and to influence it against the Anglo-Portuguese treaty. To the philanthropic section of the British public he represents his enterprise as a great humanitarian undertaking. To the commercial world of Great Britain he describes its main purpose as securing for ever Central Africa to commercial liberty,

---

[1] "The Life of Lord Granville." Lord Fitzmaurice.

free from vexatious imports and tariffs. He succeeds in raising a storm of opposition in England against the Anglo-Portuguese Treaty.

IX. Germany is in a grumbling mood, and France, encouraged by the home opposition in England, protests against the Treaty.

X. The British Government in view of these attacks at home and abroad abandons the Treaty with Portugal and henceforth supports King Leopold's scheme, for the same reason which led it to support Portugal, but, still mistrusting the king's intentions, determines that stringent conditions for the good treatment of natives and the freedom of commerce shall be secured.

XI. Agrees to participate in an International West African Conference suggested by Bismarck to settle the question.

XII. Exchanges declaration and signs a Convention with King Leopold's Association on the lines above indicated.

XIII. Takes a leading part in the Conference at Berlin which results in freedom of commerce, prohibition of monopoly or privilege, and just treatment of the natives being solemnly proclaimed.

A good many morals might be drawn from this record, but it will suffice to accentuate three conclusions, and these are :

A. King Leopold's " International Association " would have dissolved into thin air but for the separate and collective action of the Powers in allowing it to blossom from a private undertaking into a great free area under the trusteeship of the Sovereign of a small neutral European State.

B. Without British sanction, co-operation, and assistance, no such arrangement could possibly have been arrived at.

C. But for the influence exercised by King Leopold and his agents upon British public opinion, the British Government would never have given its sanction to the arrangement.

IV

A PROGRAMME IN THREE PARTS

"It appears to me that the facts I have stated afford amply sufficient proof of the spirit which animates the Belgian administration, if indeed administration it can be called."—Lord CROMER, White Book, Africa, No. 1, 1904.

THE first five years of the "Congo Free State's" existence were devoted by King Leopold to the maturing of the vast financial, military, and political programme he had been caressing—as must now be clear to the average intellect—if not from the very commencement of his undertaking, at least very shortly after its inauguration. There were many things to accomplish in the interval. One of the most important was the establishment on a solid foundation of the claim to philanthropic motive, which later on might be contested by pestilent critics, animated, of course, with the most unworthy motives. Large drafts were therefore made upon public credulity, and the resource displayed in this regard was elevated to a fine art. Royal decrees, laws, and regulations followed in rapid succession, breathing the very quintessence of philanthropy. Those which breathed another sort of essence, the King, as we shall see in a moment, thoughtfully refrained from publishing. Friendly relations were established with the unspeakable Arab whose ill-deeds were shortly to be trumpeted all over the world. Very great activity was displayed in despatching, exploring, and reconnoitring expeditions throughout the country.

24

A Programme in Three Parts

Yet, towards the end of this first period of King Leopold's enterprise, ugly rumours were already gaining currency. A policy of veiled antagonism had been set on foot in the Lower Congo towards European merchants there settled. Trade instead of being encouraged was in process of being throttled by heavy taxation. A decree was issued claiming all "vacant lands" as the property of the State; subsequent decrees whittling down the rights of the native to the area upon which his hut was built, or his cultivated patch of farm land. Another decree prohibited the hunting of the elephant "throughout the whole extent of the State's territory (three-fourths of which had not at that time been trodden by the white man's foot) without special permission," special permission being withheld; yet another decree prohibited the trade in india rubber and gum copal—*e.g.*, in the only articles ex-ivory, it was possible to trade in—in the Aruwimi district, and so on. More astonishing than aught else, perhaps, was the feverish haste with which a large body of troops recruited from the most savage tribes in the Upper Congo was being raised and equipped with modern rifles of precision.[1] By 1889, 2,200 "regulars" had been recruited. An official report of that year foreshadowed the recruiting of 5,000 in the Bangala country, and 3,000 more in the Aruwimi district. Confidential circulars which only became known last year and this, and with which not a dozen people in this country are probably acquainted, were despatched to the King's officials on the Congo. Here is an extract from one of these circulars signed by the then principal Secretary on the King's Brussels staff:

"The Congo State will allot for each recruit obtained a bonus on the following lines: 90 francs for every healthy and vigorous man considered fit for military service, and whose stature exceeds 1 metre 55 centimetres; 65 francs for every youth who stature is at least 1 metre 35 centimetres; 15 francs per male child. The male children must be at least 1 metre 20 centimetres in height, and must be sufficiently strong to be able to support the fatigues of the road. For every married man the bonus will be increased to 130 francs. The bonus will only fall due when the men

---

[1] The *Albini* rifle.

25

have been handed over to the headquarters of the various districts." [1]

The children were drafted to the "camps of military instruction," to be made soldiers of in due course.[2] The recruits were obtained by armed raids upon villages, differing in no degree from the raids of the Arabs except that they were accompanied by greater loss of life. In this way the Bangala country has been drained of its life-blood, and the population reduced in the last fifteen years by about 75 per cent., as Mr. Weeks will tell us in the next chapter; similar results have followed in the Bakussu and Batetla country— indeed, I believe, the Batetlas are practically wiped out. Another confidential circular, dated October, 1891, and signed by the Acting Governor-General in the Congo, M. Felix Fuchs, informs the District Commissioners that the Government has set aside a sum of one hundred thousand francs, which sum it is free to distribute, partly or wholly, or not at all, "with the object of rewarding the District Commissioners and their subordinates who show exceptional zeal and devotion in the accomplishment of all the duties which are incumbent upon them." The circular goes on to explain that the *sine qua non* of the allotment of these bonuses is the rigorous fulfilment of the decrees bearing upon recruiting.

"It must be well understood that no bonus will be granted in districts which do not carry out the recruiting operations provided in the decree of July 30, 1891. The maximum of bonus will be allotted only to those District Commissioners who recruit at least the number of men above mentioned for 1902. These recruiting operations are distinct from voluntary enlistments, which will continue as before. The balance of the credit not allotted will be distributed among the districts which recruit more than the number of men here mentioned."[3]

So direct and explicit a command to raid slaves, necessitated extreme secrecy, and we find the Acting Governor-General

[1] Official shorthand report, Belgian Parliamentary Debates, February–March, 1906.

[2] These were a portion of the *libérés*—so-called free slaves. See Section II.

[3] Official shorthand report, Belgian Parliamentary Debates, March, 1905.

recommending that the circular "must under no pretext be removed from your archives. You will convey to your subordinates such explanations as may be necessary in connection with this circular, *verbally*." These instructions led to a further crop of circulars, of which the following may be considered a type :—

"Coquilhatville, May 1, 1896,—Chief Ngulu of Wangata is sent into the Maringa to buy slaves for me. The agents of the A.B.I.R. are requested to inform me of the depredations he may commit *en route*. Signed, Captain Commandant SARRAZIN District Commissioner of the Equator."[1]

The humanitarian undertaking began to wear a curious aspect.

In 1890 King Leopold broke with the Arabs, and appealed to the Powers to allow him to impose import duties on merchandise in order to raise money with which to fight the wicked Arabs, those inconvenient competitors in ivory—the "Congo Free State" had already imposed an export duty of £80 per ton on ivory and £20 on rubber[2]— ostensibly to crush their slave-trading operations. This demand, coupled with the acts previously referred to—*e.g.*, exorbitant taxation of trade, prohibition of elephant hunting, partial prohibition of rubber trading, etc.,—was too much for the Dutch Government, whose subjects drove a considerable trade in the lower river. It shook the faith of the British Chambers of Commerce, and disgusted a section, at least, of the philanthropic element. Mr. F. W. Fox, for instance, made what has since become, in the light of subsequent events, a most remarkable prediction, at a public meeting, held on November 4 of that year in London. He said :

"There is an impression, very widely existing among the people in the Congo State, that when this money is voted by the Brussels Conference, there will be war and raids instead of any beneficial result, and that great evils will grow far greater than

---

[1] Official shorthand report, Belgian Parliamentary Debates, March, 1905.

[2] The West African Conference had prohibited the levying of import dues ; but had not prohibited the imposition of export dues.

the slave trade as existing at present. (Hear, hear.) We contend that it ought to be suppressed by judicious efforts, by the extension of legitimate commerce, by fair consideration for the natives, by being just to the Arabs and enlisting their sympathy, and not by exterminating the natives or the Arabs in a series of wars."

But the same old tactics were resorted to which had been used to such advantage to hound on British opinion against the Anglo-Portuguese Treaty. Public and Press were flooded with inspired articles and pamphlets representing the Dutch Government and all who shared its views as friendly to the slave trade. Finally, King Leopold got what he wanted, a mandate from Christendom to exterminate the Arabs ; and, on the strength of it, obtained £1,000,000 from Belgium as a cash-down recognition of his generosity in leaving the Congo to her in his will.[1] Thus doubly fortified, the sovereign of the "Congo Free State" brought his plans rapidly to a head. The royal programme was divided into three parts, between which there existed a close correlation.

I. The extermination of the Arabs. II. The conquest of the Soudan. III. The conversion of the Congo Basin, its economic riches, and its human inhabitants into the private property of the Sovereign. The disappearance of the Arab had a twofold advantage. It would strengthen King Leopold's reputation for philanthropy in the world, enabling him to pose more than ever as the "Godefroi de Bouillon of the nineteenth-century crusade," and, incidentally, would place in his hands not only the ivory markets occupied by the Arabs, but the vast stores of that article held by them. This was accomplished. The second was on the high road to success when at the last moment it fell to pieces. Four thousand rifles, one thousand irregulars armed with lances, and hundreds of porters, together with a considerable force of artillery, marched Nilewards after concentrating at Dungu. There were two columns. The first, under Chaltin, had only 750 rifles. Nevertheless it occupied the left bank of the Nile up to Rejaf, driving the Dervishes before it. The second, under Dhanis, met with complete disaster owing to the mutiny of

---

[1] *Vide* Section V.

the greater part of the force. Had this event not taken place, the history of the last few years might have undergone no small change, for King Leopold's objective was Khartoum ; his ambition, to play the part of " honest broker" between France and England for the settlement of the Egyptian question. The ambition was a large one, but it was seriously entertained, and the chance of success was not at all remote. As it was, his partial triumph lured Lord Rosebery into the unfortunate Agreement of 1894 over the Bahr-el-Ghazal, which alienated us from Germany in Congo matters, and nearly brought us to war with France.

The third part of the programme needs to be handled in greater detail, for, like the first it has been carried out only too completely, and to its realisation is primarily due the abomination of desolation into which the Congo territories have been plunged.

Before the birth of the " Congo Free State " a brisk trade with the natives of the Upper Congo was carried on by European merchants established on the lower river, through the native middlemen, the Ba-Congo. These Ba-Congo caravans transported goods from the European factories into the interior by the caravan road passing level with the 200 miles of cataracts which, prior to the construction of the railway by Colonel Thys,[1] separated the lower river from the upper. At the head of the cataracts (Stanley Pool) they disposed of their goods to the natives who awaited them in canoes, some of which hailed from enormous distances in the interior, receiving in exchange produce, chiefly ivory and rubber, which they brought down again to the European factories. With the advent of the " Congo Free State," Belgians, Frenchmen, and Englishmen, in the employ of a powerful trading Company registered in Belgium, *La Société Anonyme belge pour le commerce du Haut Congo*, started factories on the upper reaches of the river, dealing direct with the natives of the country. They pushed inland along the banks, and purchased ivory and rubber with European goods. They laid the foundation of legitimate business transactions with the " enterprising,

---

[1] *Vide* Section V.

high-spirited "—as Stanley called them—races of the Upper
Congo, the nucleus of a trade which would have gone on
expanding as has been the case everywhere in West Africa,
in Nigeria, Senegambia—all down the coast, in fact,
gradually penetrating inland as native enterprise grew with
the improvement of ways of communication, and the
increased accessibility of native markets. Stanley in referring—in the course of his public speeches in 1884—to the
future possibilities of the Congo trade if placed under the
auspices of a philanthropic monarch, had been positively
lyrical in his enthusiasm, and there is no doubt that had that
trade been allowed to develop, its proportions to-day would
have been very large. What a different picture we should
have had to contemplate !

But the *rôle* of supreme administrator of a tropical dependency run on lines of decency, justice and legitimate commerce, such as was understood to be the King's intention at
the West African Conference, simply did not enter into
that monarch's purview. The part would have been altogether too confined. His ideas were widely different. He
was, indeed, "a dreamer of dreams " as Stanley had described
him, but not of that sort of dream. He wished to cut a
great figure in the world, a desire impossible of accomplishment without vast financial resources which he did not
possess. So, the royal feet being now firmly planted on
African soil, the royal position in Europe being secure, the
royal will entered, with immovable determination to crush
all obstacles, on its predestined course. . . .

A secret decree dated September 21, 1891, and the
measures taken by the King's officials in Africa upon
receipt of it, changed the whole outlook of affairs in Central
Africa, and revolutionised the actual and future situation of
its millions of inhabitants. This decree laid down as the
paramount duty of the officials of the "Congo Free State "
the raising of revenue, "to take urgent and necessary
measures to secure for the State the domainial fruits (*anglicè*,
the produce of the country) notably ivory and rubber." It
was followed by a series of regulations issued by the
Governor-General through the District Commissioners,
forbidding the natives to sell ivory and rubber to European

merchants, and threatening the latter with prosecution if they bought these articles from the natives.

The merchants protested, and the King in reply defined his position. Everything in the country belonged to the "State"; the land and the produce thereof. The natives were tenants upon the "State's" property. If they interfered with that property they were poachers, and whosoever abetted them in that interference were criminals, receivers of stolen goods, and violators of the law of the land.

In that way did King Leopold by a stroke of the pen appropriate Central Africa.

To leave his officials under no misapprehension as to his intentions, other secret instructions were despatched by the King to his Governor-General. Some of these secret documents have recently come to light, but as they are practically unknown in this country—owing to the limited means of the Congo Reform Association—and as they are of transcendental importance to a proper understanding of the policy of brigandage substituted by King Leopold for the "freedom of commerce" laid down in the Conventions and at the West African Conference, from which King Leopold derives his trusteeship as over-lord of the Congo, I make no apology for giving them here.

"BRUSSELS, *June* 20, 1892.

"To the Governor General.—As I have had the honour upon several occasions of informing you, the Officials of the Congo State must neglect no means of exploiting the produce of the forests. They must succeed in keeping commerce informed of the riches of our territories, and gradually bring about a considerable traffic towards Stanley Pool for the period when the railway is opened.

"To stimulate the zeal of our officials in this matter, I have decided that in future a bonus proportionate to the cost of exploitation shall be allotted to those who are concerned with forest exploitation. These bonuses will be established as follows :

15c. bonus per kilo on rubber costing 30c.			and less per kilo.		
12½c.	,,	,,	31c. to 40c.	,,	,,
10c.	,,	,,	40c. to 49c.	,,	,,
8c.	,,	,,	50c. to 59c.	,,	,,
6c.	,,	,,	60c. to 69c.	,,	,,
4c.	,,	,,	70c. to 80c.	,,	,,

Red Rubber

"For gum copal and wax as follows :

15c. bonus per kilo on gum, &c., costing 5c.　　　and less per kilo.
10c.　　　　　　,,　　　　　,,　　　6c. to 10c.　　,,　　　　,,
5c.　　　　　　,,　　　　　,,　　　11c. to 15c.　　,,　　　　,,

"For ivory costing the State in the Congo 15 francs, I shall give no bonus.

On ivory costing 14f. I will give a bonus of 15c.
,,　　,,　　13f.　　,,　　,,　　30c.
,,　　,,　　12f.　　,,　　,,　　45c.
,,　　,,　　11f.　　,,　　,,　　60c.
,,　　,,　　10f.　　,,　　,,　　75c.
·,　　,,　　9f.　　,,　　,,　　90c.
,,　　,,　　8f.　　,,　　,,　　1f. 5c.
,,　　,,　　7f.　　,,　　,,　　1f. 20c.
,,　　,,　　6f.　　,,　·　,,　　1f. 35c.
,,　　,,　　5f.　　,,　　,,　　1f. 50c.
,,　　,,　　4f.　　,,　　,,　　1f. 65c.
,,　　,,　　3f. and less　　,,　　1f. 80c.

"For scrivelloes [1] and defective tusks, the bonus can be reduced as the Government may decide, to one half the above figures. A proportion of the bonuses due may be given to a subordinate in accordance with the lists which must be furnished me by Station Chiefs, District Commissioners, and Leaders of Expeditions. This measure will begin and will apply to all products collected from October 1st. It will not be retrospective and annuls all preceding regulations on the subject.

"The Secretary of State,
"(*Sgd.*) Van Eetvelde.

"Certified correct, Governor-General Wahis." [2]

Thus the less the Official employed by King Leopold cost his royal master in obtaining his royal master revenues, the more his royal master was pleased, and the greater his reward. The less the native got for his rubber and ivory, the larger the Official's commission! A more direct incentive to robbery and violence was never penned. There are times when the recorder of the Congo tragedy stops short with a mental gasp, and pauses before he goes on again, to wonder whether he is the victim of hallucination. On February 6, 1893, M. Felix Fuchs, Acting-Governor-General, forwards a circular to Inspectors,

---

[1] Small tusks.
[2] Official shorthand report, Belgium Parliamentary Debates, March, 1905.

A Programme in Three Parts

District Commissioners, Commanders of Expeditions, Heads of Stations—those " fine Stations" we shall hear about presently—which says :

"The State cannot assure its future unless it finds the where-withal to defray its expenditure. The exploitation of its *Domaine Privé* is in this respect an important asset. It is of paramount necessity therefore, that the State should obtain promptly there-from the necessary revenue to balance its expenditure."

This philanthropic document proceeds :

" At present it is chiefly necessary to give an energetic im-pulse to the collection of rubber and ivory. As regards the first of these products, the task of the District Commissioner, who has jurisdiction over a portion of the *Domaine Privé*, will be facilitated in large measure by the fact that no private person can buy rubber therein unless he has obtained already a con-cession of a portion of the *Domaine Privé*. . . . The Government hopes that you will do your utmost to carry out its behests, and that you will collect the greatest quantity of the various products of the Domaine." [1]

This from a " Government " to its officials.

The German Government having got wind of this singular fashion of interpreting the articles of the West African Conference, protested in the most vigorous terms through its Minister at Brussels, Count Alvensleben. Astonishing as it may seem to those who have not yet realised that Niccolo Machiavelli's precepts have been adopted and vastly extended by his modern prototype, King Leopold denied absolutely and repeatedly that any bonus was paid to his officials on ivory and rubber. Here is the letter which closes the correspondence :

" BRUSSELS, *December* 11, 1895.
" Monsieur le Comte.—In reply to the communication of your Excellency of the 7th of this month, I beg, without entering into an examination of the question of right, to declare formally that there does not exist any commercial premiums for the agents of the Independent State of the Congo, and that the Government has no intention of establishing any, either for rubber or for ivory, or for any other product whatever,
(*Sgd.*) EDMOND VAN EETVELDE."

---

[1] Official shorthand report, Belgian Parliamentary Debates, March, 1905.

Red Rubber

This official was the co-signatory with Sir Edward Grey the other day to a Convention under which the Congo forces are to evacuate certain portions of British territory they have occupied. His pledges are somewhat at a discount.

The system of paying these bonuses on revenue collected has taken various forms. Here are extracts from another circular dated Boma, January 3, 1896, and signed by the Governor-General, Baron Wahis :

"BOMA, *January* 3, 1896.

"GENTLEMEN,—By reason of the decision taken by the Government to suppress bonuses to officials connected with the exploitation of the Domaine in respect to products collected by them, the Government has decided to grant extra bonuses to officials rendering exceptional services to the State, principally in the development of the resources of the country and the bettering of the conditions of the natives (*sic*). These bonuses will be granted according to the suggestions which may be made by the Commanders of Expeditions or by District Commissioners. . . . These bonuses, however, will only be granted in districts which produce annually to the State at least 50,000 francs in taxes paid in kind by the natives—it being well understood that these taxes are to be reckoned in products sold in Europe for the benefit of the Treasury. Reports as to collection of produce must continue to be sent to me regularly to enable the Government to take note of the services rendered by our officials, and to check the arrivals of produce. But for the previous marginal notes will be substituted others, which shall consist in allotting to officials who may have contributed directly or indirectly to the collection of produce, a certain number of marks according to their respective merits, the total of the marks being represented by ten. It will not be necessary to mention in the Report the names of District Commissioners or Commanders of Expeditons, because the Government will be able, according to the produce collected, to judge of the importance of the services of these Officials. It will suffice, therefore, to follow the name of the Official with the number of marks attributed to him, according to the services he has rendered, thus :

M.X.	*Chef de Zone*	5 marks.
A.	Officer	2 marks.
B.	Non-commissioned Officer ...	2 marks.
C.	Clerk	1 mark.

Total ... 10

(*Sgd.*) Governor-General WAHIS."[1]

---

[1] Official shorthand report, Belgian Parliamentary Debates, March, 1905.

34

A Programme in Three Parts

The procedure adopted at present is as follows. Officials whose districts have produced much revenue (*e.g.*, rubber, for the ivory is becoming exhausted) receive an annual grant : District Commissioners from 6,000 to 10,000 francs, Captains in the Force Publique 4,000 to 7,000 francs; Lieutenants in the Force Publique 2,000 to 3,000 francs. Foreign officers who are inclined to be disagreeable when they return are lunched by the King, told how bad are the effects of the African sun upon the European temperament, assured that they must have been dreaming or misinformed, and if possible a *douceur* sends them away happy—not given direct of course ; that would be too vulgar, but quietly arranged in a subsequent confidential chat with one of the high officials. The grants mentioned above take the form of an entry to the grantee's credit in the register of the four per cent. Public debt (*grand livre de la dette publique*) of the Congo State, on which interest is paid. Permission is afterwards given for the conversion of this credit entry into bonds to bearer.

It is very ingenious and simple withal. The official's future is bound up with the production of revenue. He can *claim* nothing from the King ; but if his " zeal and devotion " in raiding through the country at the head of an armed rubber-hunting expedition has been sufficient, he knows that he will be rewarded. If he is wise he keeps a copy of his instructions from headquarters, which will enable him to retaliate in kind lest by any chance the royal purse strings be closed. His horizon begins with rubber and ends with hard cash—*matabiche* in Congo slang. The native is between the upper and nether millstone.

So it was in the beginning, is now and ever shall be so long as King Leopold and his financiers are allowed to pirate the wealth of the Congo forests by armed force.

Read this circular given in the White Book Africa No. 1, 1904. It is dated Boma, March 29, 1901, and is signed by the inevitable Baron Wahis.

" The quality of the rubber exported from the Congo is sensibly inferior to what it was some time ago. The difference arises from several causes, but principally from the addition to the latex [1] which is fit to be gathered, of other kinds of latex of very inferior value, or even of any dust-like matter. This cause of loss can and must be removed."

(I may here remark in parenthesis that an ingenious method of *removing* it has been practised by some of the subordinate officials. They have made the natives eat it when badly prepared.[2])

"The commissioners of districts and chiefs of zones who have all experience, know the fraudulent means which the natives often try to employ. They must take measures completely to prevent these frauds. It cannot be doubted that in those parts where the population submits to the tax it will not be impossible to lead the natives to furnish pure produce ; but in order to effect this, constant supervision is necessary, for as soon as the native notices that the supervision is becoming lax he will try to lessen his work by taking latex of a bad quality, if he obtains it easily, or by adding foreign matter. Whenever these frauds are discovered they must be put down. The commissioners of districts and chiefs of zones must examine the product at frequent intervals, in order to report in time to their heads of stations, and not to permit a condition of affairs which is most prejudicial. To this cause of the decline in the value of rubber must be added that arising from defective packing of the produce, which thus often travels during several months under the worst conditions. Much of the effort which has been taken to obtain produce in keeping with the richness of the country may be said to be lost through this neglect, for the value of the rubber may be diminished by half through this want of care. I may add that the value of rubber, even when free from all admixture, has gone down in every market for some time past. Territorial chiefs, therefore, must not only remove the two causes of loss which they can eliminate, but they must also try to neutralise the third by making unceasing efforts to increase production to the extent laid down in the instructions. The orders which I have here given will have my constant attention."

Such circulars as these from the fountain head of the Congo autocracy are accompanied as may be supposed by circulars from the subordinates to their subordinates—the men who actually get the revenue, not those whose task it is to say that the revenue must be secured ! Few of these

---

[1] *E.g.*, the juice of the vine which, coagulated, produces rubber.
[2] *Vide* Section III.

documents have ever seen light. Those that have may be taken as typical samples. Here are two in sequence from the higher to the lower rung of Congolese hierarchy :

Acting Governor-General Felix Fuchs to Commandant Verstraeten in charge of the Rubi Welle zone :

"I close by advising you that the Government firmly hopes that, inspired by the considerations set forth in the present communication, you will exhibit a fresh proof of your activity and devotion, by making the district you command produce the maximum of resources which can be drawn from it."[1]

Commandant Verstraeten to the Officials in charge of the Stations of the Rubi Welle district :

"I have the honour to inform you that from January 1, 1899, you must succeed in furnishing 4,000 kilos of rubber every month. To this effect I give you *carte blanche.* You have, therefore, two months in which to work your people. Employ gentleness first, and if they persist in not accepting the imposition of the State employ force of arms."[2]

Here are extracts from another :

"District Commissioner Jacques to the Official in charge of the Station of Inoryo :

"M. le Chef de Poste.—Decidedly these people of Inoryo are a bad lot. They have just been and cut some rubber vines at Huli. We must fight them until their absolute submission has been obtained, or their complete extermination."[3]

When the inevitable results of such appeals to pillage by violence attain too great proportions, we get a circular of this kind :

"Boma, *November 7, 1893.*

"Gentlemen, — From information which has reached the central government recently it appears that some of our agents settle palavers, make war upon the natives, burn villages without reporting their actions. Others who have gone so far as to carry out with their own hands summary executions, and have

---

[1] Official shorthand report, Belgian Parliamentary debates, July, 1903.

[2] Ibid.

[3] Official shorthand report, Belgian Parliamentary debates, February to March, 1906.

thus become assassins, have not been brought before any tribunal or court-martial. Their immediate Chiefs present in the region, could not have been ignorant of facts of this gravity, and have thus assumed serious responsibility. The government invites me to take the severest measures at my disposal to cause these deplorable abuses which sully our reputation to cease. I need not add here that this order will be executed. We have decrees and regulations. Each person must conform to them. If individual caprice was to substitute itself for law, we should become in certain parts of the territory more savage than the natives whom we have to lead to civilisation.

"(Sgd.) The Governor-General WAHIS." [1]

After this avowal, we observe the same supreme official and King's "mandatory" in Africa issuing the following instructions to the District Commissioner of Lake Leopold II. The circular is dated January 9, 1897. It reads : "Where the natives refuse obstinately to work, you will compel them to obey by taking hostages."

"Work" meaning to gather rubber for King Leopold and his financial friends, on lines laid down in the earlier regenerating circulars. It is unnecessary to add that the taking of women hostages has, since that circular, become a recognised feature of the rubber slave trade.[2]

No wonder King Leopold suppressed the documentary evidence of his own Commission of Inquiry last year.

By these measures did the produce of the Congo Basin, "lost to the world," become "a source of prosperity" to the native collector of it ! Under this system £13,715,664 of raw produce (85 per cent. rubber) has been forced out of the Congo native in the last seven years at the point of the bayonet. Furnishers of untold wealth to their absentee landlord in Europe, their own condition has steadily worsened.[3] Deprived of everything, and compelled to

---

[1] Official shorthand report, Belgian Parliamentary debates, March, 1905. Compare this circular, in which the Governor-General admits that the Congo officials are assassins, with the furious denunciations of the Press Bureau against their foreign accusers.

[2] See Section III.

[3] The total value of the imports in that period only amounted to just over £6,000,000, the overwhelming proportion of which was composed of Government material and stores.

devote their lives to gathering rubber for an alien potentate, who claims the labour of Central Africa as his personal asset.

Thus, the rubber slave trade in the *making*. We shall follow it in the *working*. We shall plunge into the equatorial forest and see how the rubber is acquired under the stimulus of force and bonuses. We shall move among the natives and realise, so far as it is possible at a distance of several thousand miles from the scene of their oppression, the daily effects of the system upon them, the system of " moral and material regeneration." And after inquiring whether this calculated plunder of a Continent possesses any redeeming feature for the plundered people, we shall pass to an examination of the revenues derived therefrom, the amount of them, and the manner of their distribution.

SECTION II

THE DEEDS

THE DEEDS

"Auferre, trucidare, rapere falsis nominibus imperium, atque ubi solitudinem faciunt, pacem appellant" (TACITUS, *Agricola*, cxxx).

("What they, by a misuse of terms, style Government, is a system of pillage, murder, and robbery, and their so-called peace is a desert of their own creation.")

I reproduce below the comments upon "Affairs of West Africa," published in 1902, in which book four chapters were devoted to the affairs of the Congo, because they are typical of the difficulties which those of us who took up this matter were confronted, difficulties which are referred to in the opening chapter of the present volume.—AUTHOR.

"The state of affairs to which he calls attention in the latter portion of the book is, indeed, so terrible, and the accusations which he does not hesitate to bring personally against King Leopold II. are so grave that, notwithstanding the unfortunately too general apprehension entertained in well-informed West African circles that there exists very solid ground for criticism, we hesitate, without independent investigation, to give further currency to his assertions. . . . *If Mr. Morel is accurately informed* there is hardly a condition of its (the Congo State's) charter that it has not broken, nor a law of common humanity which it has not flouted. The sufferings of which the picture was given to the world in 'Uncle Tom's Cabin' are as nothing to those which Mr. Morel represents to be the habitual accompaniment of the acquisition of rubber and ivory by the Belgian companies."—*The Times, December* 19, 1902.

Sir Harry Johnston in the *Daily Chronicle*, December 20, 1902 : "Mr. Morel's indictment is one of the most terrible things ever written, *if true*."

WITHIN the last few months only have the closest students of the Congo question been in a position to appreciate to

43

the full the staggering volume of records to the continuity and uniformity of outrage, AND THE ALL-PERVADING CAUSE OF OUTRAGE, on the Congo. Many of the *data* here summarised are unknown save to the comparatively few persons who are subscribers to the Congo Reform Association, in whose monthly journal they have been recorded. Others now appear for the first time. In the main the records here given are but the briefest and baldest summaries. If the whole of them were to be set down, a book double the size of the present one would hardly suffice to contain them. My object—or one of them—is to show how unbroken is the tale of horror, how dreadful the similarity. We see precisely the same scenes described by men thousands of miles apart, and with many years' interval between them.

RECORDS FROM 1890 TO 1893.

Letter from Colonel Williams, read out to a London meeting by Mr. R. Cobden Phillips, representing the Manchester Chamber of Commerce, on November 4, 1890. (Extract.) (Area : presumably upper river banks.)

"Your Majesty's Government has been, and is now, guilty of waging unjust and cruel wars against natives, with the hope of securing slaves and women to minister to the behests of your Majesty's Government. In such slave-hunting raids one village is armed against the other, and the force thus secured is incorporated with the regular troops."

March, 1891.—Letters from correspondents in the Congo read out to Manchester Geographical Society by Mr. E. Sowerbutts, the Secretary. Letters speak of atrocities by Congolese troops, women and children seized as prisoners, &c., in this " diabolical and unholy so-called civilising work." (Area : probably Cataract region.)

In 1891 the secret decree appropriating the produce of the soil, and calling upon officials to devote all their energies to collecting revenue, is issued, together with the regulations and circulars which followed it (see last chapter). The *immediate* effects of the regulations and circulars are chronicled in letters from Belgian and French traders in

The Deeds

the Upper Congo. Letters dated 1891 and 1892. *Published for the first time in* 1904.[1] (Area : river banks and central region.)

"YAMBAYA, *February* 6, 1891.—The country is ruined. Passengers in the steamer *Roi des Belges* have been able to see for themselves that from Bontya, half a day's journey below our factory at Upoto, to Boumba inclusive, there is not an inhabited village left—that is to say four days' steaming through a country formerly so rich ; to-day entirely ruined."

"GONGA DONA, *October* 20th.—Thanks to the proceedings of the State we cannot travel three hours in a canoe without coming across a hostile village. This is the way they go on. They go to a village and say to the Chief, 'If by noon three tusks of ivory are not here for us to buy, you are no longer our friend.' At noon the Chief arrives and says, 'I have only two,' or as the case may be. 'If that is the case,' replies the representative of the State, 'we will see.' The whole party then springs on shore and endeavours to make prisoners. That having been accomplished, the Chief is told, 'Come with so many tusks, and your men and women will be returned to you.'"

"BASANKUSU, *September* 17, 1892.—The villages are compelled to pay heavy taxes in rubber ; they are compelled to furnish so many kilos to the State every week. To give you an idea, the State has received 1,060 kilos in one month and a half. The State had made war upon the villages from Lulonga to Basankusu. All the villages in the Maringa suffered the same fate."

"LIKINI, *October* 15th.—After the wars with the Mambatis and the Boucoundu, when the State people took many prisoners, which the Mambatis redeemed with ivory, they have begun the same proceedings again. To buy ivory in this way does not need many goods, and has the merit of simplicity. Four days ago they started making war once more ; thirteen killed, six prisoners."

"*October* 18th.—The frequent wars upon the natives undertaken without any cause by the State soldiers sent out to get rubber and ivory are depopulating the country. The soldiers find that the quickest and cheapest method is to raid villages, seize prisoners, and have them redeemed afterwards against ivory. At Boucoundje they took thirty prisoners, whom they released upon payment of ten tusks. Each agent of the State receives 1,000f. commission per ton of ivory secured, and 175f. per ton of rubber."

"YAMBAYA, *March* 23, 1893.—The majority of natives in every village are fleeing to the forests on account of the perpetual troubles with the State."

---

[1] " King Leopold's Rule in Africa " (4½ pages).

Red Rubber

Such was the immediate result of the official instructions to raid ivory and rubber on commission ; the early beginnings of the system which was to prevail for fifteen years, and which still prevails.

RECORDS FROM 1894 TO 1898.

Glave, E. J. : an independent English traveller, formerly with Stanley, who speaks very highly of him. Crossed the Congo from the Great Lakes to the ocean in 1894–5. His voluminous diary published by the *Century Magazine* in 1896.[1] (Area : the whole country traversed.)

" The white officer at Kamambare has commissioned several chiefs to make raids on the country of the Warua and bring him slaves. They are supposed to be taken out of slavery and freed, but I fail to see how this can be argued out. They are taken from their villages and shipped south to be soldiers, workers, &c., on the stations, and what were peaceful families have been broken up and the different members spread about the place. This is no reasonable way of settling the land. It is merely persecution. . . . The brutal action of the soldiers so terrified the people that many fled into hiding, and have not since returned. . . . Not content with this, the soldiers steal everything on the plantations and in the houses. If the rightful owners object they are beaten, the women taken by force. . . . In stations in charge of white men, Government officers, one sees strings of poor, emaciated old women, some of them mere skeletons, working from ten to six tramping about in gangs with a rope round their necks and connected by a rope one and a half yards apart. They are 'prisoners of war.' . . . Expeditions have been sent in every direction forcing natives to make rubber and to bring it to the Stations. Up the Ikelemba away to Lake Mantumba, the State is perpetrating its fiendish policy in order to obtain profit. . . . War has been waged all through the district of the Equator, and thousands of people have been killed and homes destroyed. . . . Many women and children were taken, and twenty-one heads were brought to Stanley Falls, and have been used by Captain Rom as a decoration round a flower-bed in front of his house. . . . Most white officers out in the Congo are averse to the india-rubber policy of the State, but the laws command it.[2] . . . If the Arabs had been the masters it would be styled iniquitous trafficking in human flesh and blood, but

---

[1] *Vide* also " Civilisation in Congoland," by H. R. Fox Bourne.
[2] *Vide* circulars and regulations in last chapter.

46

The Deeds

being under the administration of the Congo Free State, it is merely a part of their *philanthropic* system of *liberating* the natives."

Sjöblom, a Swedish missionary of the American Baptist Missionary Union. In conjunction with an Englishman in the same Mission, Banks, Sjöblom had complained with great vehemence locally, and caused furious resentment to the Governor-General, Baron Wahis, who threatened him with five years' imprisonment. Through the intermediary of Mr. Fox Bourne he appealed to the world at a public meeting in London (May 12, 1897). His experiences cover 1895–7. (Area : central region.) The following are extracts from his statements :

"The natives in inland towns are, as a matter of custom, asked whether they are willing to gather india-rubber. The question put to them is not 'Will you live at peace together ? Will you acknowledge the Congo Government ?' It is, 'Will you work india-rubber ?' Well, many of the people are killed, and they try suddenly to disband, and refuse to bring the india-rubber. Then war is declared." Describes the usual procedure adopted. Within his knowledge 45 towns have been burnt down. Describes the sentry-system, the soldiers stationed in the villages, living on the people, and driving the adult males into the forest to gather india-rubber. Narrates how he visited a village at sunset. The people had never seen a white man and had returned from their hunt for rubber. As he was speaking to them, a soldier rushed in among the crowd, and seized an old man guilty of having been fishing in the river instead of gathering rubber ; shoots him before Sjöblom's eyes. Right hand cut off. People flee out of the town. "All except the old chiefs are forced to go away and work rubber." The sentries are "from the wildest tribes." "When they get to this work they are many times worse. They are really small kings in the towns and often kill the people for the sake of the rubber. If the rubber does not reach the full amount required the sentries attack the natives. They kill some and bring the hands to the Commissioner. Others are brought to the Commissioner as prisoners. Hundreds are constantly taken down in large steamers." . . . . "From this village I went on to another where I met a soldier who pointed to a basket, and said to me, 'Look, I have only two hands.' He meant there were not enough to make up for the rubber he had not brought.[1] He had several prisoners tied to trees. When I

---

[1] *Vide* Africa No. 1, 1904. Every cartridge expended required a right hand as tally.

came back, some of the villages were in an uproar. . . . When I reached the river I turned and saw that the people had large hammocks in which they were gathering the rubber to be taken to the Commissioner. I also saw smoked hands, and the prisoners waiting to be taken to the Commissioner. This is only one of the places in which these practices occur. There is a small island in a stream at Lake Mantumba.[1] The people had not been able to bring in the full amount of rubber. The officers with some soldiers went along there. Several of the natives were killed. I saw the dead bodies floating on the lake with the right hand cut off, and the officer told me when I came back why they had been killed. It was for the rubber. In fact the officers have always freely told me about the many who were killed, and always in connection with india-rubber. . . . In one village which I passed through, I saw two or three men on the wayside quite recently killed—about an hour before. The sentry who had to oversee the gathering of the rubber told me they had killed the men because they had not brought in the rubber. When I crossed the stream I saw some dead bodies hanging down from the branches in the water. As I turned away my face at the horrible sight one of the native corporals who was following us down said, ' Oh, that is nothing, a few days ago I returned from a fight, and I brought the white man 160 hands and they were thrown into the river.' . . . ' I have seen extracts of letters in which the writers have freely told about hundreds being killed, hundreds of hands brought by the sentries, hundreds of slaves being taken, and one of the State officials said to a resident agent, ' I have two hundred slaves here. Do you want some ?' Another agent told me that he had himself seen a State officer at one of the outposts pay a certain number of brass rods (local currency) to the soldiers for a number of hands they had brought. One of the soldiers told me the same. That was about the time I saw the native killed before my own eyes. The soldier said, ' Don't take this to heart so much. They kill us if we don't bring the rubber. The Commissioner has promised us if we have plenty of hands he will shorten our service. I have brought in plenty of hands already, and I expect my time of service will soon be finished.'" Mr. Sjöblom also gave many particulars of the monstrous demands for food, fish, &c., upon the people ; the fines inflicted upon them for shortage, their general condition of impoverishment, &c.

Campbell, Dugald, a missionary belonging, I believe, to a Scotch Presbyterian Mission. Has laboured for about a quarter of a century in the south-eastern portion of the State (Katanga). His voluminous reports to Mr. Fox

---

[1] *Domaine de la Couronne. Vide Section IV.*

The Deeds

Bourne cover a very extensive period. Those I am about to quote cover the period 1891 to 1898. Published in 1904. (Area : south-eastern region.)

Mr. Campbell sub-sectionalises his report into the "Ivory *régime*," the "Rubber *régime*," "Treatment of Natives," the "Sentry system," etc. Under "Treatment of Natives" he writes :—

"This is, and ever has been, shocking, and the cause of revolts, troubles, and when possible, exodus into the territories of other Powers. The treatment of the down-trodden natives since State occupation has brought about a moral and material degeneration. Through the gross and wholesale immorality, and forcing of women and girls into lives of shame, African family life and its sanctities have been violated, and the seeds of disease sown broadcast over the Congo State are producing their harvest already. Formerly native conditions put restrictions on the spread of disease, and localised it to small areas. But the 17,000 soldiers, moved hither and thither to districts removed from their wives and relations to suit Congo policy, must have women wherever they go, and these must be provided from the district natives. . . . Native institutions, rights, and customs, which one would think ought to be the basis of good government, are ignored."

Among the incidents he gives characterising the "Ivory *régime*," I quote the following :—

"After that Katoro, another very large chief living near the apex of the western and eastern Lualaba, was attacked. The crowds were fired into promiscuously, and fifteen were killed, including four women and a babe on its mother's breast. The heads were cut off and brought to the officer in charge, who then sent men to cut off the hands also, and these were pierced, strung, and dried over the camp fire. The heads, with many others, I saw myself. The town, prosperous once, was burnt, and what they could not carry off was destroyed. Crowds of people were caught, mostly old women and young women, and three fresh rope gangs were added. These poor 'prisoner' gangs were mere skeletons of skin and bone, and their bodies cut frightfully with the *chicotte* when I saw them. Chiyombo's very large town was next attacked. A lot of people were killed, and heads and hands cut off and taken back to the officers. . . . Shortly after the State caravans, with flags flying and bugles blowing, entered the mission station at Luanza, on Lake Mweru, where I was then alone, and I shall not soon forget the sickening sight of deep baskets of human heads. These baskets of 'war

49

Red Rubber

trophies' were used . . . for a big war-dance, to which was added the State quota of powder and percussion-caps. . . . I made a journey myself to the copper hills in the west, to the caves, to Ntenke's, Katanga's, Makaka's, and Kateke's, all in South Lamba, and found the sentries everywhere living like kings, plundering, killing, and burning villages in the name of the State. I append a list of the villages and chiefs at 'Sentry Posts' known to me, and each manned by two black soldiers. [Here follow twenty villages, with their localities, etc.] Each of these posts was manned, as stated, by two black soldiers to look after State interests, chiefs, and ivory. . . . Perhaps you will say, 'Why did you not speak out and report all this?' My first experience in Katanga was Captain X's threat to imprison my colleague for denouncing these doings. Every time I made representations they were declared impossible, or the answer was, 'I will ask my head sentry to make inquiries,' the head sentry being one of the worst blackguards in the country. Nothing was ever proved. He would not believe his soldiers could be guilty of such misconduct, or, 'Well, they must have *carte blanche*, or the natives would not respect the State.' Sometimes 'Might is right,' would be the curt reply. What could one say? There were no judges or courts of appeal, and the officer, often at his wits' end, would say, 'What can I do? I MUST get ivory. I have no law or regulation book. I am the only law and only God in Katanga.'"

Under the "Rubber *régime*" similar stories are given, always with an abundance of names, places, etc.

Here are a few short extracts :—

"Meanwhile, on the Luapula similar abuses existed, and women were raped and made to serve both white and black, until many of the best and biggest villages crossed into British territory, where they live in peace. [Follows a long list of the villages which have migrated.] The wholesale exodus is due to Belgian raiding, the sentry system, and the maltreatment of the natives."

Under the "Sentry system" Mr. Campbell says :—

"I have known them tie up chiefs for a week in ropes, and keep them tied until a sufficient ransom was brought. . . . I have met them on the road on plundering expeditions, travelling in hammocks with from twenty to thirty carriers—these, of course, impressed into the work—besides other carriers who carried their pots, cloth, provisions, and guns wherever they went. . . . It was a common practice to remove sentries who were unsuccessful in securing sufficient ivory and to replace them by others more ruffianly disposed, whose ivory-extorting powers had been previously tested."

50

The Deeds

Banks, of the American Baptist Missionary Union, reporting locally from Bolengi in 1896 (Area: central region) :—

Describes raid of State troops upon the villages of Bandaka Wajiko. Cause, poor quality of rubber. Questions soldiers, and is told fifty people have been killed and twenty-eight taken prisoners. Sees the prisoners taken through the mission station. Counts "sixteen women tied neck to neck." Some of these women carrying their tiny children. Several "young children were walking on before who were also prisoners." Visits the raided village. "In a little shed lay one of my late school children, a promising young lad. I lifted the leaves by which he was covered, and saw his right hand cut off. I then went through the village and saw the people burying their dead. I counted over twenty bodies and newly filled-up graves. All the bodies had the right hand cut off."

Kenred Smith, of the British Baptist Missionary Society, testified before the Commission of Inquiry in 1904, as to atrocities committed in 1893. Extract from letter to the Author; published this year in C. R. A. organ. (Area: central region.)

"I thought that all evidence submitted to the members of the Commission would be given in due course to the public, and was not, therefore, too careful in making manuscript notes of my remarks before it. Happily I have notes. I submitted them to them and now send you the substance of my remarks." Details. Expedition sent on June 2, 1898, by local agent of the *Anversoise*, (*vide* Section IV.), to punish people who sought to escape the rubber "tax." Villages of Mika and Bosomakuma attacked. Men, women and children killed and mutilated. Village of Bosolo then attacked and became, according to native evidence, "a veritable shambles." Visited Mika, and "saw mutilated bodies or parts of bodies representing some twenty people, and new-made graves bringing up the number to at least thirty." Native evidence placed before him showed two hundred people killed. "A cannibal feast followed the slaughter." Complained locally. So far as he knows no action taken.

Clark, Joseph, of the American Baptist Missionary Union. Extracts from his diary, personal correspondence, and reports to local officials from 1894 to 1899. The complete documents were handed to the Congo Commission in 1904, and suppressed together with all other documentary evidence brought home by that Commission. They are

Red Rubber

now made public for the first time here, with Dr. Barbour's permission. The area from which Mr. Clark writes is the *Domaine de la Couronne*, and this account, together with Mr. Scrivener's, which will be referred to later, will show an appreciative Public how the regenerator of Africa obtains his revenues !

Ikoko [Clark's mission station] represented in diary and letters in 1893, as a large town "beautifully situated in a bay with, say, four thousand people within a radius of 1½ miles from the mission station." The people are "fine looking, bold and active." In 1894 the district first came under the influence of the philanthropic monarch Leopold II. Large demands for rubber principally are made; also for fish and forced labour for the State plantations at Bikoro. Outrages commence.

"*November* 15, 1894.—Seven Irebus were foully murdered about half an hour from here. They had been tied and brutally shot when unable to move away from their murderers. . . . My only hope under present rule is for us to try to put the information into the hands of the American Ambassador, and try to get him to personally lay the reports before Leopold II. I do not think he can know of what is being done in his name." (To a correspondent.)

"*November* 28th.—The State soldiers brought in seven hands and reported having shot the people in the act of running away to the French side." (To a correspondent in Scotland.)

"*December* 8th.—A year ago we passed or visited between Irebu and Ikoko the following villages. [Here follow the names of eight villages with "probable population" of each : total 3,180.] A week ago I went up, and only at Ngero (one of the villages in the list) were there any people ; there we found ten." (To a correspondent.)

"*April* 12, 1895.—I am sorry that rubber palavers continue. Every week we hear of some fighting, and there are frequent 'rows' even in our village with the armed and unruly soldiers. During the past twelve months it has cost more lives than native wars and superstitions would have sacrificed in three to five years. The people make this comparison among themselves. It seems incredible and awful to think of these savage men armed with rifles and let loose to hunt and kill people, because they do not get rubber to sell at a mere nothing to the State, and it is blood-curdling to see them returning with hands of the slain, and to find the hands of young children amongst bigger ones evidencing their bravery." (To a correspondent.)

"*May* 3rd.—The war was on account of the rubber. The State demands that the natives shall make rubber, and sell same

The Deeds

to its agents at a very low price. The natives do not like it. It is hard work and very poor pay, and takes them away from their homes into the forest where they feel very unsafe, as there are always feuds among them. The rubber from this district has cost hundreds of lives, and the scenes I have witnessed while unable to help the oppressed have been almost enough to make me wish I were dead. The soldiers are themselves savages, some even cannibals, trained to use rifles, and in many cases they are sent away without any supervision, and they do as they please. When they come to a town no man's property or wife is safe, and when they are at war they are like devils. Imagine them returning from fighting some rebels(?) see on the bow of the canoe is a pole, and a bundle of something on it. These are the hands (right hands) of sixteen warriors they have slain. 'Warriors!' Dont you see among them the hands of little children and girls? I have seen them. I have seen where the trophy has been cut off, while the poor heart beat strongly enough to shoot the blood from the cut arteries at a distance of fully four feet." (To a correspondent in America.)

"*May.*—All the fighting about us on the Lake for say eight months has been on account of the rubber." (To a correspondent in America).

"*May 17th.*—Nearly all Ikoko is in the bush—this everlasting rubber palaver is sending lots into eternity, and many to live like wild beasts in the woods, where they are afraid to make a fire for fear of attracting the man-hunters" (*i.e.*, the soldiers). (To a correspondent.)

"*May 28th.*—Kindly let me appeal to you again on behalf of Ikoko that the tax of rubber may be taken off." (To Commissaire Fievez).[1]

"*June 5, 1895.*—There is a matter I want to report to you regarding the Nkake sentries. You remember some time ago they took eleven canoes and shot some Ikoko people. As a proof they went to you with some hands, of which three were the hands of little children. We heard from one of their paddlers that one child was not dead when its hand was cut off, but did not believe the story. Three days after we were told that the child was still alive in the bush. I sent four of my men to see, and they brought back a little girl whose right hand had been cut off, and she left to die of the wound. There was no other wound. As I was going to see Dr. Reussens about my own sick-

---

[1] In the Official Bulletin for June, 1896, there is an eulogistic report on the admirable assiduity of this official in obtaining rubber. It tells us that the district under his administration produced in 1895 "650 tons of rubber bought at 2½d.—European price—and sold at 5s. 5d. per kilo in Antwerp!"

ness, I took the child to him and he has cut the arm and made it right, and I think she will live. But I think such awful cruelty should be punished." (To M. Mueller, Chef de district, Bikoro).

"*June 7th.*—How many people have been slain for the sake of rubber I cannot tell, but the number is large." (To a correspondent.)

"*March 25, 1896.*—This rubber traffic is steeped in blood, and if the natives were to rise and sweep every white person on the Upper Congo into eternity there would still be left a fearful balance to their credit. Is it not possible for some American of influence to see the King of the Belgians and let him know what is being done in his name? The Lake is reserved for the King—no traders allowed—and *to collect rubber for him hundreds of men, women, and children have been shot.*" (To a correspondent.)

The Congo "Government" in Brussels—*e.g.*, the King—denied the existence of this royal preserve—until 1902! The proceeds are handled by the King exclusively, and are not paid into the so-called public revenues of the Congo State. *Vide* Section IV. The exasperated natives turn upon their destroyers.

"*April 15th.*—Two white men and about fifty soldiers killed by the Montaka natives on the Lake. Ikoko and Ngero are the only important villages not in arms—all caused through the rubber demand and mode of operation." (To a correspondent.)

"*Nov. 2, 1898.*—Some fighting in Ikoko two weeks ago. Two old men, one old woman, one girl, and two children killed. The old woman's hand was cut off. I saw the body. One child of about two and a half or three years of age had been struck over the stomach with the butt of a gun, and then thrown into the water, and a younger child had been no doubt treated in the same way, but its body was not found. A young girl (about ten) was with them, and she had been beaten and thrown into the water and died. The woman had been stabbed after being taken prisoner—the old woman was shot." (To a correspondent.)

We have seen that in 1893 Ikoko had a population of 4,000 souls. I complete these particular extracts with the following appeal to Lieutenant Dubreucq, Commissaire, dated May 5, 1899 :—

"I desire to pray you that some alteration be made in the present State demands on Ikoko, or before long there will be no people here but those attached to the mission. . . . Now probably there are not over six hundred of all ages of people in the town and fishing camps. There is not one native chief of influence.

The Deeds

While I have been here there have been four chiefs of considerable 'force,' but two of them were shot, and the other two were several times in the chain, and at last died in the town here. At present the death rate is very great because the people are badly nourished."

Such is the story of Ikoko and neighbourhood.

Weeks, John, of the British Baptist Missionary Society. Extract from a Report to the District Commissioner of the Bangala region, dated Monsembe, November 6, 1897, handed to the Commission of Inquiry in January, 1905; published in full in the C. R. A. organ for July, 1905. (Area: river banks and central region.)

"Last year the country all about here was flooded, yet you levied your cassava tax month after month upon the people, in addition to your oil, fowls, and goat tax, etc. The people here had not enough to eat, and as their cassava was destroyed by the flood, they had to buy it at an exorbitant price from more fortunate districts. This year again the country is flooded and the farms spoilt, but I suppose you will enforce the cassava tax, and the people have to starve again; and why? To feed and strengthen the State soldiers, to raid them again in their weakness! You take away the sturdy young men, leaving only the old people and children, so that every steamer that stays here loots the town, because the proper defenders have been taken off by the State."

Mr. Weeks, reporting to the District Commissioner and to the Governor-General in June, 1903, deals with the depopulation of the country since 1890. His full letter is published in the *West African Mail*, October, 1903. It covers thirteen years.

"It distresses me very much to see and hear that this town, and others of this and neighbouring districts, are in a more deplorable state than they were two years ago (when Mr. Weeks returned to Europe on furlough). When we came to settle in Monsembe, in 1890, there were over 7,000 people between here and Bokongo. In 1900 there were very few over 3,000, and now there are not many over 1,000. If the decrease continues at the same rate, in another five years there will be no people left." Proceeds to set forth the causes. Continual deportation of young men to serve as soldiers and workmen, and of young women for other purposes. Demand for men levied without "any regard to population." Flight to get away from oppressive taxation. Sleeping sickness; thinks that this disease "would

55

Red Rubber

never have taken such a hold upon the people if they had not had their spirit crushed out of them by an ever-increasing burden of taxation." Taxation in food stuffs becoming heavier and heavier. Imposition of fines "sapping the life of the people." "Heartrending to compare this district now with what it was in 1890."

In letters to friends in England, dated June and July, 1903 :—

"I say, without any fear of contradiction, that the condition of the people is, to put it mildly, one hundred per cent. worse than in 1893." . . . "The entire population of the district is now 9,400, and quite half has recently been driven from the bush to the river to repopulate its banks. Stanley, in 1885, reckoned this same district at 80,000 people. In 1890 Mr. Stapleton and myself, in search of a site, landed at a very large number of towns, and concluded that the figures of 1885 were too high, and put the population down at 50,000. The population has dropped in 13 years from 50,000 to under 5,000. . . . This is not the only district which has gone down in population. Starting from Stanley Pool, Bwembe, has about 100 for every 1,000 it once had ; Bolobo has not a third of its former population. . . ." (Here follows an enumeration of towns with their old, and former population.)

Morrison, William, of the American Presbyterian Mission. Reports outrages in the Kasai district, beginning in 1898. They are given in the next record.

Murphy, of the American Baptist Union. Describes in *Times* of 1895 the raids and atrocities carried on by Congo troops in his district from 1893-5. "The hands—the hands of men, women, and children—were placed in rows before the *Commissaire*, who counted them to see that the natives had not wasted cartridges." Area : *Domaine de la Couronne* (Lake Mantumba).

Casement, Roger, British Consul in the Congo. It is difficult to dissect, from the point of view of time, the long and detailed disclosures of Consul Casement, which disclosures cover the past as well as dealing with the present. But here and there are passages which can be selected as showing how the present day situation is the outcome of long years of oppression. Consul Casement's Report was published in 1904. (Area : *Domaine de la Couronne.*)

The Deeds

" The population of the Lake-side towns would seem to have diminished within the last ten years by 60 to 70 per cent. It was in 1893 that an effort to levy an india-rubber imposition in this district was begun, and for some four or five years this imposition could only be collected at the cost of continual fighting."

Area : river banks.

" The station at Bikoro has been established as a Government plantation for about ten years. It stands on the actual site of the former native town of Bikoro, an important settlement in 1893, now reduced to a handful of ill-kept, untidy huts, inhabited by only a remnant of its former expropriated population."

" We touched at several points on the French shore, and on the 25th July reached Lukolela, where I spent two days. This district had, when I visited it in 1887, numbered fully 5,000 people ; to-day the population is given, after careful enumeration, at less than 600.

" Bolobo used to be one of the most important native settlements along the south bank of the Upper Congo, and the population in the early days of civilised rule numbered fully 40,000 people, chiefly of the Bobangi tribe. To-day the population is believed to be not more than 7,000 or 8,000 souls. The Bolobo men were famous in former days for their voyages to Stanley Pool and their keen trading ability. All of their large canoes have to-day disappeared, and while some of them still hunt hippopotami—which are still numerous in the adjacent waters—I did not observe anything like industry among them. Indeed, it would be hard to say how the people now live . . ."

" Perhaps the most striking change observed during my journey into the interior was the great reduction observable everywhere in native life. Communities I had formerly known as large and flourishing centres of population are to-day entirely gone, or now exist in such diminished numbers as to be no longer recognisable. The southern shores of Stanley Pool had formerly a population of fully 5,000 Batekas. These people some twelve years ago decided to abandon their homes, and in one night the great majority of them crossed over into French territory. Where formerly had stretched these populous native African villages, I saw to-day only a few scattered European houses. In Leopold-ville there are not, I should estimate, one hundred of the original natives or their descendants now residing."

Area : *Domaine de la Couronne.* In the notes to his report Consul Casement gives details of native evidence showing how the " Lake-side " people were extirpated :—

" I decided to visit the nearest settlement of these fugitives. I

Red Rubber

asked first why they had left their homes and had come to live in a strange, far-off country where they owned nothing and were little better than servitors. All, when the question was put, women as well as men, shouted out, 'On account of the rubber tax levied by the Government Posts.' . . . I asked them how this tax was imposed. . . . 'From our country each village had to take twenty loads of rubber. These loads were big ; they were as big as this (producing an empty basket which came nearly up to the handle of my walking stick). . . . We had to take these loads in four times a month.' 'How much pay did you get?'— (Entire audience) 'We got no pay. We got nothing.' . . . 'It used to take ten days to get the twenty baskets of rubber. We were always in the forest, and then when we were late we were killed. We had to go further and further into the forest to find the rubber vines, to go without food, and our women had to give up cultivating the fields and gardens. Then we starved. Wild beasts—the leopards—killed some of us when we were working away in the forest, and others got lost or died from exposure and starvation, and we begged the white man to leave us alone, saying we could get no more rubber, but the white men and their soldiers said, "Go ! You are only beasts yourselves ; you are nyama (meat)." We tried, always going further into the forest, and when we failed and our rubber was short the soldiers came up our towns and shot us. Many were shot ; some had their ears cut off ; others were tied up with ropes round their neck and bodies and taken away. We fled because we could not endure the things done to us. Our chiefs were hanged, and we were killed and starved and worked beyond endurance to get rubber. . . . The white men told their soldiers, "You kill only women ; you cannot kill men." So when the soldiers killed us' (here he stopped and hesitated, and then, pointing to the private parts of my bulldog—it was lying asleep at my feet) he said, 'then they cut off those things and took them to the white men, who said, "It is true you have killed men."' 'You mean to tell me that any white man ordered your bodies to be mutilated like that, and those parts of you carried to him?'—(All shouting) 'Yes, many white men.' 'You say this is true? Were many of you so treated after being shot?'—(All shouting) 'Nkoto ! Nkoto !' (Very many ; very many)."

Mr. Scrivener in his diary confirms this last statement. He heard it from the lips of the sentries themselves, and in the Mongalla massacres of 1899 the agents of the Anversoise confessed to ordering sexual mutilations.

Dealing in a long enclosure with the appalling depopulation of this region, Consul Casement gives as the primary ⌐n thereof :—

The Deeds

"War," in which children and women were killed as well as men. Women and children were killed not in all cases by stray bullets, but were taken as prisoners and killed. Sad to say, these horrible cases were not always the acts of some black soldier. Proof was laid against one officer who shot one woman and one man while they were before him as prisoners with their hands tied, and no attempt was made to deny the truth of the statement. To those killed in the so-called "war" must be added large numbers who died while kept as prisoners of war. The irregular food supply has been another cause, says the Consul. The native is "without ambition because without hope." He does not attend to his plantations owing to the sense of insecurity. "When sickness comes he does not care." A third cause is the "lower percentage of births." Weakened bodies brings this about, also "women refuse to bear children and take means to save themselves from motherhood." They "give as the reason that, if war should come, a woman big with child or with a baby to carry cannot well run away and hide from the soldiers." With regard to the mutilations practised by the soldiers and referred to by Mr. Clark and others, the Consul says, "Of acts of persistent mutilation by Government soldiers of this nature I had many statements made to me, some of them specifically, others in a general way. Of the fact of this mutilation and the causes inducing it there can be no shadow of doubt. It was not a native custom prior to the coming of the white man ; it was not the outcome of the primitive instincts of savages in their fights between village and village ; it was the deliberate act of the soldiers of a European administration, and these men themselves never made any concealment that in committing these acts they were but obeying the positive orders of their superiors."

Whitehead, John, of the British Baptist Missionary Society. Extracts from letter to Governor-General, dated Lukolela, July 28, 1903. Published in Africa No. 1, 1904 (White Book). (Area : river banks.)

"The population of the villages of Lukolela in January, 1891, must have been not less than 6,000 people, but when I counted the whole population in Lukolela at the end of December, 1896, I found it to be only 719, and I estimated from the decrease, as far as we could count up the known number of deaths during the year, that, at the same rate of decrease, in ten years the people would be reduced to about 400 ; but judge of my heartache when on counting them all again on Friday and Saturday last to find only a population of 352, and the death rate rapidly increasing."

Red Rubber

With the year 1898, the great Trusts of the central region came into being, and to the horrors of the *Domaine de la Couronne* and all that had been up to that time *Domaine Privé* were added the horrors of the Trust area, as the agents of these concerns (which are the King under varying labels—*Vide* Section IV.) struck new ground, or, as was the case with the A.B.I.R., carried further devastation into districts already "tapped."

Lacroix and other agents of the Anversoise Trust; confessions of. (Area: central region, Mongalla.)

Fighting in the Mongalla district had been continuous since 1898. On April 10, 1900, the *Niuwe Gazet*, of Antwerp, published the confessions of Lacroix. Instructed by his superiors to attack a certain village for shortage in rubber, he had killed in the course of his raid many women and children. "I am going to appear before the Judge for having killed 150 men, cut off 60 hands; for having crucified women and children, for having mutilated many men and hung their sexual remains on the village fence." Other confessions followed, published in *Le Petit Bleu* and other papers. The Congo Courts inflicted long terms of imprisonment. The men never served them, and have long since been released. The defence was identical. They had acted under instructions— to force rubber by any and every means. The "superiors" were not troubled. Later on, as we shall see, the trial of the man Cauldron, also an agent of the *Anversoise*, showed, four years later, a precisely similar state of affairs existing in the district.

Weeks, John (see above).

Letter of protest to District Commissioner of Bangala, dated Monsembe, November 30, 1903. Published in the *West African Mail* in 1904. Describes punishment of towns of Bokongo, Bongondo, etc., for shortage in food stuffs by a force of 150 soldiers under an officer; gives names of eleven women, ten men, and a girl slaughtered unresisting: "It is very evident from the different places in which these people were shot down that there was no armed resistance": "have you neither mothers nor sisters that you can treat women in this brutal way." Mr. Weeks proceeds to give particulars of increasing wretchedness of people owing to scandalous taxation; people compelled to sell their rela-

The Deeds

tives into slavery to meet it ; gives names of people sold into slavery to provide food stuffs for State stations. Lieutenant in charge was allowed to return to Europe, although a subsequent inquiry confirmed the truth of Weeks' charges. So admitted by the Commission of Inquiry.

In a letter to the author, dated December 24, 1903, published in the *West African Mail*, 1904. Gives abundant and detailed statistics of taxation in food stuffs : shows that the 820 natives of all ages and both sexes in the four sections of Malela, Bongondo, Mungundu, and Bokongo must supply each year to the State food stuffs aggregating £1,605 16s. 8d. in value.

"I need scarcely point out that young children, very old people, and invalids cannot earn a wage, or even farm or fish ; consequently the burden falls heavier on those who can, and the vision before them is one of unceasing toil in order to comply with the demands of the State. Is it any wonder the natives die under the burden ? The wonder to me is that so many are alive after these seven years of oppression and taxation. Death has less horror than this constant grind, this perpetually trying to fill a bottomless sack, this everlasting paying of heavy taxes, meeting exorbitant fines, being shot down untried, or forced to work in the chain on a State station. Death is kinder than this sort of living. . . . My colleague has just returned from spending a week among the Ndobo towns, and his comment on what he there beheld was ' Death and decay in all around I see.'"

Tilkens, Lieutenant, officer of the *Force Publique.* His letters read in the Belgian House in July, 1903 ; cover 1897–1900. At the time he wrote them Tilkens was carrying out his duties as fixed by his superior officers. (*Vide* Sections I. and IV. Area : north - eastern region. *Domaine Privé.*)

Letter to Major Lenssens of the Belgian Army on July 20, 1898.

"The Chef de Poste of Buta announces the arrival of the steamer *Van der Kerkhove,* which is to be floated upon the Nile. He will require the colossal number of 1,500 carriers. Unhappy blacks ! I do not like to think of it. I ask myself, where I can find them. If the roads were good it might be different ; but they are barely cleared, crossed repeatedly by marshes, where many will find a certain death. Hunger and the fatigues of an eight days' march will account for many more. What blood this

61

transport had not caused to flow! Three times already have I been forced to make war upon chiefs who refuse to co-operate in the work. Unfortunately they are but poorly paid for such arduous labour—5d. worth of cowries for the upward journey, and a piece of American cloth for the homeward journey. If a chief refuses it is war, and that atrocious war—perfected weapons of destruction against spears and lances. . . . A native chief has just come to tell me, ' My village is a heap of ruins ; all my wives have been killed. Yet what can I do ? When I tell my people to carry the white man's goods they flee to the woods, and when your soldiers come to recruit I can give them no one because my people prefer to die of hunger in the woods rather than do transport work.' . . . Often am I compelled to put these unhappy chiefs in the chains, until some 100 or 200 carriers are obtained, which procures their liberation. Very often my soldiers find the villages deserted ; then they seize women and children and capture them."

To his mother in 1898 :

" Commandant Meeus, my District Commissioner, is about to return and Commandant Verstraeten, the friend of Major Lenssens, replaces him. It is he who inspected my station and who complimented me highly. He told me that the nature of his report would depend upon the quantity of rubber produced. When he left me he told me to employ myself actively in collecting rubber and from 360 kilos in September, my production rose to 1,500 kilos in October, and this month I trust it will be over 2,000 kilos. . . . By January I shall be making 4,000 kilos per month, which makes 500 francs profit above my salary. . . . I really am a lucky fellow, and if I play at rubber for two years I shall make 12,000 francs over and above my salary."

On January 26, 1899, Commandant Verstraeten wrote to the Governor-General :

" I draw the Government's attention to Lieutenants Tilkens, Landeghem, and Verslype. These agents have specially distinguished themselves in putting in train the exploitation of rubber. To them is due the surprising results obtained in the area allotted to their action."

Tilkens to Major Lenssens, May 12, 25, July 11, and August 10, 1899 :

" I expect a general uprising. I think I warned you of this, Major, in my last. The motive is always the same. The natives are tired of the existing *régime*—transport work, rubber collecting, furnishing live stock for whites and blacks. . . . For three months I have been fighting, with ten days' rest. . . . I have 152 prisoners. For two years I have been making war in this country, always accompanied by forty or fifty *Albinis*.[1] Yet I cannot say I have subjugated the people. . . . They prefer to die. . . . What can I do? I am paid to do my work, I am an instrument in the hands of my chiefs, and I obey the orders which discipline exacts."

Verstraeten was never punished. Nay, he has been promoted in the Belgian army which he continues to adorn.

Ruskin, of the Congo Balolo Mission. Declarations before Judicial Officer Rossi, April 12, 1902. Minutes taken down by Mr. Jeffery of the same mission, in shorthand. Confirmed before Commission of Inquiry, and accepted as correct, 1904. Published in 1904 by author. Area: A.B.I.R. concession ; central region (extracts) :

" In the early months of 1899 M—— had a large number of prisoners[2] at the factory. They were improperly fed and cared for and died at the rate of from three, five, and sometimes ten a day. They were dragged by a piece of *ngoji* tied to the foot out into the bush, and only a little earth and a few sticks thrown on top of them. Hands and feet were left sticking up and the stench was awful. . . . On July 18, 1899, four were released. An old man was found in the mission station. We gave him food and water which he ate ravenously, the director came up . . . and released one hundred and six prisoners. We saw them pass our station, living skeletons. Some were so much reduced that they had to be carried home. Among them were old greyheaded men and women. Many children were born in prison.

" They also seized Balua, the wife of Bontanga, and M. F—— had her flogged giving her two hundred *chicotte*. So severely was she dealt with that blood and urine flowed from her. She died shortly after. . . . One man had bad rubber ; M. G—— compelled him to lie on the ground and Ilunga, one of the sentries, gave the man *chicotte*. G—— then struck the man with the flat of a machet, and he jumped up. G—— drew his revolver and shot him through the leg. . . . M. F—— thought that his men were not strong enough and, therefore, could not compel the people to bring in what he considered sufficient rubber. Once when he was away his men stole some rubber, and for this he had them tied up right in the sun to stakes for a day and a night. Mrs. Cole (now Mrs. Harber) when passing on her way to the schools saw the men there from a distance. They were naked and without food and water all day, and so great was their agony that their tongues were hanging out."

---

[1] *E.g.*, soldiers armed with the *Albini* rifle.
[2] *E.g.*, hostages.

Red Rubber

Didier, French explorer attached to the Bourg de Bozas Expedition, passed through the Lado *enclave* in October, 1902, reports the neighbourhood of the Congo State Fort at Dufile " deserted by its former inhabitants." Along the whole course of the route the natives had fled " fearing the white man's impositions." (Area : north-eastern region ; *Domaine Privé*.)

Cromer, Earl of, reporting to British Government of the same region in 1903 (White Book, Africa, No. 1, 1904) says :

"The reason of all this (deserted condition of the country, oppression, etc.) is obvious enough. The Belgians are disliked, the people fly from them, and it is no wonder they should do so, for I am informed that the soldiers are allowed full liberty to plunder, that payments are rarely made for supplies. . . . I understand that no Belgian officer can move outside the settlements without a strong guard."

Grogan, independent English explorer, says of the whole eastern frontier [1] (*Domaine Privé*) :

"From the north of Lake Albert to Lake Mweru there is a perfect state of chaos. Whole districts are administered by incompetent officials, often non-commissioned officers, and the troops are the lowest type of natives, almost invariably cannibals. . . . The people were terrorised and living in marshes. . . . The Belgians have crossed the frontier, descended into the valley, shot down large numbers of natives—British subjects—driven off the young women and cattle, and actually tied up and burned the old women. I do not make these statements without having gone into the matter. . . . Every village has been burnt to the ground, and as I fled from the country I saw skeletons, skeletons everywhere ; and such postures, what tales of horror they told ! . . . Thus a tract of country about 3,000 square miles in extent has been depopulated and devastated. . . . This was the Congo Free State ! . . . When in Mboya the Balegga told me similar tales ; here I was repeatedly given accounts that tallied in all essentials, and further north the Wakoba made the same piteous complaints ; and I saw myself that a country well-populated and responsive to just treatment in Lugard's time is now practically a howling wilderness.

Baccari, Captain-Surgeon in the navy, royal Italian envoy to the Congo in regard to a bogus emigration scheme

---

[1] " From the Cape to Cairo," 1900.

The Deeds

fostered by the King Leopold to throw dust in the eyes of the Italian public. Passed through the eastern district (*Domaine Privé*) in 1903. Report suppressed by Italian Government ; a bald, very bald summary, only allowed to appear :—

> " As to the natives those nearest to the proposed Italian settlements are nearly all in revolt against the Belgians. Everywhere the blacks are terrorised and suspicious. . . . The natives have to be compelled to work, so we have all the ghastly scenes of the slave trade, the collar, the lash, and the press-gang."

Interviewed by the *Giornale d'Italia*, Captain Baccari stated that the :

> " Italian officers employed in the Congo were intended to be used in the enslavement of the natives, but that they had refused to carry out this design, and had in consequence become objects of persecution."

Many reports of the Italian officers employed in the Congo army were published by the Italian papers in 1905, covering their experiences chiefly in the Eastern district. Summing up these reports the *Corriere della Sera* says : " Slavery nominally established is rampant, cannibalism exists, and the sole desire of the native is, if possible, to flee from the white man." *Vide* also statement in Section IV.

Lloyd, A. B., independent English traveller, crossed the Congo from the Semliki to the ocean in 1899. (Area : north-eastern region, *Domaine Privé*.)

> " In the afternoon I was walking through the potato fields when I came upon sixty or a hundred women, all with hoes cultivating the ground, and close at hand a native soldier with a rifle across his shoulder mounting guard. I inquired where all the poor creatures had come from, and was told a sad story—alas ! not uncommon in the Belgian Free State. A Wakona chief had been told to do some work for the Belgians, and when he refused, soldiers were sent, and upon the least resistance the men were shot down and the women captured. It was a sad sight to behold these poor creatures driven like dogs here and there and kept hard at their toil from morning till night. One of the Belgian soldiers told me that there had been many killed, including the chief, and when I said what a terrible thing it was, he

Red Rubber

merely laughed and said, 'Washenzi Bevana' (they are only heathen)." [1]

Scrivener, A. E., of the British Baptist Missionary Society, traversed a tract 150 miles long, on foot, in the *Domaine de la Couronne* in July, August, and September, 1903. Allowed the author to make full use of his diary ; printed in full in the *West African Mail,* in 1905. It is very voluminous and the briefest summary here given :—

"In the afternoon we passed a ruined mud house, and were told that this had been a rubber post with soldiers in charge, but that since all the people had run away it had been given up. Later on we saw still more numerous sites where only recently thousands of people had been living. Cassava was still growing in the plantations, and bananas were rotting on the trees. . . . All as still as the grave. . . . A little further on we found another deserted rubber post. Just as the sun was setting we reached a large and imposing State post. . . . All round were plentiful signs of the former population. Later I heard from a white official that the remaining population did not number a hundred all told. . . . For hours we walked through a deserted country, though here and there on both sides were frequent signs of a recent population. . . . Three chiefs came in with all the adult members of their people, and altogether there were not three hundred. And this where not more than six or seven years previously there were at least three thousand ! It made one's heart heavy to listen to the tales of bloodshed and cruelty. . . . We passed through miles and miles of deserted sites, and on all sides were groves of palms, and bananas, and many other evidences of a big people. . . . A man bringing in rather under the proper amount of rubber, the white man flies into a rage and seizing a rifle from one of the guards shoots him dead on the spot. Men who had tried to run from the country and had been caught, were brought to the station and made to stand one behind the other and an *Albini* bullet sent through them. 'A pity to waste cartridges on such wretches.' . . . On M—— removing from the station, his successor nearly fainted on attempting to enter the station prison in which were numbers of poor wretches so reduced by starvation and the awful stench from weeks of accumulation of filth that they were not able to stand. . . . In due course we reached Ibali. There was hardly a sound building in the place. Why such dilapidation ? The commandant away on a trip likely to extend into three months, the sub-lieutenant

[1] "In Dwarf-land and Cannibal Country," 1899.

66

The Deeds

away in another direction on a punitive expedition. In other words the station must be neglected and rubber-hunting carried out with all vigour. I stayed here two days, and the one thing that impressed itself on me was the collection of rubber. I saw long files of men come, as at Mbongo, with their little baskets under their arms, saw them paid their milk-tin full of salt, and the two yards of calico flung at the head men ; saw their trembling timidity. . . . So much for my journey to the Lake (Lake Leopold II.). It has enlarged my knowledge of the country, and also, alas ! my knowledge of the awful deeds enacted in the mad haste to get rich. The Bulgarian atrocities might be considered as mildness itself when compared with what has been done here."

Bond, Charles, of the Congo Balolo Mission, in a letter published in December, 1903, says of the A.B.I.R. concession territory :—

"I have the evidence of a number of men working for us at the present time that at their town on the Bosombo River numbers of men have been killed outright, and others have died from having their hands cut off because they would not submit to demands."

Casement, Roger (see above). To give a summary of Consul Casement's report describing the condition of affairs observed by him in 1903 which would convey to the reader a just notion of its cumulative force, would be impossible without devoting to it more space than I can afford. The area affected is the river bank region on the main highway of "Leopoldian civilisation." Here are a few short summaries :—

A village of 240 people all told, compelled to produce one ton of "carefully prepared food stuffs" every week at a price far below the current figure. Other villages in much the same situation forced to carry their "tax" long distances. A group of villages whose population in 1887 was 5,000, now reduced to 500. Raids and slaughter for delay in paying food taxes (p. 26). Insufficiency of food accountable for much of the sickness prevalent (p. 28). Monstrous and illegal fines for shortage in food supplies, or rubber, impoverishing the people, and leading to general wretchedness and despair. Natives fleeing from the white man, where formerly they greeted him with open arms. Villages taxed in gum copal to an almost incredible extent. A group of villages working all the year round, and subject to the usual punishments for shortage, producing per town £300 *per annum* value in gum copal, receiving

Red Rubber

£10 *per annum* as a return ! A native of Montaka—a typical case—produces some £12 of gum copal *per annum,* and receives in exchange 1s. 4d. for his "entire year's work," the value of an adult fowl according to local prices? Mutilation and outrage frequent and habitual. Slavery forced upon the people—that is, selling relatives—in order to meet State demands. Women taken to hostage houses before the Consul's eyes. Their men-folk guilty of shortage in rubber, etc., etc.

I would earnestly beg every reader of this volume to spend 8½d. and write to Messrs. Harrison and Sons, St. Martin's Lane, for a copy of the Report (Africa, No. 1, 1904).

Berthier, Léon, Frenchman, visited the Upper River, and spent some time in the country (1899 to 1901). His diary was published by the Colonial Institute of Marseilles in 1902. (Area : river banks, north and central region, *Domaine Privé.*) Here are short extracts :—

"Belgian post of Imesse well constructed. The *Chef de Poste* is absent. He has gone to punish the village of M'Batchi, guilty of being a little late in paying the rubber tax. . . . A canoe full of Congo State soldiers returns from the pillage of M'Batchi. . . . Thirty killed, fifty wounded. . . . At three o'clock arrive at M'Batchi, the scene of the bloody punishment of the *Chef de Poste* at Imesse. Poor village. The *débris* of miserable huts. . . . One goes away humiliated and saddened from these scenes of desolation, filled with indescribable feelings."

Gilchrist, Somerville, of the Congo Balolo Mission, in a letter of protest to the Governor-General on the condition of the people of the Lolanga District, July, 1903. (Area : river banks and central region, *Domaine Privé.*)

Describes exorbitant fines and monstrous taxation levied upon these people by the State.

"Eight years ago there was a population in these towns of at least 5,000 people, compared with the 1,200 to-day. . . . The people themselves are literally starving to keep up these supplies."

There was the usual bogus inquiry which came to nothing.

Frame, W. B., of the British Baptist Missionary Society, in a letter to the author dated March 10, 1904, describes the state of the country as noted by him in a trip up-river in 1903 :—

The Deeds

"I am convinced that, with the exception of this very limited district (Lower Congo), and, perhaps, that of Stanley Falls, the title of 'Slave State' is very fitting to the *régime* that exists. . . . As I traversed the old caravan road to the Pool my eyes were opened. Crowds of people passed me every now and then, bearing heavy loads of *kwanga* (cassava puddings) for the State. Some were little girls of twelve years of age carrying eight and ten ; some were women converted into sweating beasts of burden, for besides the twelve *kwanga* on the head, they often had a baby on the back ; some were men and some were little boys. . . . What the State demands is that such and such a town shall bring in, say, 250 *kwanga* every fourth, eighth, or twelfth day, according to the distance. What it means to the people is nothing to the State, and the cry of the women, who have to grind from morning to night to provide and often to carry, is not heard by the State officer. The labour is forced. . . . The natives have no time for anything else. They are slaves. All up the river is the same thing. . . . At one place where crowds of people ought to have been on the beach we found the whole town had fled. Young and old, male and female, were hiding in the bush because the fish tax was not complete. . . . We visited a town near Lisali where the people had recently come from inland to escape the cruelties of the rubber tax."

Frame, W. B., Howell, John, Kempton, S. C., Kirkland, R. K., all missionaries of the British Baptist Society, were descending the Congo on the missionary steamer *Goodwill* when, on October 29, 1903, they came across, when turning a bend of the river, the following scene at the native village of Yandjali, where the steamer was wont to call for fuel :—

"The town was occupied by a party of Congo Government soldiers under two white officers. The four missionaries on board were horrified to see the native soldiers of the administration, under the very eyes of their officers, engaged in mutilating dead bodies of natives who had just been killed. Three native bodies were lying near the river's edge as the *Goodwill* put into the banks, and human limbs were lying within a few yards of the steamer as she sought to make fast. One of the slaughtered natives was a child. A State soldier was seen drawing away the legs and other portions of a human body. Another soldier was seen standing by a large native basket in which were the viscera of a human body. The missionaries were promptly ordered off the beach by the two officers presiding over this human shambles."

Red Rubber

Mr. Frame, in a letter to the author, confirms the accuracy of the above account :—

" Time can never wipe the barbarous scene from our memory. The mutilated dead, the mad rushing and firing of the soldiers let loose, and the hasty flight of the poor people hunted from their homes like wild beasts, made us sick at heart, and when we looked into the faces of our black crew we were ashamed, for were not these things done in the name of the State, and under the eyes of its white officers."

It is advisable to bear in mind that this incident occurred three years ago, on the *main pathway of "civilisation!"* Imagine what must take place in centres removed from prowling missionaries !

Williams, A. R., of the Christian Missionary Alliance of New York, and Mr. Hall, a West Indian missionary of good family, trained at the Calabar College, Kingston, Jamaica, attached to the Baptist Missionary Society of Boston, describe in letters to the author published in 1904, the impoverished condition of the natives of the Lower Congo, whose condition is one of Elysian bliss compared with their tortured and oppressed brethren in the vast upper region. " They live on, getting more impoverished every year," says Mr. Hall. " The soldiers," says Mr. Williams, " are a perfect terror to the whole place. They rape the women, clear the villages of live stock, and generally behave in the most oppressive manner."

De Lamothe, ex-Governor of French Congo, testifying before the Cotelle Commission held in Paris in 1900 to inquire into the working of the *concessionnaire* system, stated in reply to questions that thirty thousand natives had crossed from the Congo State into French territory owing to the ill-treatment meted out to them.

The American Memorial to Congress presented through Senator Morgan on April 19, 1904, contains long accounts from several American missionaries working in the Congo as to the state of affairs prevailing. It is always the same story. Here are some extracts. (Area : central region, *Domaine Privé.*)

Layton, A. E., reports on children forced to work for the State, and the system of hostages or prisoners to compel labour.

The Deeds

Dr. Lyon writes : " A close acquaintance with the conditions shows the cogency of the natives' contentions that they are no less than slaves to the State. And as slaves I have observed they must sometimes make bricks without straw, as when one must furnish fish nearly the year round, and he can catch fish only at certain seasons. Then one is forced to buy in other parts, paying in this way ten to forty times what will be received in return from the State Post. To meet these obligations one of the remaining members of a once large family had to pawn, *i.e.*, sell into slavery, a younger member of his family. ' The poor people of this section (Bolengi, near Coquilhatville) are broken-spirited and poverty-stricken by an arbitrary and oppressive system of taxation.' "

Billington, A. E., reports from Bwembu : " Men are first applied for, and if they do not present themselves, a soldier or soldiers are sent, who tie up the women or the chiefs until the workmen are forthcoming."

Clark, Joseph, reports : " I have seen men and women chained by the neck being driven by an armed soldier. . . . The native has no desire for the improvement of his surroundings. He will not make a good house or large gardens because it will give the State a greater hold on him. His wife refuses to become a mother because she will not be able to run away in case of attack. Twice this week the people of Ikoko have been rushing off to the bush to hide on the approach of a large canoe of soldiers."

And so on *ad infinitum et nauseam.*

Morrison, William (see above), 1898–1902. First accounts made public in 1900. Morrison sent a private personal appeal to King Leopold on October 21, 1899. (Area : south-western region, Kasai.)

Describes raiding by State officers and soldiers round Luebo ; efforts being made to compel the Baluba population of Luebo, consisting of several thousands, to remove to Luluabourg, the State station, five days distant " where they would have to work." In July, 1899, heard that a large body of Zappo-Zaps, a cannibal tribe, armed and utilised by the State to force rubber from the natives—as irregulars in fact—were forcing rubber tribute in the Bena Pianga country. Similar information reached Sheppard, Morrison's colleague, at a station nearer the scene of the disturbances. A number of the prominent chiefs of the region had been invited by the Zappo-Zaps to a conference and treacherously murdered. Sheppard went to the spot. He was received in a friendly way by the Zappo-Zaps. Saw many burnt villages. In the raiders' stockade where the slaughter had taken place Sheppard " saw and counted " eighty-one human hands slowly drying over a fire. Outside the stockade more than two score bodies he counted. Some of the flesh had been carved off and eaten. Some of the Zappo-Zaps were armed with the *Albini.*

On May 5, 1903, Morrison addressed a public meeting convened by the Aborigines Protection Society, and gave a number of details of the reign of terror in June, July, and August, 1902, in his district, chiefly dealing with man-hunting by State officers and troops to recruit soldiers.

Gilchrist, Sommerville (see above), in comments on the Report of the Commission of Inquiry. Published in C. R. A. organ, December, 1905. (Area : river banks, central region, *Domaine Privé.*) Gives in abundant detail effects of State " taxes " upon the people covering many years.

" With regard to the causes of depopulation in the Lolanga district where I have lived for fourteen years I emphatically affirm that for one who has died of sleeping sickness there have been twenty deaths due to lung and intestinal diseases ; and for one death due to smallpox, there have been forty due to lung and intestinal troubles. . . . The lung and intestinal troubles are without doubt due, in a very large proportion of the cases, to exposure involved in collecting the taxes, and in hiding from the soldiers in the forest, as well as the miserable huts the natives now live in, because they have neither time nor heart to build better. And all the diseases mentioned with others find ready victims in the half-fed people, and produce their fell work with the greater rapidity and effect. . . . So strong is the passion for rubber and copal that the companies and the State on the various rivers are continually having disputes about their respective boundaries, and overlapping in what they claim to be each other's territory in the interior between the tributaries and the main Congo. It was one of the commonest occupations of the *Commissaires* to be settling these disputes. And it was a very frequent cause of bloody affrays between the natives serving the various companies or State—the trespassing on each other's parts of the forest while out gathering the rubber to meet the respective demands made upon them."

Whitehead, John, of the British Baptist Missionary Society, testified before the Commission of Inquiry on the history of his district (Lukolela). Evidence suppressed ; part published in the C. R. A. organ for December, 1905.

Mr. Whitehead's statement traces the history of the district from 1891 to 1905. First food taxes, then rubber taxes *and* food taxes.

The Deeds

"Until then there had been no demand for rubber. When that demand was made and the people objected, an expedition went inland about the end of 1901. The prowess of the State force was exhibited, chiefs killed, villages destroyed, and the payment of the tax enforced." Gives depositions of chiefs and much evidence. Protesting to the Governor-General in a letter dated April 19, 1904, he calls attention to the system prevailing forcing lads to "sign on" for twelve years as "labourers."

Ruskin, Mrs., of the Congo Balolo Mission in comment upon the Report of the Commission of Inquiry. Published in C. R. A. organ for December, 1905. She describes the beginning of the rubber traffic in the A.B.I.R. concession :—

"It is interesting to hear the Bongandanga people tell of the beginning of the rubber trade. How wonderful they thought it was that the white man should want rubber, and be willing to pay for it [that was in the days antecedent to the decree of 1891. —AUTHOR]. How they almost fought for the baskets in order to bring them in and obtain the offered riches. But they say, 'We did not know, we never understood what it would become in the future.' Now it is looked upon as the equivalent of death ; they do not complain so much of want of payment, as that there is no rest from the work, and no end to it except death. . . . I have known women to be taken (as hostages) without any regard to their condition, during pregnancy or the period of lactation. They were made to work in the sun at grass work or weeding ; some were confined in the common prison or hostage house without any privacy, and obliged to be at work again in a few days with their babies at their backs. The hostage house was described to me by a woman who had been imprisoned there ; and the details would be unprintable. . . . Only two epidemics of smallpox have been known in the memory of living natives at Bongandanga, one in 1901, and the other fifteen or twenty years before. Sleeping sickness was absolutely unknown until about four years ago. The people are easy victims to it, because of lack of food and rest, and exposure to damp, rain, and cold. Also they are fast losing any desire to live, and therefore do not try to throw off the terrible lethargy which so soon overcomes them."

Messrs. Gilchrist, Weeks, and other missionaries are unanimous in describing the ravages of diseases—sleeping sickness, intestinal trouble, pneumonia, etc., to the wretched condition of the people owing to the grinding tyranny under which they live, to supply King Leopold and his financiers with revenues, and his soldiers and their crowd of retainers with food-stuffs.

Lower, Mr. and Mrs., of the Congo Balolo Mission at Ikau. A.B.I.R. concession. Described to the Commission of Inquiry in 1904 innumerable outrages perpetrated upon the natives in 1902 and 1903. Evidence suppressed. Published by the C. R. A. last year. Summary :—

Natives flogged and shot for shortage in rubber. Names, dates, etc., given in great detail. They are all specific cases, of which this is a type : " Went to report murder of his mother by sentries . . . cruelly treated by sentries in consequence. . . . Beaten by sentries during a two weeks' stay in prison ; sent back to village ; died two days later." Men, women, and children given in the lists of the murdered—punishment for delay in rubber production.

Harris, J. H. ; Mrs. Harris ; Padfield, Charles ; Stannard, Edgar, all testified before Commission of Inquiry of atrocities and general oppression and ill-treatment antecedent to 1904. Evidence suppressed, published in summarised form by C. R. A., 1905.

RECORDS IN 1904 AND 1905.

1904 was chiefly remarkable for the voluminous and appalling accounts sent home by the missionaries on the A.B.I.R. concession, Messrs. John Harris, Herbert Frost, Edgar Stannard, and Charles Padfield—all of the Congo Balolo Mission. Voluminous, detailed, and terrible narratives from the first three named of these gentlemen were published in the C. R. A. organ for August, 1904, and for many months to come information was regularly supplied by them to the author, and supplied by the author to the world's Press. The public is sufficiently familiar with these reports—which have, moreover, been confirmed by the Report of the Commission of Inquiry—to absolve me from quoting from them. It suffices to say that they are concerned exclusively with the atrocities committed by the A.B.I.R. "Company" in forcing rubber from the natives of the country. At the close of 1905 the Commission of Inquiry began its ascent of the upper river, and Messrs. Billington,

The Deeds

Clark, Grenfell, Scrivener, Gilchrist, Mr. and Mrs. Harris, Stannard, Ruskin, Gamman, Mr. and Mrs. Lower, Mr. Padfield, and Weeks testified before it. Their evidence was suppressed; but summaries, in some cases lengthy summaries, were published in 1905 by the Congo Reform Association.[1] On August 4, 1905, Sir Charles Dilke again brought the Congo question forward on the Foreign Office vote. Earl Percy, replying for the then Government, stated that Consul Mackie was not allowed to see the depositions of the witnesses, but that he "had sent home extracts from some of the evidence given at the later sittings." This report of Consul Mackie's was suppressed by the British Government, and every attempt to have it produced has hitherto failed; an incident which is curious to say the least.

Further evidence was supplied in the course of 1904 from other regions. Writing to the author on May 17, Mr. Weeks gave details of the treatment of three prominent chiefs of his district in connection with incidents arising out of the food taxes. Two or three chiefs were placed "in the chains," and died in them from ill-treatment after a few weeks' incarceration. The third was a fortnight "in the chains," and was fined £10 because his village had failed to trap a bush pig, part of the fortnightly tax levied by the adjoining Government station. On May 27th Mr. Scrivener, in a letter to the author, described another journey into the *Domaine de la Couronne*, peopled by some wretched survivors of the rubber hunting orgies in the Lake district. He gave abundant details (as usual) of men and women shot, women tied up and thrown into the river, etc. "Then ensued a series of massacres which would be incredible were it not for so much of a like character that has been proved only too true. The district is now a waste."

Mr. Whiteside, of the Congo Balolo Mission, sent a long letter to the *Belfast News* (21st October), describing the condition of the Lolanga towns.

---

[1] "Evidence before the Congo Commission of Inquiry." Price 2d. Four editions were published.

Red Rubber

Much Italian evidence was produced in 1905; chiefly from the Eastern District, and led to stormy scenes in the Italian Chamber.

A long letter to the author from a missionary correspondent in the Katanga district also came to hand. Unhappily the writer was terrified—not unnaturally from the details given—lest his name should appear; which deprives his evidence of some of its weight in the public estimation. The letter was published in the C. R. A. organ for September, 1904. It describes the usual proceedings. Girls raped and carried off by King Leopold's officials; chiefs degraded and shot; forced labour; oppression and cruelty rampant.

A further memorial to Congress from the American Missionary Societies, dated January 16, 1905, contains more evidence from American missionaries.

Mr. Charles H. Harvey reports :—

> "The dreadful form of rubber collecting has, among other evils, introduced a form of slavery of the worst possible kind. No man's time, liberty, property, person, wife, or child is his own. His position is worse than that of the sheep or goats of the white man. . . . Even the dreadful horrors of the 'middle passage' are completely put in the shade by deliberate, demon-like acts of atrocity."

Mr. H. W. Kirby reports :—

> "I have just returned to Lukunga after visiting our 15 mission stations. The population is decreasing, and during the last twenty years has decreased very rapidly." The first cause of the decrease he attributes to "Fighting with the State." He says : "The further away from publicity the greater the atrocities. I have heard much. I could tell much, but you know enough. A white officer forcing a native to drink from the water closet; shooting down hand-cuffed men ; the employment of fierce cannibal soldiers that terrorise the people ; shooting down twenty men to pay for a lost dog."

The judgment of the Boma Appeal Court in the Caudron case was published by the Congo Reform Association in May, 1904. It showed the state of affairs prevailing in the territories of the Anversoise Trust to be similar in all respects to that which obtained when Lacroix and his coadjutors were performing their civilising deeds; and it showed the complicity of the Supreme Executive in these deeds. (*Vide* Section IV.)

Letters from the Kasai to the author disclosed further risings of the natives against the rubber ·demands made upon them. These risings have since assumed larger proportions.

Mr. T. Ackermann, a Swiss, described in a report sent to Herr Ludwig Deuss (a highly respected merchant of Hamburg, who has laboured manfully in Germany for the cause of Congo reform), atrocities committed in 1902 and 1903 at Flambi, Fakisuli, etc. (Lomami district). Each case stated in great detail, and some of them peculiarly horrible :

> "If the chief does not bring the stipulated number of baskets, soldiers are sent out, and the people are killed without mercy. As proof, parts of the body are brought to the factory. How often have I watched heads and hands being carried into the factory."

Herr Duess sent a copy of the report to the German Government, and I transmitted a copy to the British and American Governments. Published, minus the names of individuals, in the *West African Mail*, March 3, 1905.

1905 was notable also for the publication of confidential circulars and regulations issued by the agents of the A.B.I.R. Society "Company" to their agents; proving the complicity of the Home Administration in the taking of hostages and other concomitant of the rubber slave-trade.

EVIDENCE TO HAND SINCE THE COMMISSION OF INQUIRY VISITED THE COUNTRY.

No sooner was the back of the Commission of Inquiry turned than the *régime* they had described as wholly "illegal" and atrocious was again in full swing, and continues to-day all over the Congo, as it must do, of course, just as long as England and Europe allow it. King Leopold's claim to the land, its products, and its people have not been abrogated, but declared afresh ; hence the system under which those claims are upheld has not altered one iota, except, for the worse.

The latest information may be briefly summarised. Of course, and unhappily, it only touches a tiny fringe of the vast Congo. For the rest, where there are no informants, the student is thrown back for positive evidence upon the admissions of the Belgian papers. These testify to a grave rising in the Ituri region, where "gold" has recently been discovered. Private information received by the author is to the effect that three months ago troops were concentrating from all sides at Stanley Falls to deal with this rising. French advices from the Congo state that King Leopold's troops have been repulsed with the loss of two officers and 80 men. Belgian papers tell us that 500 soldiers are being despatched. Those papers also admit risings on the Kasai, the Kwango, and the Busira. In short, the same situation obtains as has existed since the Decree of 1891, which inaugurated the rubber slave-trade.

*　　　*　　　*　　　*　　　*

On January 17, 1905, Mr. Harris writes to the Vice-Governor General—who committed suicide[1] when the Commission returned to Boma from their investigations—giving a long list of atrocities perpetrated in the Nsongo Mboyo district which he had just visited ; also the names of seventy-three adults (including many women) and a number of children killed by sentries in that district. On April 4th Mr. Stannard writes to the author stating that the Director of the A.B.I.R. had repudiated the Commission's findings, and intends to continue as before. Mr. Harris writes to the District Commissioner on April 10th, pointing out a recrudescence of the rubber slave-trade, giving details of raids by sentries upon villages. Vain protests ! Matters go on in the old way. Mr. Stannard, writing to the author in the same month, says, "the devil's work is in full swing again." Further letters from Harris to the District Commissioner

---

[1] The Senior Governor-General is just now reposing in Brussels amid bowers of orchids and roses. *Vide* a recent interview.

The Deeds

describing the raiding of Bolumboloko, massacre, hostage taking, rape, and so on.

All last year, and during the present year, up to a few days ago, the author, as Hon. Secretary of the Congo Reform Association, has been engaged in sending reports to the Foreign Office,[1] proving the prevalence of the same condition of things, and not only from the A.B.I.R. district ; but from the river banks in the *Domaine Privé*. The journey of Mr. Whiteside and Mr. Stannard in the Upper Lomako will be fresh in the public mind. There have been visits of " High Commissioners," " Inspectors," and the Governor-General, since the Commission left the Congo. The only result has been an aggravation of existing ills ; the one new feature, the persecution of the missionaries in a determined effort to brow-beat them into silence. Massacre, outrage, rapine, the river of blood flows on, and the river of gold flows in.

$$* \qquad * \qquad * \qquad * \qquad *$$

Since the above was written, evidence has continued to accumulate. The *Times* publishes a long letter from Mr. Freshfield, covering extracts of letters received by him from the British and Italian expedition now exploring Ruwenzori, and showing oppression, misrule, and brutality in the Semliki region (N.E. area : *Domaine Privé*). A considerable amount of information has reached me from the Tanganyika region (Katanga Trust) proving beyond doubt the existence, with the knowledge and complicity of the officials, of the old-fashioned slave-trade by Arabised chiefs protected by the Authorities. In the name of humanity, will not the German Government disclose the reports it has received from its officials in East Africa on this subject ?

Mr. Charles Bond (see above) sends detailed reports of an aggravation of the food taxes round Lolanga since the Governor-General's visit.

---

[1] All the correspondence exchanged between the Foreign Office and the Congo Reform Association is sent to the public press, and published in full month by month in the official organ of the Association.

SECTION III

IS THERE A REDEEMING
FEATURE?

I

THE ARAB AND THE LIQUOR TRAFFIC

"The Free State did not flinch before its perilous task (the destruction of the Arab power), and it has reaped the fruits of its energy."—DESCAMPS, *New Africa.*

"The suppression of the liquor traffic with the suppression of the slave trade is the finest title to glory which the Congo State possesses."—*Report of the Congo Commission of Inquiry.*

WHAT in the face of this history can be urged on behalf of the Congo Administration which shall be held to extenuate in any essential respect the havoc it has wrought?

In an interesting article which appeared in the *Quarterly Review* for January last, and whose authorship entitles it to the most careful attention, it is suggested—after a generous acknowledgment of the present writer's justification for his charges—that I have "perhaps stuck too exclusively to one side of the picture," that I have been disinclined to admit a "redeeming feature."

That criticism struck me very much.

I had never thought that there was a redeeming feature which could be urged in the same breath with deeds too infamous to be forgiven by mercy itself. I had never realised sufficiently until I saw that article that the matter was one of debate. I have never until this day attempted to argue it. If I do so now I beg the reader to believe that it is wholly from an impersonal point of view. If the Congo Administration has any virtues let them be set forth ; by all means let their claims be proclaimed and the foundations upon which they rest subjected to analysis.

What, then, is the "other side of the picture"? What is its relative value to the side we have gazed upon?

The Congo Administration claims to have suppressed the

83

Red Rubber

slave-raiding carried on by half-caste Arabs [1] in a portion of the Congo Basin about one-fifth the size of the territories over which it now asserts dominion.

The Congo Administration claims to have prohibited the liquor traffic in its territories.

The Congo Administration claims to have built railways, put up the telegraph and telephone in certain districts, placed steamers on the upper river, built a large number of "fine stations," and in this manner established "civilisation" in the heart of Africa.

The Congo Administration claims to have introduced a regular system of "Justice" in its territories.

Travellers have borne witness to the good treatment of the natives in specific areas.

That, I think, fairly covers the ground.

Some of these assertions are true : some are partly true and partly false. Some are altogether false. Even were they all literally true and could bear the test of examination, could they palliate, much less excuse the wrong-doing of the past fifteen years?

The Congo Administration extirpated the Arab slave dealers. It did.[2] The policy pursued by these semi-barbarians was atrocious. But was it so atrocious as the civilised barbarism which has replaced it? If not, what becomes of the virtues attributed by the Congo Administration to itself as a consequence of its action?

If you knock down a foot-pad who is ill-treating some one, and after having driven the aggressor away, proceed to deal more severely with his victim, what claim have you to righteousness?

A British officer—Major A. St. H. Gibbons—who has

---

[1] The Arabs never got further West than the head waters of the Maringa. It was the Congo State Administration itself which brought them as far West as Stanley Falls. Tippoo Tib was King Leopold's first governor of the Upper Congo. That was before the struggle for political supremacy and the ivory markets, which the Arabs possessed, began.

[2] I thought it had completely when I wrote this sentence. In point of fact, documents which have only just now reached me, prove that the old-fashioned slave-trade is still rife west of Tanganyika (see p. 79).

travelled through the region where these half-caste Arabs formerly held sway, and whose references to Congolese administrative methods have been in some respects so impartial that King Leopold's Press Bureau has quoted him in its publications [1] as a friend and defender, has written in this respect.[2] "To say that the status and lot of the native population has been in any way improved by the Belgian occupation seems to me more than doubtful." Remember that the above passage refers to that part of the Congo where the Administration claims to have conferred untold blessings upon the natives by delivering them from Arab tyranny. Major Gibbons continues : " Under Arab influence the freedom of organised native communities was not interfered with. These people came to trade—to give and take, not to take only. Morally speaking I will content myself here with the bare assertion that the natives are not the gainers by the Belgian occupation." What a tremendous indictment of the Congolese position as regards the Arab contention in these few lines ! The Arab did not *take only.* The Congolese official does, and the natives " are not the gainers " under the change. This condemnation comes with added force when read with the accounts issued by the Press Bureau relating to the treatment of the natives under Arab rule. If they are worse off *now*, what, in the light of those accounts, must their condition be ?

No man is probably more competent than Dr. Hinde, who served with the Congo forces in the Arab campaign, to speak of the characteristics of their occupation before its downfall, and passages from his famous book are also quoted by the Press Bureau in substantiation of the claim to virtue. What is the verdict of Dr. Hinde ? " Despite," he writes, " their slave-raiding propensities during the forty years of their dominion, the Arabs had converted the Manyema and Maleba countries into some of the most prosperous in Central Africa." The military and other operations conducted by the Congo Administration on its eastern frontiers

---

[1] For the matter of that quite unjustly. (As he has himself pointed out in a letter to the *Times*.)
[2] "Africa from South to North," 1904.

Red Rubber

have necessitated the head-carriage over the great caravan routes, formerly utilised by the Arabs to convey their ivory to the East coast, of a gigantic mass of stores of all kinds. One of those great trade routes, that leading to the western shores of Lake Tanganyika, crosses the heart of the Manyema country mentioned by Dr. Hinde as one of the most prosperous, under Arab rule, in Central Africa.

What does the Report of King Leopold's own Commission tell us on the present condition of the native peoples in the territories traversed by this route? It tells us that the native peoples are " exhausted " through the demands made upon them for head-carriage in the transport of Government material, and are threatened with " partial destruction."

Captain Baccari, the King of Italy's envoy, travelled through that region three years ago.

What has he placed on record? " We have all the ghastly scenes of the slave trade, the collar, the lash, and press-gang." A lieutenant in the Italian army, whose official military records I have seen, and of whose *bonâ fides* I have personally assured myself, has recently returned to Italy after spending nearly three years in this—the Eastern Province of the " Congo Free State." Like so many of his compatriots he entered King Leopold's African army without the faintest idea of its habitual tasks, or of the nature of the Congo Administration itself.[1] He writes :

"The caravan road between Kasongo and Tanganyika is strewn with corpses of carriers, exactly as in the time of the Arab slave trade. The carriers, weakened, ill, insufficiently fed, fall literally by hundreds; and in the evening, when there happens to be a little wind, the odour of bodies in decomposition is everywhere noticeable, to such an extent, indeed, that the Italian officers have given it a name—' Manyema perfume.' "

After fifteen years of " moral and material regeneration " *à la Leopold*—" Manyema perfume " !

---

[1] The Italian Government, owing to the protests of its officers on the Congo, has prohibited any further recruitment for the Congo army even among officers on the retired list. None will be allowed to renew their contracts. In twelve months from now there will not be a single Italian officer on the Congo.

The Arab and the Liquor Traffic

Where is the "redeeming feature" here?

One might add a very great deal more in this connection, on the ethics of Arab *versus* Leopoldian slave raiding and trading. One could point to the fact that a brisk trade in slaves is carried on to this day by the revolted soldiery of the Congo State, through territory which the Congo Administration professes to control, with the Bihean caravaneers from inland Angola. One could point to the testimony of Italian officers to the effect that in the Arabised villages of a portion of the Eastern Provinces "the old markets for women slaves exist to-day as they did before," and that the inmates of the harems of Congo officers in that province have been bought and sold. One could point, *inter alia*, to Consul Casement's Report and to the evidence placed before the Congo Commission of Inquiry showing that the monstrous demands for food-stuffs levied upon the natives in certain districts under direct administrative influence, compel the wretched people to sell their relatives into slavery in order to meet those demands.[1] One could recall—as I have done—those official circulars signed by the supreme Executive, and torn from the abysmal and secret darkness of Congo infamy, after many years, by Monsieur Vandervelde, the Belgian Labour Leader, fixing a bonus payable to officials for every man captured and forced into the Congo army and military camps, so much per head for a man of a certain stature, so much for every youth, so much "per male child." One could assert and demonstrate abundantly that the raids upon villages by Congo officials and troops, to seize recruits and labourers : that the raids upon villages by Congo officials and troops to capture women—"delicate operations . . . to seize hostages," as the Report of the Commission of Inquiry puts it, to punish and terrorise communities short in their supply of rubber, raids in the course of which massacres wholesale and atrocities unspeakable are the habitual accompaniments, constitute proceedings indistinguishable from the raiding of Arab bands. One could prove—did not one feel that the reader is already sick with proof—

[1] Africa No. 1, 1904. (White Book.)

Red Rubber

that the "Congo Free State" in its basic claims, practices, and methods is primarily a huge slave-owning and slave-raiding corporation, and that compared with the cold diabolicism of its policy, Arab excesses extending over an infinitely smaller area were tame.

The slave-raiding, slave-dealing Arab was, at least, constructive. He destroyed, but to build again. He was a coloniser—a ruthless one, but still a coloniser ; witness the huge centres of economical activity, of agricultural production he created. He belonged to the land ; he had permanent interests in it. To have played the *rôle* of mere destroyer would have been to make waste of his habitation and his substance.

But his successors, wielding absolute power in the country, are not attached to the soil. The objects of their employers in Europe are purely financial and foreign to Africa. Those employers seek a rapid accumulation of riches, and they spend those riches out of Africa. Africa—the people of Africa—play no part in the ends to which those riches are put. For the preservation of the races of Central Africa it would have been better if Islam—which, as the leading authorities on Africa, British and French admit, breeds union for mutual aid among the black peoples—had thrown deep and abiding roots among the Bantu races of the eastern section of the Congo Basin. It would have given them that co-operation and adhesion by which alone they could have withstood the ravages of the special compound of slavery and "regeneration" patented by King Leopold in the name of Christianity. Civilisation went frantic over the cruelty of the uncultured Arab half-caste. It has allowed the cultured European to impose upon an infinitely greater number of human beings a yoke more unbearable than the Arab laid.

And that yoke remains.

* * * * *

From the Arab to the gin bottle and the demi-john of rum. The Congo Administration claims to have prohibited the liquor traffic in the Upper Congo. The claim is untenable. The Act of Berlin, it was, which

88

formally prohibited [1] the importation of alcohol into the Upper Congo just as it prohibited it in Northern Nigeria. The Act of Berlin did not prohibit the import of liquor into the Lower Congo, and the Congo Administration has not suppressed it there, nor put on duties as high as in some other West African Dependencies. The two foremost Belgian authorities on the Congo question—Mr. A. J. Wauters, Editor of *Le Mouvement Géographique*, and Professor Cattier, of the Brussels University—pointed this out soon after the publication of the Report of the Commission of Inquiry, in which the Commissioners are made to say that the Congo Administration deserves the thanks of the civilised world for sternly waving aside the temptation of paying its labour with gin. As that fine humanitarian and excellent wit—a rare combination—*grand chasseur devant l'eéternel*, Pierre Mille, remarks in his and Challaye's " *Les deux Congos* " :

" It is perfectly true that the Congo State does not pay the natives with a drink of brandy : it does not pay them at all ! It is excessive to praise it *even for that*, because the Berlin Act explicitly forbids the import of alcohol ! But no doubt the Commissioners, seeing that the Congo State had violated all the other clauses of the Act, were amazed at its having respected this one."

Apart from the inaccuracy of the claim historically considered, the fusel oil of hypocrisy is present in larger proportions here than in all or nearly all the other philanthropic protestations of the Congo Administration. This is not the place to discuss the African liquor traffic with any thoroughness. Personally I have written against it very

---

[1] It may be argued that the Congo Administration has violated other clauses of the Act. So it has, of course, but always by a subterfuge. Thus it has suppressed commerce by appropriating the elements, which, in Central Africa, constitute it. But it claims that those elements are *in esse* the property of the Administration, and that trade is perfectly free . . . in other things ! But by no conceivable ingenuity could it have declared that a bottle of gin was, really, a bottle of eau-de-Cologne : to admit of its importation would have been too patent a violation for the most subtle of jurists to explain away.

strongly. But the more one studies the accessible data, and the brighter the light which is thrown upon the various factors concerned, the more is the problem of the liquor traffic in Africa as in Europe seen to bristle with complications and difficulties. And without being converted thereby, one is impressed with the character and the weight of conviction of some of those [1] who have opposed the general view as to the positive hurtful effects European imported liquor has upon the primitive swamp-and-forest-dwelling communities of West Africa ; the more one is inclined to the belief that the true lines of reform are in the direction of improved quality, and progressive rises in customs duty whenever the import is seen in a given period to average out above its normal and virtually stationary figure.

Be that as it may, the attempts of the Congo Administration to wash away its sins by dragging in (on an historically false issue to begin with) the liquor traffic argument, can only fill the mind of an ordinary person who knows something of the facts with disgust. It is better, it seems, for the " regeneration " of the native that he should be subjected to all the Congo Administration subjects him to, rather than be allowed to spend a portion of his earnings in the luxury of a drink. He has been robbed of all he possesses which is marketable against European or American merchandise. He can buy nothing, neither drink to drown in temporary oblivion his misery, nor aught else, for he owns nothing with which to buy, and his labour belongs to King Leopold. And the Administration which has robbed him calls heaven to witness that it has forced him, with moral and material suasion, to take the pledge. Similarly might the highwayman justify the rifling of his victim's pockets lest the latter were tempted to spend their contents on liquor at the nearest inn, and by the same process of reasoning the highwayman could claim superior virtue in knocking his victim on the head as the best means of placing him, for ever, out of the reach of temptation.

---

[1] Mary Kingsley and Sir William Macgregor, for example.

II

PUBLIC WORKS AND THE PRICE THEREOF

"What does the native receive in return for all this taxation?
I know of absolutely no way in which he is benefited. Some
point to the telegraph. In what way does the telegraph benefit
the native? Those who live near the line have to keep the road
clear for nothing, and in tropical Africa that is not an easy task.
Others point to the scores of steamers running on the Upper
Congo. In what way do they benefit the native? Here and
there along the river natives are forced to supply large quantities
of firewood for an inadequate remuneration. Others, again, point
to well-built State stations. In what way do they benefit the
native? They were largely built and are now largely maintained
by forced labour. Then others point to the railway. It is a
splendid achievement of engineering skill and pays large dividends to shareholders, but in what way does it benefit the
thousands of natives on the Upper Congo?"—J. H. WEEKS, for
twenty-five years a missionary in the Upper Congo, in a letter to
the author, dated Monsembe, December 24, 1903.

I COME to the third claim. The Congo Administration
has undertaken the construction of public works and
buildings. "Elegant"[1] stations have been erected along
the banks of the upper river. That is quite true. No
one has ever denied it. Some of the public edifices at
Boma and Matadi on the lower river are quite as
substantial as those which are to be met with in other
administrative centres of the West Coast of Africa. But
who has paid for their erection? The Congo native.

---

[1] *Vide* Report of the Commission of Inquiry.

Red Rubber

Whose labour is it which has reared them from the ground?
The labour of the Congo native. Whom do they benefit
now that they are there?

The Congo native? The Congo native who is "entitled
to nothing"?[1] The Congo native who owns neither his
land, nor the fruits of the soil (which he alone can gather),
nor his labour?

If the Congo native does not benefit from the existence
of these fine buildings which his labour has constructed and
paid for; if their existence merely facilitates the plunder
of his country and the exploitation of his person by the
occupants of them, in what sense can their construction be
claimed as evidence of "civilisation"?

To maintain such a thing would be to make use of an
argument which no longer passes muster in the world. It
is out of date by two thousand years.

Go *behind* those fine stations, those camps of military
instruction, those Government-run plantations. Go *behind*
them into the forest and the bush. Mingle with the people
of the land. Witness their abiding desolation, their daily
griefs. Wander among ruined homes and poverty-stricken
hamlets, where once flourished prosperity and ease. Look
how the grass almost conceals the village paths once so
clear and clean; weeds overhanging the now crumbling
huts; sud invading the river frontage once filled with
cassava steeping-pits—that sud where the mosquito and the
tsetse love to breed, the purveyors respectively of malaria
and sleeping sickness, whose dread ravages sweep increasingly
through the land, finding ready victims in a broken-spirited
and ill-nourished people, broken by long years of grinding
tyranny, ill-nourished through the workings of a system
which demands for its multitude of agents the staple food-
stuffs of the country. Where are the stores of brass rods,
the numerous live-stock which were once the pride and
wealth of these primitive communities? Arbitrarily seized,
the Commission of Inquiry is fain to admit, as it records
the "incontestable impoverishment of the villages." Where
are the native industries which once gave pleasure and

---

[1] M. Smet de Naeyer, the Belgian Premier.

occupation to these people—iron-ware, brass-ware,[1] rude pottery, basket-making? They have "decayed," says the report of the Commission—decayed, as everything worth preservation has decayed and withered beneath the breath of Leopoldian civilisation. "It is hard to tell how these people live." [2]

See these men in whom the very manhood seems stamped out dragging themselves back from the bush at the day's end after a weary search through partly submerged forest, knee-deep, waist-deep in fœtid swamp, for the accursed juice of the rubber vine, that vine which they must find and tap in all seasons, in all weathers, whether the sap is rising or falling, always, ever, day after day the year round until death in some form—by violence, exhaustion, exposure, or disease, or mere weariness and sorrow—closes the term of an everlasting and—to them—mysterious visitation. See them at night in the forest, far from home, wife, and children, their interminable search not yet over, huddled together shivering under a few palm-leaves with a scrap of fire in their midst. The nights are cold in the equatorial forest. The rain invades their scanty shelter, and the night-wind chills their naked bodies racked with rheumatism and fevers, their minds a prey to superstitious fears in the impenetrable gloom made by the giant trees and matted creepers through which the sun never pierces, where malignant spirits are abroad—exposed, unarmed and helpless, to the attack of some roving leopard.

What thoughts are theirs! In the distant village wives and children live at the mercy of the capriciousness, cruelty, and lust of the armed ruffians set there by the white man : men fierce, all-powerful, speaking another tongue, tribal enemies perchance, or maybe the worst malefactors in the community, specially selected for that very reason as the most fitting instruments of oppression : men whose lightest word is law, who have but to lift a finger—they and their

---

[1] If you want to see the high level of art to which some of the Congo races can rise, pay a visit to the entrance hall of the Constitutional Club, London, and look at the collection of beautiful spears, battle-axes, and knives hanging on the walls.

[2] *Vide* Consul Casement's report.

Red Rubber

bodyguard of retainers—and death or torture rewards protest against the violation of the sanctuaries of sex, against the rape of the newly-married wife, against bestialities [1] foul and nameless, exotics introduced by the white man's "civilisation" and copied by his servants in the general, purposeful, satanic *crushing* of body, soul, and spirit in a people—crushing so complete, so thorough, so continuous, that the capacity of resisting aught, however vile, slowly perishes.

Out there in the forest, the broken man through the long and terrifying watches of the night—what is his vista in life ? Unending labour at the muzzle of the *Albini* or the cap-gun : no pause, no rest. At the utmost if his fortnightly toll of rubber is sufficient, if leaves and dirt have not mingled in too great proportion with the juice, he may find that he has four or five days a month to spend among his household. If so he will be lucky, for the vines are ever more difficult to find, the distance to travel from his village greater ; then the rubber must be taken to the white man's fine station, and any number of delays may occur before the rubber-worker can leave that station for his home. Four or five days' freedom per month—that is the very *maximum* he can expect. Five days to look after his own affairs, to be with his family, and always under the shadow of the sentry's rifle. But how often in the year will such good fortune attend him ? Shortage on one occasion only will entail the lash, or the chain and detention ; worse, perhaps, if the white man has a fever or an enlarged spleen that day. And if he flinches ? If, starting from an uneasy sleep there in the forest, when shapes growing out of the darkness proclaim the rising of another day, he wakens to the knowledge that his basket is but half full and that he must begin his homeward two-days' march betimes, not to miss the roll-call, his heart fails him and he turns his face away, plunging further into the forest, fleeing from his tormentors, seeking only one thing blindly, to get away from his life and all that it means—what will happen ?

---

[1] Sodomy, publicly forced upon chiefs or influential head-men whom it was necessary to humiliate in the eyes of their people, has been resorted to in certain territories at the point of the sentry's gun. The practice is unknown among the natives.

Public Works and the Price Thereof

Well enough he knows. Has he not seen the process with his own eyes? Father, mother, or wife will pay for his backsliding in the hostage-house. And whither shall he flee? The forest encompasses him on every side, the forest with its privations by day, its horrors by night. There he must live seeking such nourishment as roots and berries will afford. Shall he gain some other village in the hope that it may be a friendly one? But there will the sentry be also, and his doom as a " deserter " is sure.

$$*\qquad*\qquad*\qquad*\qquad*$$

Go *behind* those " coquettish " centres of " civilisation " where the superior Congolese official drinks, keeps his women, and superintends the shipment of the rubber in the river steamers bound for the Pool, the railway, and the ocean steamers. Go behind those outlying " Posts " where the subordinate Congolese official or agent of the Government-controlled rubber trusts lives in discomfort and solitude —unless his posse of savage and often cannibalistic auxiliaries can be called company—eating out his soul, losing hold on decency and dignity with the months, harried by perpetual objurgations from the superior person in the fine station for rubber, more rubber, still more rubber.

Go *behind* them—those out-stations—and in some covert place near at hand in a clearing, surrounded by bush, hidden from prying eyes of prowling missionary or chance traveller, you will come across it. A small, low-roofed building, opening into another, where a guard of sentries keep watch and ward. This is the hostage-house, one of the recognised institutions of the Upper Congo, like the *chicotte*, the *collier-national*—otherwise the chain-gang—and the *matabiche*—otherwise the rubber bonus. Inside, herded like cattle in a pen, cramped and suffocated, unkempt, grovelling in filth and squalor—men, women, and children, chiefly women. Half-starved, wholly starved at times—what a story the records of the Congo Courts will tell if a substantial number of them are ever dragged to light! For the pestered, unwrought subordinate white man in the out-station, grown callous, and habitually, almost unconsciously, cruel, has other things to think about besides his hostages and their victual-

95

Red Rubber

ling. It is as much as he can do, often enough, to feed himself and his soldiers. Taught by his superiors to look upon the people of this regenerated land as brute beasts ere he sets foot among them, the daily task assigned to him has bred a total disregard for human suffering. His mind has become simply non-receptive to such ideas. Rubber is his god! His salary is a mere pittance, but every ton of rubber from his out-station spells *matabiche*, and every month that passes means possession coming nearer, and with it release from his surroundings. Censure, if the out-put falls below the stated figure. Praise and advancement, if he succeeds in maintaining or increasing it; . . . and *matabiche*. Rubber is his god! The natives are but means to an end—and them he loathes. Ah! how he grows to loathe them! Are they behindhand in their quota? Then they are robbing *him*: he who has power of life and death over hundreds or thousands of men, women, and children! Do they tremblingly urge that the vines are exhausted? They are defying *him*! He knows it, and his fever-haunted brain devises fresh measures for their coercion. He re-reads his instructions, couched in terms of mingled cajolery and warning, and he hardens his heart. Fevers, solitude, discomforts, excesses, the sense of omnipotence grafted upon an indifferent *morale*[1] and pernicious ideas inculcated by his employers, the sense of mingled irritation and vanity excited by seeing fear, and the deceit born of fear, in every face, the iron chains of the whole system of which he has become the tool, and, in a sense, the victim—a system implacable, unalterable, machine-like, whose motive power, controlled and directed with genius from a far-away European city, operates in the Equatorial forest with passionless regularity—all this has made of him what he is, what he needs must be, lost to all moral sense, impervious to emotions of pity or compassion.

"When an official begins to realise the *coulisses* of the Administration, he is stupefied to have fallen so low in the social scale. He cannot ask for his resignation because the *Recueil administratif*

---

[1] The type of Belgian—they are not all Belgians, of course—who goes to the Congo is usually a very poor one.

does not admit it.[1] If he insists, and leaves his station, he can be prosecuted for desertion, and, in any case, will probably never get out of the country alive, for the routes of communication, victualling stations, etc., are in the hands of the Administration, and escape in a native canoe is out of the question—every native canoe, if its destination be not known and its movements chronicled in advance from post to post, is at once suspected and liable to be stopped, for the natives are not allowed to move freely about the controlled water-ways. The official must therefore finish his term, always obeying the *ukases* of the Governor-General and the District Commissioner, without the hope of being able to make known the miseries he is undergoing to the outside world, because in Boma there is a *Cabinet noir*[2] for correspondence."[3]

Look inside that hostage-house, staggering back as you enter from the odours which belch forth in poisonous fumes. As your eyes get accustomed to the half-light, they will not rest on those skeleton-like forms—bones held together by black skin—but upon the *faces*. The faces turned upwards in mute appeal for pity : the hollow cheeks, the misery and terror in the eyes, the drawn parched lips emitting inarticulate sounds. A woman, her pendulous, pear-shaped breasts hanging like withered parchment against her sides, where every rib seems bursting from its covering, holds in her emaciated arms a small object more pink than black. You stoop and touch it—a new-born babe, twenty-four hours old, assuredly not more. It is dead, but the mother clasps it still. She herself is almost past speech, and soon will join her babe in the great Unknown. " The horror of it, the unspeakable horror of it."[4]

Every station, every " post," every " factory " of the rubber districts of the Upper Congo, and many in the food-taxed districts, has its hostage-house. The number of hostages detained is inscribed upon registers, and—so

---

[1] " Every one knows that the Congo Government will not allow its officers to return home."—*Signor Santini*. Deputy for Rome in the Italian Chamber, November, 1905.
[2] That is a Department which examines outgoing and incoming correspondence. I have had experience of that.
[3] Letter to the author from an Italian officer.
[4] The Reverend S. Gilchrist (nine years' experience on the Congo) to the author, describing his visit to a hostage-house at Mampona.

Red Rubber

far as the out-stations are concerned—monthly statements on forms printed for the purpose and entitled, "*Etat des indigènes soumis à la contrainte par corps*," are forwarded in duplicate to headquarters.[1] By careful reckoning of the number of stations and out-stations, the authorised number of hostages detained *per mensum* in each, and documentary evidence showing how that number is exceeded, it has been possible to compute that ten thousand human beings pass through the hostage-houses of one only of the vast rubber preserves of the Upper Congo in a single year. How many remain to die, or leave them only to die, is more difficult to compute.

The hostage-house is one of the most efficacious assets of the rubber slave-trade.

Sometimes with shameless boldness, but with some attempt at outward decency because the site is a more public one, the hostage-house flaunts itself openly and is a more pretentious and commodious building. This, on the premises of one of the " fine " and important central stations. And here you can see the prisoners as they march, roped, through the station to the abode which a beneficent Administration has caused to be erected for the purpose of stimulating a healthy desire to work among the natives of Central Africa. Slowly the procession winds its way through the station buildings—officers' bungalows, drying sheds for rubber, and so on. At its head walk four sentries fez on head, and cap-gun or *Albini* slung from their brawny shoulders. Behind them eighteen women— mothers, those whom motherhood will shortly claim, maids, girls of tender age. Some carry babies, or hold tiny children by the hand, for who shall feed these if left in the village behind? Faltering they come, casting fearful glances to left and right, " so terror-stricken that they cannot control the calls of nature." [2] What is their offence? It is an offence by proxy, and a very grave one.

---

[1] I have these documents in my possession. *Vide* also particulars given in the next chapter.

[2] Letter to the author from a correspondent who has seen these familiar sights on the Congo. For further particulars the reader is referred to the White Book, Africa No. 1, 1904.

Public Works and the Price Thereof

The husbands, or the brothers of these women have failed to trap the weekly antelope required as part of the tax for the white man's table ; or their supply of fresh fish is short —fish are not always abundant in all seasons in the same locality, but the Congo official and his soldiers require fish, and fish they must have ; or the rubber has been of bad quality and insufficient in quantity. It is necessary to take these measures. The husbands will require their wives, and they will trap the antelope, they will find the fish, and they will improve their rubber supply. They are lazy that is all. If they do not —— well the women will remain in their pleasant abode, fed generously by an Administration full of concern for their moral and material welfare. Should delay prove exaggerated and indefensible, it will be the painful duty of the official in charge to send a number of sentries to visit that village. Merely to visit it, of course. They will take their guns ? Yes, but for self-protection. These people are wild, very wild. But, rest assured, the guns will not be used save under deliberate provocation ; it would be contrary to the regulations. Ah ! of course, if the regrettable necessity presented itself—why, then these poor brave sentries would have to defend their lives. The women in the house of detention ? Well, no doubt they would be very happy to join the sentries' *ménage*. And who knows ? You observed the fifth in the line, she with the brass anklets ? No ? You English are strange people. She was pleasing, quite pleasing. " Distinguished magistrates " assured the Commissioners of Inquiry—says their Report—that the detention of women in hostage-houses was the most " humane form of coercion." Perhaps it is on the Congo, for there are many worse. But the Leopoldian conception of humanity, is the humanity of the human tiger thirsting, not for blood, but for rubber which presently—when flung from the hold of an ocean carrier (owned by an Englishman, plentifully be-starred and be-medalled) upon the Antwerp quay—shall be converted into gold.

Gold to pour into the lap of some favoured friend.[1]

---

[1] *Vide* the revelations published widely throughout Belgium during the last few months.

Red Rubber

Gold to be invested in undertakings "from China to Peru." Gold to rear palaces, pagodas, and monuments to the Emperor of the Congo in Belgian cities. Gold to purchase properties under brilliant Mediterranean skies. Gold to be hoarded in private treasure-chests of which none but the Royal owner holds the key. Gold to corrupt consciences and manufacture public opinion : to disseminate lying literature throughout the world, even on the seats of continental railway carriages.

I have stood on that quay of Antwerp and seen that rubber disgorged from the bowels of the incoming steamer, and to my fancy there has mingled with the musical chimes ringing in the old Cathedral tower, another sound—the faintest echo of a sigh from the depths of the dark and stifling hold. A sigh breathed in the gloomy Equatorial forest, by those from whose anguish this wealth was wrung. *They* knew not their merciful Emperor. Yet that echo took form of words in my mind. "Imperator"—it has seemed to whisper—"Imperator ! Morituri te salutant ! " (We who are about to die, salute thee, Emperor !) Perhaps it was because thoughts flew backwards five hundred years when to the sound of the same gentle pealing from the old Cathedral tower, the ancestors of this same people, which permits to-day its foreign monarch and his financial body-guard to plagiarise in Africa the infamies committed upon its own citizens by the hirelings of another foreign monarch, fell in mangled heaps in the narrow streets of this very city. If there be a spirit in that tower which never dies—as legend somewhere has it—one can picture the cynical smile that flits across its shadowy features as, contemplating at once the rubber-laden quay and the escutcheon of the city with its severed hands, and thinking of the Congo toll—the toll of the handless stump—reflects of the world and its ways, " Plus ça change : plus c'est la même chose."

Yes. Go *behind* those fine stations cemented with the blood of black humanity, and see into the lives, read into the hearts of the people. Witness the degradation to which native life has sunk—that elderly Chief honoured in the eyes of his subjects, flogged and put to menial tasks, made

100

to drink from the white man's latrine.[1] In the social
system of the African native the person of the chief is
at once the father of the clan, its rallying-point, the centre
to which it looks for guidance, the symbol of all that the
clan venerates and regards as holy. The deliberate policy
of " Bula Matadi "[2] has been to break down that influence,
in nine cases out of ten an influence for good, and of course
put nothing in its place. Every feature of indigenous life
which made for self-respect has been dragged in the mud
of grinding tyranny and foul imaginings : natural instincts
of dignity and decency undermined : indigenous laws for
the localisation of disease rendered of no avail through the
wholesale deportation of women, and the moving hither and
thither of masses of soldiery.[3] Public incest[4] as a pastime
to the brutal soldiery : things nameless, unprintable. Watch
that procession wending its way through the tortuous bush
track. Mourners—sons carrying the body of their father,
murdered by one of the village sentries in a fit of caprice, to
the white-man's station. The slain man was the chief of
that primitive community. Moreover he was a "medal-
chief." Surely in this case justice could be secured against
the assassin. Impatiently the white man hears the story,
and bids the bearers, through an interpreter, depart. The
rubber was insufficient. It was not the first offence. The
chief was responsible. "It is enough." As the men delay
somewhat in taking up their burden, he sets his dog upon
them.[5] Watch, too, this son of a murdered father, begging
from the murderer, permission to untie the body from
where it hangs on yonder sapling, and give it decent burial.
That permission will be granted him eventually, but on
it will be founded a further pretext for extortion, and a
goodly portion of the remaining family goods will pass into

---

[1] White Book. Africa No. 1, 1904.
[2] Native name for the Congo Administration. It means the
breaker of stones. It should be changed to the breaker of
hearts.
[3] *Vide* in this respect, and more particularly, the long report of
Mr. Dugald Campell sent to the Foreign Office, by Mr. Fox
Bourne.
[4] Evidence before the Commission of Inquiry.   [5] Ibid.

Red Rubber

the sentry's hands. Note the gait of that youth as he limps painfully into the village square. He is a fine muscular specimen of humanity. What ails him? As he turns, the cause is clear enough. Down his broad naked back and loins, the blood slowly runs and drips upon the ground. Flies are buzzing round his shoulders. He has been flogged by the white man's orders for shortage. Fifty blows of the rhinoceros hide whip. He fared better than Bokoto of Wala, he explains to his aged mother as he reaches his hut —*he* got a hundred strokes, and had to be carried away.

*　　　*　　　*　　　*　　　*

Go *behind* those "fine" stations, which figure in the illustrated publications so obligingly scattered broadcast by the Press Bureau. Get from the lips of survivors the story of the "breaking" of their village. The narration takes you back to the Middle Ages, to the exploits of the Spanish *conquisitadores* in the West Indies. Go from village to village : from district to district. Leave the rubber zone and visit that fishing centre where the old men—the young are away getting in their fortnightly "tax"—will tell you, in their primitive simplicity, "our young men have no time even to make children. There is nothing before us but death." Get from the lips of the people everywhere the same story of misery and woe : here, when the weekly tax in food-stuffs have been paid there is nothing left but leaves to eat : [1] there the chant of mourning for relatives slain in an affray with the sentries. Pass on through swamp and brushwood. There is another hamlet not far off and from its direction a confused noise arises, quickly to be distinguished as cries of terror, shouts, execrations. A man dashes past you running swiftly down the bush path you are now entering. Seeing you he doubles back and plunges into the forest. You come upon the scene. It is typical and commonplace. A white man in dirty clothes and straggling beard sits upon a stool. Before him stand several soldiers surrounding, or holding five women and a man, whom the official is angrily interrogating through an interpreter. He is taking the census of the village, and

Evidence before the Commission of Inquiry.

Public Works and the Price Thereof

apportioning its "taxation," that is all. Other soldiers are busy looting the huts, coming out with armfuls of spears and knives, cutting down the plantations, or chasing with loud shouts the villagers who have fled panic-stricken to the bush. Multiply such scenes, such tales, such tragedies ten thousandfold, and you will only touch the fringe of a people's misery.

To men who have lived among them for many weary moons, and whose existence would long ago have been intolerable but for their faith in the Almighty, to a man who for years has been receiving the outpourings of these men's hearts in letters and in speech, and whom circumstances have given an insight—granted to few—into the European side of this unparalleled scandal and colossal human tragedy, until their hideousness has burned itself into his soul and scorched it, there is no "redeeming feature" in the public works constructed by King Leopold on the Congo, or in Brussels.

On the Congo, every mile of railway, every mile of road, every new station, every fresh stern-wheeler launched upon the water-ways means a redoubling of the burden on the people of the land. First because their labour and their labour alone, supplies the needed moneys and the needed muscles. Secondly, because these material evidences "civilisation" serve but one purpose, that of facilitating the enslavement of the inhabitants, of tightening the rivets in the fetters of steel within whose pitiless grip they groan and die.

As for the handsome edifices raised by King Leopold in Brussels with the proceeds of this rubber slave-trade, I can find no words more fitting than those of Mr. Vandervelde uttered in the Belgian Chamber last March, to characterise them :

"I tell him that this money, these profits, these presents are shameful things because they are the result of the exploitation of a whole people."

III

JUSTICE AND THE FRIENDLY CRITIC

"The administration of justice in the Congo is of such an impartial and protective character, and is so highly appreciated by the natives themselves that they come in ever-increasing numbers and from great distances to submit to the jurisdiction of the whites" (sic).—DESCAMPS, *New Africa.*

THE Congo administration claims to have introduced "Justice" into its territories. Justice! The virtue which consists in giving every one his due! Clearly, it is not a claim to this sort of Justice on the Congo which requires discussion. No. What is contended by and for the Congo State is that it has instituted a *judicial system*, which is a very different thing. A *judicial system* can be pure, or impure. It can be an instrument of protection to the weakest. It can be an engine ot tyranny under which the weak are ground to powder with every appearance of strict legality. It is claimed for the judicial system of the Congo State, in that familiar and inimitable language of lofty sentiment studded with rhetorical flowers, that "it corresponds with the double mission to be fulfilled by the Government, to solve the essentially judicial litigation which can arise in social life, and to punish in conformity with the law the violation of social order." [1]

There exists in the capital of the Congo State, Boma on the lower river, a Court of First Instance, and an Appeal Court, and there are thirteen territorial tribunals scat-

---

[1] Descamps, " New Africa."

104

Justice and the Friendly Critic

tered throughout a country some 800,000 square miles in extent. For all criminal cases the Appeal Court at Boma is supreme, beyond it there is no appeal. The "Superior Council" in Brussels, whose members are appointed by the King and which never meets, is theoretically a Court of Cassation for civil cases.

The first essential of a pure judicial system is a magistracy independent of executive influence or control. Under a *régime* of absolute autocracy such conditions are unlikely. In the Congo State they are obviously impossible, and it is one of the many amazing things in the Report of the Congo Commission of Inquiry that, having seen the Congo system at work, having noted the breaking of the paper laws of the land by the Executive and by individuals throughout the length and breadth of their peregrinations,[1] the Commissioners should have pleaded earnestly and strenuously for a magistracy free from Executive interference, a plea which has necessarily been rejected by the Sovereign autocrat.

The members of the Congo Magistracy are, from highest to lowest, nominated by the King. The Governor-General is the King's "mandatory" and the Public Prosecutor's office is exercised under the Governor-General's authority. The latter can stop prosecution in criminal cases, and can suspend proceedings in criminal cases at any stage after they have been instituted. He does so habitually, as the Report of the Commission of Inquiry admits. It could not be otherwise, seeing that the Executive itself is the supreme violator of the "law." The Public Prosecutor and his assistants are, consequently, the servants of the Executive, that is to say of the Governor-General; and the judicial system of the Congo State exists only to give an appearance of legality to what is indefensible, to invest the

---

[1] To take one instance, "forced labour" was applied by the Administration for eleven years, illegally, from 1892, when the King drafted his famous decree requiring the "Secretary of State" to "take all measures which he may deem necessary or useful to ensure the exploitation of the products of the *Domaine Privé*," until September, 1903, when daily and impending revelations caused the drafting of a forced labour law, regularising its application.

rubber slave-trade in the eyes of Europe with the garb or respectability, to make the world believe that a legal machinery exists to protect the native, when that machinery is used, in point of fact, to minister to his oppression.

With such a system the effective administration of justice is, of course, impossible, and it is not the least of the negligences of British Governments, that they should have permitted for all these years, British subjects on the Congo, whether white or black, to be subject to the jurisdiction of the Congo Courts. Moreover that situation still obtains. Under it one Englishman was hung out of hand. English missionaries are now being harried for speaking the admitted truth before the Commission of Inquiry, and a very considerable number of British coloured subjects have suffered, and doubtless now suffer, the gravest wrongs.[1] I refer to this subject again in Section V.

There is some little difficulty in conveying to the ordinary mind the moral atmospheric conditions prevailing on the Congo. They are so charged with chicanery and deceit, so utterly abnormal in every sense of the word, that long experience alone can properly assimilate them, and the knowledge thus acquired is not communicable in a couple of sentences. One can only ask the reader to bear in mind that the Congo State surrounded itself from the earliest days with the trappings, not of an ordinary colonial undertaking, but of a professedly philanthropic institution, and that when it started out on its career of piracy and brigandage—in 1892—these trappings clung about it, forming a raiment well-nigh impenetrable to criticism. In the succeeding years, King Leopold, himself highly proficient, uniquely so, indeed, in State-craft of a certain order, has attached to his interests by various means men schooled in all the subtleties of the law. Never, probably, has greater ingenuity been displayed to give black the semblance or white—or at least of grey. Laws innumerable have been drafted, and flourished in the eyes of Europe, securing to the

---

[1] *Vide* Chapter I.

Justice and the Friendly Critic

Congo native freedom, absolute and entire, ensuring for him such beatitude in this life and such a quasi-certitude of salvation in the next that as Lord Fitzmaurice, speaking in the House of Lords in July last, wittily put it, " some of your Lordships on leaving this House might almost be disposed to take a ticket immediately for the Congo." The torchlight of truth has finally succeeded in reducing these trappings to dust and ashes, but the atmosphere is not yet rid of the particles.

So it is that in considering the judicial system of the Congo—which cannot be separated and treated as a thing apart from other sections of the Congo system—this factor must ever be present in the mind. When in diplomatic correspondence, official publications and in the emanations from the Press Bureau, King Leopold's secretaries and scribes dwell with emphasis upon " La Justice Congolaise," as though the Congo judicial system was by them regarded as the greatest proven tribute (with the suppression of the Arab and the gin bottle) to administrative genius, one has to point out that the Congo Administration does not, and never has *administered* in any known acceptance of the term. As Professor Cattier truly says, " after twenty years it has not even begun to administrate ; . . . everything must be begun afresh."

An early duty of a civilised administration in tropical Africa is to recognise, uphold, and strengthen where required the existing native courts—the chief sitting in council with his elders—the machinery for the preservation of law and order founded upon indigenous customs (whose essential justice and suitability, investigation seldom fails to reveal). Bound up in this a careful and constant study by the administrative officials of the laws and usages of the people, their practices in regard to chieftainship, hereditary succession, marriage, tenure of land and other property, their entire social fabric in short, is the necessary, indeed the principal business of the administration of a tropical African dependency. But such trivialities as these find no part or lot in the Leopoldian conception. They are absolutely foreign to it. There is not a recognised native court from one end of the Congo territory to the other. If you speak to a Congolese official about native customs, laws and what not, he simply laughs at you. He has no time for that sort of thing. His duty is to maintain the revenue, and if possible increase it, if he is stationed in one of the revenue-producing districts, and revenue means rubber, ivory, and gum copal. If he is stationed in one of the great food-producing districts, his duty is to superintend the output, distribution and despatch of supplies, and to see that every village within the taxable area delivers, fortnightly or weekly as the case may be, its fixed quota. This is a task of considerable magnitude.

There are tens upon tens of thousands of soldiers (and their women and retainers), workmen, labourers of all sorts, etc., engaged directly or indirectly in different branches of the rubber slave-trade. They must be fed, and the Congo Administration, unlike civilised administrations, does not import large quantities of dried fish, rice, and so on, for the consumption of its retainers. Therefore those retainers live on the land, and as the overwhelming proportion of the get-at-able native population in the rubber districts is employed from January 1 to December 31 in searching the forests for that article, the food supplies for the great station centres in those districts (the out-stations are supplied locally and the sentries in the villages look to the village women —not their own—to support them) have to come from a distance, from other districts. When the enormous number of mouths to be fed is considered, and the continuous nature of the demand, it will be readily understood how vital to the working of the system it is that the supply should be kept up without a hitch, what dangers would be incurred if a break of any duration occurred. The Report of the Congo Commission of Inquiry points this out, and states explicitly that its remarks are of general application to all the great station-centres. It admits, indeed, that "sometimes a portion of the workmen, soldiers, *and prisoners*, are often deprived of food for twenty-four hours." No surprise need be felt that the hostages, *e.g.*, prisoners, are "sometimes" forgotten ! It will be seen, then, that an indispensable feature of the rubber slave-trade is the forcible maintenance of a considerable section of the population under pressure for the production of food-stuffs, as unrelaxing as the pressure for revenue.

Between these two primal needs—revenue (*e.g.*, rubber) and food, the Congolese official has time for nothing, everything else lying outside the sphere of what is really required of him, save in a few and strictly exceptional cases where, owing to a variety of causes, different conditions prevail.

With what does the Magistracy in the Congo concern itself? In the Europeanised towns of Boma and Matadi, a number of trumpery little cases of litigation—rather encouraged than otherwise—occur. In the true Congo—the vast upper region stretching from Stanley Pool to the Nile and the great Lakes—there is no litigation to speak ot. There are no competing commercial firms and there is no room for litigation between master and slave ! The wretched native has been taught by bitter experience to shun Bula Matadi in whatever guise he appears before him. The Commission of Inquiry sorrowfully recognised that the " evangelical missionary " has come to be regarded by the native as the " only representative of equity and justice," [1] thus conferring upon him a prestige, the Commissioners add, which " should be invested in the magistrates." In the " distinguished magistrates," who opine that to drag mothers, wives, and young girls from their homes and thrust them into hostage-houses is "the most humane form of coercion"? The Commissioners are silent on this point.

The truth of the matter is that the principal employment of the Congo magistrates consists in dealing with the crimes committed by Europeans upon the natives ; in dealing, that is, with the fatal and inevitable accompaniment to the system of which the supreme local Executive is the inspirer or rather the transmitter and applier, inspiration emanating from Brussels, whence " comes every initiative," as Professor Cattier rightly says. If this is the principal employment of the Magistrates, the chief object is to make an impeccable outward simulachre of stern activity compatible with securing immunity for the criminal. The task is easier than it sounds,

---

[1] Which explains the laudable desire of the Congo Administration to browbeat him into silence.

for the simple reason that there is no publicity. Out of the innumerable judgments delivered by the Congo Courts in cases of atrocity during the course of the last decade,[1] no complete text, and extracts from one judgment only, has ever been published in Belgium! It sounds incredible. It is, however, strictly true. The Government of M. de Smet de Naeyer has been a very complaisant one for the Sovereign of the Congo State. Were those judgments accessible to the Belgian public, now that its eyes are partly open to the verities of this awful business, the effect produced by the Report of the Commission of Inquiry would be slight by comparison. Only two complete texts have ever reached this country, that of the Appeal Court in the Caudron case, and that of the Territorial Tribunal of Stanleyville in the case of John Brown, a native of Lagos. The former was, and remains, with the exception of the official circulars, Consul Casement's Report, and the Report of the Commission of Inquiry, the most revealing document connected with Congo affairs, which has ever seen the light of day. It was the first official document—from the Congo side—of any importance which we had been able to acquire,[2] and not only did it show the complicity of the supreme Executive in the rubber slave-trade, but it convicted the Governor-General himself of violating the laws of the land.[3] The other judgment is evidential of the kind of "justice" which a British coloured subject—even one with Brown's exceptional position and record on the Congo—can expect if he comes to loggerheads with the "superior official."

Hence it is not difficult to understand that this absence

---

[1] As many as forty-five Europeans have been at one time either in prison or under arrest at Boma on varied charges, from "contravention aux décrets sur les armes à feu" (anglice, arming sentries with rifles, which is against the law), to "mutilation de cadavres" (anglice, hand lifting).

[2] The secret circulars only became accessible later.

[3] "No argument," wrote Lord Lansdowne, with the reticence of a statesman in office, to H.M. Minister in Brussels on June 6, 1904, "can be entertained to the effect that acts of violence are improbable or impossible under a system, such as that revealed by the judgment pronounced by the Court of Appeal at Boma in the Caudron case."

Justice and the Friendly Critic

of publicity facilitates very greatly the object to which I have referred. The Public is informed now and then that numerous arrests have taken place, and that several agents have been sentenced. The Press Bureau circulates a cleverly-worded despatch to the Continental and American journals affiliated to it, in which "individual excesses inseparable from every colonising enterprise" are deplored, and the magnificent independence "notwithstanding the odious calumnies of Mr. Morel and his gang" of the Congo Magistracy proclaimed. There the matter ends, so far as the public is concerned. Of the subsequent fate of these men—who are all subordinate agents from the outstations in the bush—nothing ever transpires. I have been able to trace one or two, not without considerable difficulty. Their history is a little diversified, but one characteristic is common to all. After serving an infinitesimal part of their sentence they come back very quietly to Belgium. Here a mysterious Providence ensures their keeping quiet. Sometimes a local job is found for them. One man, for instance, who was a bootmaker's assistant by trade, before being given unlimited power over men and women in the Congo forests, was comfortably set up in a comfortable little shop of his own. His sentence in the Congo was ten years. He served eight months. Another, who has married and settled down in the haberdashery line, was given a life sentence on the Congo for burning an old woman alive. A foreign appointment—preferably in Egypt it would seem—is rather usual. No one knows of course who the fairy godmother, or father, is ; but the effect is potent. Silence is ensured— that is the main point. I have received some very curious letters from Belgium in the last few years, some with appeals, some with offers of the most varied description. One professed to be from the father of a young Belgian sentenced to ten years. A curious sequel attached to it. The writer stated that he had appealed to one of the Congo State Secretaries in Brussels, on his son's behalf, on the plea that the latter had merely carried out the instructions of his superior. This high official had replied that a reprieve would be difficult to arrange just now in view of the agitation in England, but he would consider what might be done. Six months had passed since this meeting, but the youth still lingered in Boma gaol. The writer added that he had not told the high official in question one thing. That was that he, the writer, possessed documentary proof of his son's obedience to orders, in the shape of a letter from his chief, an officer of high rank in the Congo army. Would I like to see the letter? I answered that it would be very interesting to see the letter, repeating in my reply the name he had mentioned. I did not expect an answer, and I was not disappointed. But two months later I noticed in a published passenger list of the latest homeward bound Congo mail-steamer, the name of my correspondent's son. My letter, as I anticipated, had evidently been used to some purpose with the high official aforesaid!

Does this absence of publicity and the advantages it entails for the Congo Administration mean that the Congo Magistracy must be regarded as individually and collectively corrupt? Not at all. That, as a body, it is innoculated with the virus of the system, one need seek no better indication than that afforded by the views quoted in the Report of the Commission of Inquiry of some of its " distinguished " members on the subject of women-hostages. That in itself is about the most damaging revelation which could well be imagined, especially when we are told in the publications of the Press Bureau that the taking of *women*-hostages is contrary to the *written law*. I have a letter before me from one of the Assistants of the Public Prosecutor at Boma, offering for a consideration the documents which in his capacity of Magistrate he possesses, " documents which would astonish the world." The world has ceased to be astonished at King Leopold and all his works. Truly the usual type of European on the Congo, whether fulfilling the rule of magistrate or not, is worthy of his royal master!

I have no doubt that there are honest individuals among the Congo Magistracy, and the particulars given in Father Vermeersch's recent book throw a flood of light on the way in which the honest magistrate is hampered at every turn by the Executive, when engaged in gathering evidence for the prosecution of a European criminal. But, assuming for the sake of argument that every Congo magistrate were above suspicion, there would still be a barrier which neither the Public Prosecutor nor *a fortiori* his assistants can cross.

The publication of the Caudron judgment [1] and the events which followed it illustrated this very forcibly. That publication, as I have remarked, was a staggering blow to the Congo Administration, and King Leopold sought to parry it by issuing a special Manifesto, addressed to the Governor-General and calling upon the Public Prosecutor and his Assistants, the *Substituts* or " Deputy-Attorneys," to " search for all officials, no matter who they may be " who had participated in the particular rubber-raids the scapegoat Caudron had been concerned in. The Manifesto further stated that " the Government " (that is, the King) " intends that there shall be no indulgence shown towards any of its officials who may participate in blameable acts towards the native people." With that nicety of expression and enthusiasm for righteousness which is impressed so forcibly on these royal promulgations, the Manifesto proceeds to anticipate that " all officials no matter who they may be " have been triumphantly dragged out of their hiding places by a noble and perspiring Public Prosecutor, and declares :

" If the constituent elements of participation do not exist, and if the prosecution fails, it will remain for the superior authority to examine if the agents of the State whose administrative responsibility appears, nevertheless, to be implicated in these cases either by their acts or by their inaction, shall not be the object of disciplinary measures of a seriousness proportionate to the faults which they have committed."

To the uninitiated this evidence of pained surprise, barely-concealed indignation, and resolute intent on the part of the Emperor of the Congo conveyed sincerity, and the Press

---

[1] The case had nothing unusual about it, at all. The only trouble was that the British Consul in the Congo—Mr. Nightingale I think it was—and myself managed to secure a copy of the minutes of the judgment, and that, by a purely fortuitous chain of circumstances. I hope the Consul will not take it amiss from me if I remind him that I got my copy first !

Bureau hastened to improve the occasion. The judgment of the Appeal Court was such, of course, that had the instructions in the King's Manifesto to the Governor-General been carried out, the first warrant of arrest issued by the Public Prosecutor would have been against the Governor-General, whom the judgment clearly indicated for the committal of an illegal act involving in its train cruelty and outrage upon natives ! The next person to be arrested would have been the District Commissioner, *i.e.*, an official ranking, with two exceptions, next to the Governor-General. The third would have been the Officer in command of the Government troops who assisted Caudron in his raids ; then the Manager in Africa of the " Company " whose servant Caudron was, and so on all down the scale. The prison at Boma would have had to have been enlarged.

It is hardly necessary to add that the Magistracy was powerless to do anything of the kind. Caudron was defended—a rare occurrence in the Congo—and the prosecution did not, and, could not deny that Caudron was merely a servant of the Executive ; that he received, with the consent of the Executive, which took three-fourths of the profits derived by the " Company "[1] from its rubber operations, 3 per cent. commission on all the rubber he secured ; that the " Company " had no lands of its own, and was merely acting as rubber-collector for the Executive ; that its raids were conducted with the open assistance of Government officers and troops ; that the arms and munitions of war utilised by the " Company " constituted in itself the proof that the Executive recognised the right of the " Company " to employ them, since they could, by law, only be placed in the hands of those specially so authorised by the Governor-General ; that every rifle, and cartridge, in the possession of the " Company " was passed through the Custom House and conveyed to the " Company's " station in Government vessels ; that in the year 1903—the year of Caudron's raids—these Government vessels had conveyed 40,000 rounds of ball cartridge to the " Company " ;

---

[1] Caudron was an agent of the *Anversoise*. *Vide* Section IV.

and, finally, that, for the results of such illegal raids, the Executive itself was solely responsible.

Particulars of the trial of the man Van Caelcken—an out-station subordinate of another of the rubber "Companies"[1]—on December 9, 1904, which have reached me, are merely a replica of the Caudron business. His performances had been denounced by the missionaries. They included the seizing of women-hostages, arming sentries[2] with *Albinis*, etc. Van Caelcken conducted his own defence, in the course of which he made no attempt to deny taking hostages, and produced as his justification for doing so a letter from his District Commissioner, and a circular signed by the Governor-General. The latter document deplored the decrease in the rubber output from the concession, and reminded the "Company's" agents that they were entitled to exercise " bodily constraint " upon the natives. The defendant pointed out that he was not concerned with the legality or illegality of such measures.[3] He merely carried them out, as he was bid. As for the detention of hostages, there was no secret about it, and every agent was called upon to furnish, in writing, monthly lists of his prisoners, one for his manager, the other for the Executive. Needless to say, the penalty inflicted upon Van Caelcken was not severe, and he has long since returned to Europe. Needless to say, also, that proceedings against the Governor-General and the District Commissioner for their illegal instructions were not taken ! [4]

The defence of de Tiège, another subordinate agent, whose sentence of 15 years by the Court of First Instance

---

[1] The A. B. I. R. *Vide* Section IV.

[2] These sentries—why they are called so no one seems to know—are irregulars armed by the "Companies." Consul Casement estimates their number at 10,000.

[3] The taking of hostages was authorised as far back as 1897, by Governor-General Wahis in a letter to the Commissioner at Lake Leopold II., entirely contrary to law.

[4] The defence of the black soldiers on the rare occasions when missionary exposures have compelled action is much the same. " Why do you give me a rifle, if it is not to shoot with ? Why am I given cartridges, if I am not to use them ? If you tie me up, why don't you tie up the white man ? "

was reduced to 10 years by the Court of Appeal in November, 1904, ran on much the same lines. This case was notable for an incident which makes one rub one's eyes and wonder whether one is living in the twentieth century. A favourite pastime of de Tiège consisted in forcing natives, who brought him badly prepared rubber, *to eat it.* The Court held that the "introduction into the stomach by the mouth of an elastic substance" (*ingérence*) was not productive of after ill-effects, and that the subsequent illness and death of the men who had been compelled to eat the badly-prepared rubber could not, therefore, be attributed to this. The charges included other counts— that of murder and complicity in murder—but the reduction of the sentence was on the grounds stated above.

When the Commission of Inquiry entered the Maringa territory, they found a state of affairs which dismayed them. Here were established missionaries who were determined that the Commissioners should drink the cup of horrors which was their daily experience to the dregs. From a radius of fifty miles, multitudes of natives flocked to the river side and told their stories of unspeakable woe before the visibly impressed Court, held on board a specially chartered Government vessel. Wholesale massacres, murders, torture, rape, mutilation, depopulation, impoverishment, misery profound—the shameful tale flowed on, until at the end of the week—· when but a tithe of the tragedy had been unfolded—the Commissioners, sickened and appalled, said they had heard enough. Their verdict is on record. Yet the Managing Director of the "Company" on the spot, directly responsible for this welter of abomination, was allowed to leave the country untouched, while the Commission was still in it. The Assistant-Manager stepped into his shoes. The District Commissioner and his assistants were not troubled. The officer commanding the troops in the Concession was retained, promoted, and has since been engaged in prosecuting one of the missionaries for libel ; and one of the Directors in Europe was appointed by the King a member of his "Commission of Reforms"! The European management of that "Company" includes the Grand Marshal of King Leopold's Court, and several high Congo officials. Its President is a Senator. The Congo Government holds half the shares, and the net profits of the concern in six years have amounted to £730,000 on a paid-up capital of under £10,000, each share of a nominal value of £20 (of which the Congo Government possess 1,000) having received in that period dividends totalling £295.[1]

Where in history will you find such a record, and what can be said of the judicial system under which such a record is established?

We have seen how the Governor-General controls the judicial machinery, that he can interfere in prosecutions, suspend them, and what not. Executive interference with the " Law " takes many forms, and is further freed from impediments by the abnormal relations pertaining between Belgium under the present Government (which has been in power for twenty years) and the King's autocracy on the Congo. Everything, as I have said, connected with the Congo is abnormal. The officers of the Belgian army serving in the Congo army continue to draw their salaries from the public funds of Belgium. Strictly speaking, no such officer accused of committing crime on the Congo, can be tried there. A Belgian tribunal is alone entitled to try the case, and he should be immediately recalled. The " Congo Free State " stands towards Belgium in the light of a " Foreign Power." Its headquarters are in Brussels, true, but legally it is non-existent in Belgium, and no tribunal outside the Belgian Courts could sit in Belgium upon a Belgian subject accused of crime abroad without violating the Constitution of Belgium. As the majority of the high officials of the Congo Executive, District Commissioners, Inspectors, *Chefs de Zones*, and so on, are military men, it will be seen how important from King Leopold's point of view, as Sovereign of the Congo State, it is that the responsibility for atrocities should not be brought home to them personally. In this he is assisted by the character of the Congo judicial system on the one hand, and the complicity of the present Belgian Govern-

---

[1] For further particulars, *vide* Section IV.

117

ment on the other. An interesting light was thrown upon this aspect of Congo abnormity by the Tilkens case, in 1903. Tilkens was a sub-Lieutenant in the Belgian army, and a Lieutenant in the Congo army. He was in command of one of the sub-posts in the Rubi-Welle rubber district,[1] and secured in three years £40,000 worth of india-rubber. After he had returned to Belgium, charges of atrocity were preferred against him in the Congo. After consulting the senior Governor-General, who at that particular time was on leave in Brussels, he returned to the Congo to meet them. Although his indictment included charges of a terrible—though not unusual—nature, he was let out on bail of £200. Convinced that he would not obtain justice on the Congo, but would serve as a scapegoat for the sins of his superiors, he "stowed away" on a home-coming steamer. There is little doubt that his departure was facilitated by the local Executive, which was not at all anxious to try him. Upon his return to Belgium he demanded a public trial. His demand was refused. He was tried by default on the Congo and sentenced to 10 years. He thereupon handed his *dossier* to M. Vandervelde. It contained written orders from his superior officers on the Congo— high Executive officials—demonstrating conclusively that the usual pressure had been exercised upon him to increase his. rubber output, with the habitual result. These M. Vandervelde read out to the House, and rightly regarding this as a test case, called upon the Belgian Government to grant Tilkens's request, for a trial in Belgium. The Minister responsible to the Department of Justice made no sign, however. What would have transpired at a public trial? Tilkens's defence would have been the plea of military obedience to instructions—required of all soldiers[2] —which rendered atrocities upon a population already maddened by monstrous demands and only kept down by main force, necessary and indeed requisite. The letters of Commandant Verstraeten (see Section I.) would have been put in. In the cross-examination of this official and his

---

[1] *Domaine Privé.*
[2] His district was under martial law, moreover.

predecessor in office, Commandant Meeus, the letters received by them from the Acting Governor-General, M. Felix Fuchs, and their letters to him must necessarily have been produced, and he himself cited to appear. But this correspondence would have been sufficient, and more than sufficient! It would have had the effect of the explosion of a powder magazine under the edifice of moral and material regeneration. Responsibility for the rubber slave-trade would have been traced to its fountain head.

Thus it is that Belgian officers—Executive officials of the Congo Administration—are prosecuted on the Congo only when circumstances make prevention absolutely impossible, as in the case of Lieutenant Massard, whose arrest the Commission of Inquiry itself demanded by telegraph to Boma after hearing the evidence of M. Scrivener and native witnesses at Boma.[1] Thus it is that not a single Belgian officer has ever been sentenced by the Congo Courts save by pre-arranged default. Thus it is that not a single Belgian, even accused of the most abominable crimes on the Congo, has ever been proceeded against in Belgium. Thus it is that when missionaries denounce the atrocities of some Commandant or officer in the Congo army, either the accused party is given a kindly hint and proceeds down-river on sick leave *en route* for Europe, while with great ostentation a judicial commission ascends the river to inquire into the charge ; or if matters—owing to the action of some honest magistrate—have reached the stage when to save the face of the law the officer has been summoned to Boma, surveillance is relaxed by " superior order " pending the examination of his *dossier*, and the accused discreetly embarks for Europe ; or if a stage still further advanced has been reached before Executive interference can be exercised with befitting secrecy and decency, the accused is liberated on bail, stows away—unbeknown of course to all!—and when the same steamer reaches the Congo on her next voyage, the face of the law is saved by a summons being taken out against the captain for harbouring a passenger not noted on the official passenger list, a

---

[1] Lieutenant Massard was acquitted.

Red Rubber

fine of 20 francs inflicted, and a judiciously edited report of the proceedings finds its way into the European Press through the usual channel, providing yet another example of the impeccability of the Congo Courts. This judicial pantomime is not played for the benefit of officers of the Belgian army only. Officials of the Rubber Trusts who are believed to possess incriminating documents, are beneficiaries equally with the former. In one recent case, the departure of an official from a particular spot on the upper river synchronised with the arrival of an "Assistant Attorney" with a criminal *dossier* concerning him. He had left for Europe long before the investigation was complete.

A final illustration of the methods of criminal jurisprudence on the Congo may be briefly touched upon. The native has been taught by sad experience to avoid the Congo Courts as a pestilence. Natives who have been induced by the missionaries to testify against some official have been compelled to travel immense distances, in some cases upwards of one thousand miles, to Boma. There they have been detained for months—in the case of one recent batch for eight months—and there most of them have died, or come back only to die. Change of diet, home-sickness—to both of which the native is peculiarly susceptible—coupled with neglect and lack of nourishment, have been mainly attributable for this mortality, deplored in the Report of the Commission of Inquiry. So disgraceful has been the treatment of native witnesses even at Boma, that in a published communication to the Congo Reform Association, dated August 17th last year, Lord Lansdowne, after referring to the reports " of the severe privations from which these natives are suffering," received by His Majesty's Government from the Acting British Consul at Boma, intimated that instructions had been sent to that official " to give the native witnesses such assistance as he properly can in their efforts to obtain work during their detention at Boma." A kindly act very greatly to his lordship's credit. Thus from a sentiment of ordinary humanity, allied to a sense of philanthropic responsibility, insomuch as the charges brought by

Justice and the Friendly Critic

a British subject against a Congo official had led to the summoning of native witnesses to Boma, a British Foreign Minister instructed a British Consular officer in the capital of the "Congo Free State" to try and find work for these natives (in order that they should procure the wherewithal to feed themselves), whom the Public Prosecutor had caused to be conveyed four hundred and fifty miles from their homes as witnesses for the prosecution in the public trial of a Congo official! These men were the relatives of victims of the rubber slave-trade from which the Congo Executive reaps millions, but that Executive could not afford to feed them while serving as witnesses on one of its farcical trials!

"The mere word Boma terrifies them. Thus at the present moment it is very difficult, if not impossible, in many regions of the Upper Congo to induce the natives to testify before the Courts. The inhabitant of the Upper Congo summoned as a witness flies to the forest. He must be treated as a criminal, hunted, chained sometimes, in any case subjected to force, to conduct him from his village to the Court."

It is not I who wrote that. It is the Commissioners of King Leopold. Personally, I can see no "redeeming feature" in the "justice" which the Congo Administration has introduced into the Congo Basin, where impunity for the guilty is ensured, and where the mere act of complaining spells for the native exile or death.

Rather do I agree with Professor Cattier, that "it is organised and systematic protection of injustice," and I fail for my part to see how any reasonable human being can arrive at an opposite conclusion.

*　　*　　*　　*　　*

I now come to the fifth and last point, viz., the statements of travellers and others, favourable to the Congo State as regards its treatment of the natives, which have been given to the world. A year ago an extensive analysis of this evidence would have been necessary. Happily, it is no longer so, for the report of the Congo Commission has put the blatant section of the Congo State's defenders out of Court. We have our revenge for the contumely they sought to throw upon us, in the ridicule which the Report of the Commission of Inquiry has cast upon their "impartial investigations." With that class of apologist and defender of the Congo State British public opinion has done for good and all. To recall their travesty of facts would be to do them too much honour. They had their brief term of self-advertisement, they succeeded for a time in helping to confuse the public mind, they delayed a little the manifestation of the truth, and so helped to prolong the agony of a people. Their consciences are, doubtless, satisfied.

Apologists and defenders of the class which, producing no evidence, chose, for reasons best known to themselves, to re-echo the mendacities issued by the Press Bureau, or in the official publications of the Congo Administration, are no better off. The Report of the Commission of Inquiry has disposed of them also.

A section of the Catholic priesthood and laity, especially the former, which, in a measure quite sincerely, saw in our campaign of mercy an attack upon Catholic institutions and upon a Catholic country, must now be convinced of their double error by the statements of the religious press of Belgium, the debates in the Belgian Chamber, and the Report of the Commission. If not, it must be either because these documents are inaccessible to them, or because they refuse to admit that they were misled. In either case further attacks upon the reform movement from that quarter would be deprived of *raison d'être*.

A section of Irish feeling is hostile, and probably always will be hostile. Men whose judgment is as distorted as Mr. Mackean's, who would prefer King Leopold to Lord Aberdeen at Dublin Castle, are beyond the reach of argument. But they do not count. Whatever feelings Irishmen may entertain towards England and Englishmen in the abstract or in the concrete, the cause of Irish Nationalism has nothing to gain by identifying itself with the beneficiaries of the rubber slave-trade. Distrust, suspicion, even hatred of England, is permissible in an Irishman. But love for the Emperor of the Congo in the Irish breast is an incongruity. Moreover these Irish admirers of the

Justice and the Friendly Critic

Sovereign of the Congo State are destitute of evidence. They merely re-echo the absurdities which reach their hands through the ramifications of the Press Bureau. The only evidence we owe to an Irishman is the evidence of a gallant gentleman and man of honour—Roger Casement.

The lucubrations of certain Continental and Irish-American journals subsidised by the Press Bureau are similarly innocent of evidential value, and beneath discussion.

The area of controversy, so far as contradictory evidence is concerned, is indeed narrowed down to a few, a very few, observers who have journeyed through or sojourned in parts of the Congo State not visited by the Commission or Inquiry, and who have personally seen nothing to complain of. This in any case is not, one may remark, a matter which is in the least surprising. It would be quite possible to travel from London to Stanley Falls and back again, and observe little or nothing offensive—particularly if you happened to be a person of some distinction, average superficiality, and no experience of African conditions. Travelling from Antwerp to Boma in one of Sir Alfred Jones's steamers you would be perfectly comfortable, and any unfavourable opinions you might have formed of the bulk of the African regenerators on board (especially if you were conversant with the French tongue) would be dissipated by the courtesy of the higher officials, and the geniality of the English captain. Arrived at Boma you would be impressed with the " fine buildings," the " coquettish " air of this administrative centre, the general signs of activity and military punctiliousness prevailing. At Matadi, the termination of your ocean journey, this impression would strengthen at sight of the railway skirting the arid *flancs* of Palabala, the workshops, the engineering establishments, and so on. A two days' journey on the narrow-gauge line winding in amazing curves amid fine scenery would probably fill you— and rightly so (I have ever "rendered homage," as they say in Belgium, to the perseverant energy and determination of the Belgian engineer, Albert Thys, who constructed this line in the teeth of great obstacles ; it was a triumph of individual skill and of individual enterprise—it was not

123

the Congo Government which built that railway, but a private company) — with admiration. The uninhabited country-side might set him wondering, but he would probably be ignorant of the fact that what is now desert was once a thriving and populous region, and no one certainly would enlighten him. The end of his railway journey would bring him to Leopoldville, another centre of considerable activity—with many sternwheelers, more engineering shops, churches, etc. He would not pause to think how its 3,500 inhabitants were fed, and he would not be told that the people within a radius of sixty miles were rapidly disappearing under the crushing burden of the food-taxes.[1] And so on up to Stanley Falls in a Government vessel, passing not a few " fine stations " on the river-side, not a few steamers and other tokens of " civilisation."

To return from this digression to the "favourable evidence " existing. In the Lado Enclave, the strip of territory on the Nile leased to King Leopold by Lord Rosebery twelve years ago, a large force of troops is stationed. Several forts have been erected. The soldiers are there, a smart body of men, mostly commanded by Italian officers. Their barracks are substantial and commodious. The stations are well kept. Two British officers visiting these Congolese military and political posts have commented favourably upon their appearance. Their remarks have been spread broadcast by the Press Bureau, and made the most of. Curiously enough, no one in this country had suspected the existence of an evil state of affairs in this tiny strip of territory until Lord Cromer's scathing comments appeared in the White Book of 1904. Since then information has reached me from unquestionable sources that the history of the construction of these military edifices was characterised by the usual proceedings. The Foreign Office can throw light upon it whenever it chooses to do so. I observe that Sir Charles Eliot in his recently-published volume speaks rather favourably of these Congolese stations on the Nile and adds : " It is generally said that our officers can always

---

[1] *Vide* Report of Commission of Inquiry.

reduce natives to obedience by threatening to deport them to the Belgian side of the river. It is certain that there are no villages for many miles round the Belgian stations." In short, it is quite possible to speak in commendation of the armed Congo camps on the Nile without affecting the question of the wrongs of the Congo natives in the very slightest degree; and from such commendation the Congo Administration is welcome to any consolation it can derive.

What remains then, as positive evidence, favourable to the Congo State? The experiences of Mr. Grey and one or two other Englishmen in the employ of the Tanganyika Concessions, Limited, which is engaged in exploiting the copper mines of South-Eastern Katanga, and the experiences of Sir Harry Johnston, who penetrated thirty miles into Congo State territory from Uganda in 1900, and visited other parts previously. I need say no more on this point beyond mentioning that as these lines are written I understand Sir Harry Johnston will be good enough to contribute a short notice to this volume, and adding that the Congo Reform Association is proud to number him among its supporters. As for Mr. George Grey's experiences, his distinguished brother, the present British Minister for Foreign Affairs, referred to them with perfect frankness in the last debate on the Foreign Office vote. He confirmed their favourable nature, and explained that they were "carefully limited" to the "southern extremity of the Congo State," where it might be added there is no rubber, and where the presence of a number of Englishmen—and especially an Englishman known by King Leopold to be related to the British Minister for Foreign Affairs—is in itself calculated to keep excesses in check.

I will make a present to the Press Bureau of another favourable piece of testimony. It comes from a missionary acquaintance of mine, who, writing from Upoto in the early part of the present year, states : " Happily Upoto has been under the rule of Commandant Scardino for the past three years. It is no secret that he is not in accord with Congo State methods. Consequently Upoto district has not been terrorised to such an extent as other parts.

Commandant Scardino has ever shown himself as inclined to leniency rather than oppression, and taxes have been more frequently modified than increased." I am happy to print that paragraph concerning an Italian officer and gentleman who, like other of his compatriots, has had the breeding and the strength of will to endeavour, amid great difficulties, to rise above the system whose unwilling servants he and they have been, and who as a result are detested by the supreme Congo Executive as much as the British missionaries almost. Nor are such exceptions wholly confined to Italian officers. Captain Lemaire of the Belgian army is another, and a very notable one. Poor Dooms was another, but he disappeared. The officials who fall foul of the Executive are curiously apt to disappear on the Congo. In the case of Dooms, the agent of disappearance appears to have been a hippopotamus. The Danish Lieutenant S—— very nearly did.[1] I hope that officer's experiences may some day be published. He is highly connected, and his story would be especially interesting from the point of view of the treatment by the Congo Executive of the foreign officers who have accepted appointments in the Congo army under a complete misconception of the state of affairs, and who have endured all the indignities, privations, dangers, and moral sapping which an Italian officer in a letter to me—after describing "La traite des noirs," the black slave-trade—rightly describes as "la traite des blancs," the white slave-trade. These solitary exceptions are the one bright spot in a sea of blackness, for all the rif-raff of the European armies, the "lost souls," as the Italians say, have been recruited by King Leopold's agents to carry out his infamous policy. Blackguards were required to perform that dirty work, and the Congo Basin has been flooded with blackguards, converted in many instances to fiends incarnate by the tasks they have been set to do. Nor is it only among army officers that exceptions have occurred. Who shall tell the tale of the miseries of the wretched Belgian clerk or artisan,

---

[1] The case of Captain Baccari, the King of Itaty's envoy, will be present in the minds of all.

Justice and the Friendly Critic

ill-bred, ignorant, but with decent instincts, who has gone out to the Congo to the tune of the *Brabançonne*,[1] filled with patriotic imaginings, only to find himself thrust into some out-station and told to get rubber, plunged suddenly into an earthly hell ? Missionaries have had such men coming to them half-frantic after a few weeks' stay, begging and imploring their assistance ; and a shot, self-inflicted, has often enough abruptly terminated a career which in Europe might at least have been respectable. No one who has probed deep down into this cesspool of iniquity and naked human passions, or who understands the workings of the monstrous growth which civilisation has allowed to spring up in Central Africa, blames the agents of the system, but the system itself. The miserable tools are to be pitied—brutes as many of them are, the *déclassés*, the failures, the off-scourings of Europe. It is the beneficiaries that should be pilloried, the modern slavers of Africa who sit at home and pocket the dividends. Above all, that one Will—the will of a megalomaniac—which controls, rules, dominates every wheel and rivet of the Machine ; drunk with absolutism, impervious to every feeling of humanity, who drives his daughter from her mother's death-bed ; flaunts with ostentation the irregularities of his private life before all men, and rakes in millions from the anguish of his miserable African slaves.

---

[1] The Belgian national anthem.

BARNEGO CHIEFS

Showing Their Emaciated Condition

SECTION IV

THE BENEFICIARIES

THE BENEFICIARIES

" Bondage under the most barbarous and inhuman conditions, and maintained for mercenary motives of the most selfish character."—The MARQUESS OF LANDSDOWNE in House of Lords, July, 1906.

" But this labour which is said to be instead of a tax in the Congo State, do we know that it goes into the pockets of the State or to the public revenue? There are no public accounts, and as long as that is so, and so long as this taxation or this labour is levied by companies working for private individuals, the Congo State must remain open to the reproach that it is imposing not taxes but forced labour for the purposes of private profit."—Sir EDWARD GREY in House of Commons, July, 1906.

" Let us repeat, after so many others, what has become a platitude ; the success of this work is the result of an autocratic government—that is to say, of the prescience of a single man guided by a single thought ; it is the work of one sole directing will."—ALFRED POSKINE, *Bilans congolais.*

"To procure for the sovereign a maximum of revenue, such has been the object of administrative activity."—Professor F. CATTIER, Royalist and Annexationist, Teacher of Colonial Jurisprudence at the University of Brussels.

THE preceding sections have dealt with the history of King Leopold's Congo enterprise and the deeds which have characterised it, more especially during the last decade, as the effects of the system elaborated in the royal decrees of 1891–2 have made themselves felt with increasing force throughout a steadily widening area. An examination of the arguments advanced in favour of that enterprise, or in extenuation of its offences, has enabled us to pass successively in review the general condition of the native peoples under King Leopold's absolutism, the relative criminality of the Arab ivory slave-trader and the European rubber slave-

131

trader, the validity of the liquor traffic contention, the nature and the working of the judicial system introduced into the country, and, finally, the value and extent of the positive evidence favourable to the treatment of natives by Congolese officials.

We have now to consider for whom, in whose interests, this martyrdom of the races of Central Africa is being inflicted and endured, who are the beneficiaries of the rubber slave-trade, what is being done with the profits accruing therefrom.

*   *   *   *   *   *

Before coming to that point, it may be useful to summarise in a few passages the conclusions of the Report of the Congo Commission of Inquiry in regard to the two main direct causes from which the miseries of the natives spring, and as such affecting particularly the efforts made n this country to compel exposure and redress, viz., the requisitions in india-rubber and the requisitions in staple food supplies.

So far as the rubber "taxes" are concerned, the Commission found that "everywhere on the Congo, and notwithstanding certain appearances to the contrary, the native only gathers india-rubber under the influence of direct or indirect force" (p. 266), and made sundry allusions to what is implied by the word "force" on the Congo, viz., indiscriminate massacre, settlements of soldiers in rubber-producing villages, uncontrolled and unhampered in the execution of their instructions, taking of hostages, imprisonment of women and children, flogging, illegal fines and punishments, and so on. It thus described the condition of the rubber gatherer :—

"In the majority of cases he must, every fortnight, go one or two days' journey, and sometimes more, to reach the place in the forest where he can find in fair abundance the rubber vine. There the gatherer passes some days in a miserable existence. He must construct an improvised shelter which cannot obviously replace his hut ; he has not the food to which he is accustomed ; he is deprived of his wife, exposed to the inclemencies of the weather and to the attacks of wild beasts. He must take his harvest to the station of the Government or the company, and it

132

The Beneficiaries

is only after that that he returns to his village, where he can barely reside two or three days before a new demand is upon him" (p. 192).

In other words, the native in the subjugated rubber districts of the Congo must, on the Commission's own showing, under pain of suffering the various methods or retribution alluded to by the Commission, devote over three hundred days—under the above-named conditions, conditions obviously involving enormous loss of life—per annum to the gathering of rubber in order to pay his "obligatory tax" either to the Congo Government or to its Trusts.

So far as the taxes in staple foodstuffs are concerned, the Commission found that around Leopoldville (pp. 174–5) and "all the great centres" (p. 177) the population is compelled to bring in every four, seven, or twelve days considerable supplies of native-prepared bread, sometimes from enormous distances.

"As the bread (kwanga) only keeps fresh for a few days, the native, even by doubling his activity, cannot free himself from his obligations for any length of time. Even if the tax does not claim his whole time, he is perpetually obsessed by the thought of the next near payment, which causes the tax to lose its true character and to be transformed into an incessant *corvée*" (p. 176).

The results noted by the Commission from this "taxation" were depopulation (p. 174), the abandonment of the villages (p. 177), the "general misery reigning" (p. 177). The Commission found that the same conditions characterised the riverine tribes "taxed" in fish (p. 179)—the same recurrent demands, the same depopulation (p. 179), the same methods of coercion for shortage (p. 180).

Beside these admissions, which are here very briefly summarised, the remainder of the report is of secondary importance. They show us, broadly speaking, the population of the subjugated area of the Upper Congo divided into two great groups or sections, the rubber gatherers and the food suppliers—the first the direct suppliers of revenue, the second the indirect suppliers of revenue, labouring to feed the army of officials, agents, soldiers and their retinue (quartered upon the direct suppliers to compel the incessant output of rubber), and to feed the workmen, labourers, woodcutters, station hands, and others engaged in various ways in handling, preparing, and shipping the rubber to Europe. The admissions of the Commissioners show us these two great sections of the populace doomed to a perpetual enslavement, working out their cruel destiny for alien taskmasters without pause, without rest, without hope, growing fewer in numbers, impoverished and miserable, and subjected to inhuman punishments. To use Professor Cattier's words : " The impositions in rubber and foodstuffs which weigh upon more than half the territory—that is to say, over an area three or four times as large as France—subject the natives to a well-nigh continuous slavery . . . to a slavery more severe than that imposed by the Arabs."

*   *   *   *   *   *

Why? Why this enslavement and destruction of a people ?

The same old motives which from the beginning have been responsible for all the great world tragedies : human ambition, greed, and selfishness ? Yes, but let us narrow responsibility to its just limits. To arrive at the truth by process of questioning is a sound method handed down to us by the ancients.

What in reality is the " Congo Free *State* " ?

Is it a " *State* " ?

The fundamental principle of a "State" is the participation of the people of the land in the government of their country. It must be clear to the meanest intelligence that the people of the Congo "State" do not participate in the government of the country. The people of the Congo are divided into a number of separate communities and tribes, and there has been no attempt to weld together into one state-form any of these communities or tribes. Hence the word "State" in connection with the Congo enterprise is a complete misnomer.

Is it an African Protectorate or a Dependency ?

An African Protectorate or Dependency implies the establishment or over-lordship by a European nation in a

The Beneficiaries

portion of Africa, for its protection against external aggression, and for its internal administration through the development of the country in the interests of the people of the land and of the European nation which has assumed over-lordship. No European nation has assumed over-lordship of the Congo, but, with the assent of the Powers, a single man, King Leopold II. of Belgium, attributed to himself the title of " Sovereign " over the communities and tribes of the Congo basin. The country is not being developed in the interests of the people of the land, nor in the interests of a European nation. Hence the Congo enterprise is neither Protectorate nor Dependency.

Then what is the Congo enterprise ?

It has no precedent : nothing with which it can be compared. It is unique. Its component parts are :

I. A European King (monarch of a small European State whose neutrality was guaranteed by the Powers) who claims sovereignty over twenty millions of negroes in Central Africa.

II. A staff of Executive officials who direct the exercise of that Sovereignty from a European capital.

III. A staff of Executive officials who exercise that sovereignty in Central Africa through

IV. A considerable force of native troops, workmen and labourers.

What interpretation has the Sovereign given to his claim of sovereignty over those twenty millions of African men, women, and children ?

He has interpreted—without the consent of the Powers —the word sovereignty to mean *possession*.

How has he interpreted the word possession ?

He has interpreted it by an immense appropriation and expropriation. He has interpreted it by conveyancing the land of these twenty millions of negroes to himself, and all vegetable and mineral products which that land contains. This gigantic property he has divided into various parts for the purpose of raising and classifying its revenues. One part he has set aside to provide the sums necessary for the remuneration of the Executive staff in Brussels and on the Congo, the construction of dwelling-places for the staff on

135

the Congo, the construction of public works and other undertakings required to ensure the working of the property. This part of the property (A) he has called *Domaine Privé*, which by a recent manifesto he has altered with fine irony into *Domaine National*. Another part (B) he has handed over for stewardship, on various terms, to financiers from whom he has borrowed money, or to personal friends and officials of his European Court ; these, with his assistance, have raised capital to work the property thus entrusted to them, and formed " Companies " which they have floated on the Belgian Stock Exchange : in these " Companies " the Sovereign holds shares, usually one-half the total number issued. A third part (C) he has declared inalienable from himself and his heirs for ever : its revenues accrue to him. This part is termed *Domaine de la Couronne*.

Of what do the assets, or the revenues of this property consist ?

They consist (1) of the produce of the soil which has commercial value on the European markets after paying expense of handling and transport ; (2) the people of the land. The climate of the Congo being what it is, the produce of the soil is only obtainable by the people of the land, and the conveyancing of the former by the sovereign to himself would have been but a meaningless operation without the services of the people.

And how are the services of the people secured ?

The Commission of Inquiry has told us—by " FORCE," and force spells, in practice, as the Commission of Inquiry has also told us, and as the evidence we have produced shows us, the enslavement and destruction of the people of the land.

The " Congo Free State " is, therefore, not a State, nor an African Protectorate or Dependency, but an estate in Africa covering nearly one million square miles, and inhabited by perhaps twenty million human beings. This estate is claimed by one man—although he has never set foot in it—living in Europe, as his exclusive property, he having dispossessed the native inhabitants of their land, and the produce of the land which they alone can gather, and

The Beneficiaries

enslaved them in their homes to collect that produce for himself, and generally to work his property for him.

And I beg you to recollect that we are not living in the times of the Pharaohs, but have entered the twentieth century of the Christian era.

* * * * * *

From henceforth let us dismiss from our minds, our speech and our writings, the idea that the administration, or the maladministration, of an African "State" or Dependency is in question. King Leopold is the "State," and King Leopold, absentee landlord of a vast African property, is alone in question.

Above all, let us refrain from referring to the Congo as a Belgian Colony, let us avoid writing of "Belgian misrule," and let us keep from saddling the Belgian people with responsibility which is not theirs, save morally, and in that respect only a few degrees more so than it is of the British and American peoples.

Until the report of the Congo Commission of Inquiry appeared—after eight months' procrastination—shorn of all the evidence placed before it [1] the Sovereign of the Congo enterprise had with considerable skill manipulated Belgian public opinion entirely in his favour. Foreign criticisms directed against his enterprise had been invariably represented as an attack upon the Belgian people, and the scandals of that enterprise sheltered in the folds of the

---

[1] Lest the wicked Mr. Morel should make good use of it! "He (M. de Cuvelier, King Leopold's principal Secretary in Brussels) seemed to think that the renewed demand for publication had been suggested to you (Sir E. Grey) with some such sinister design by the Congo Reform Association."—Sir A. Hardinge, British Minister in Brussels to Sir E. Grey, March 29 1906. "Allow me to remind you that the step taken by Sir Constantine Phipps (Sir A. Hardinge's predecessor) on January 11 last followed close upon the letter Mr. Morel addressed to the Foreign Office, 'to suggest that pressure should be brought to bear upon the Congo Government to give full publicity to the evidence laid before its own Commission,' and I cannot but believe that that suggestion, coming from Mr. Morel, whose *rôle* is known to you, was aimed at the Congo State."—M. de Cuvelier to Sir A. Hardinge. April 19, 1906. White Book, June, 1906.

Red Rubber

Belgian flag and beneath the cloak of Belgian patriotism. The Press Bureau persistently fanned this legend, and as nearly all the Belgian newspapers were influenced by it, and the Belgian people largely ignorant of the true state of affairs, the scheme worked with wonderful success. "The publication of the Report of the Commission of Inquiry" says Professor Cattier in the preface to his notable volume,[1] "has transformed as by a magic wand the nature of the discussion of Congo affairs, . . . whoever should have alleged a year ago one-tenth of facts which to-day are definitely established would have run the risk of prosecution." To-day the situation in Belgium has, indeed altered, and is discussed with greater fulness in the last section of this book.

Here we will be content with tracing so far as is possible under present circumstances how the revenues from the Congo enterprise are distributed, and the amount of them. Figures are always indigestible to the average reader, but it is absolutely necessary in this instance to deal with them. We have drunk deep from the well of human misery : the well of human greed has now to be explored.

The King, the reader will remember, has divided his self-constituted property, so far as the revenues derived therefrom are concerned, into three parts :

A. Revenue to cover general working expenses of the property : termed "Government" or "Public" revenue.

B. Revenues acquired through the allotment of portions of the property to "Companies" or Trusts for the collection of india-rubber.

C. Personal revenues, inalienable.

Retaining the fiction of a "State," an official bulletin is issued several times a year by the Brussels section of the King's Congo staff : and in this official bulletin is given each year what purports to be the revenue and expenditure of the "State." These figures are *estimates* only, and printed as such. The actual returns are never issued. They are the estimates, be it well understood, of the

---

[1] "Etude sur la situation de l'Etat Independant du Congo." Brussels, 1906.

The Beneficiaries

revenues derived from the part of the Congo marked A, *e.g.*, the *Domaine Privé* or *National.* They profess to be the estimated revenues and expenditure of the "Government." Until 1903 they were supposed to represent an estimate of the *total* revenues derived by the "Government" from the "State," the very existence of part C.—with its inalienable personal revenues—having been systematically denied, although created in 1896.[1] These *estimates* have been issued since 1891, and for the fifteen years, 1891–1905 inclusive, figure out as follows :

Receipts, 250,353,590f.

Expenditure, 277,491,569f.

Excess of expenditure over receipts, 27,137,979f.

According to the above figures, then, the general management of the Congo enterprise has entailed in fifteen years an *estimated* working loss in round figures of £1,085,000. These figures being estimates only are valueless. They are not only valueless in the present instance, but deliberately misleading. To what extent will never be known probably, unless one of King Leopold's Congo staff in Brussels should turn "King's evidence." In so far as they are used in argument as indicative of the profit and loss on the management of the Congo enterprise, they are fraudulent.

Very few persons have succeeded in ascertaining the amount realised by King Leopold's brokers from the sale of the rubber and ivory, which constitute the principal items in the estimated revenue obtained from this part A. or *Domaine Privé* of the Congo. M. A. J. Wauters has published the figures of the sales effected on the Antwerp market for 1895–6–7. Dr. Anton, Professor at the University of Jena, was able to give those for 1898. The present writer secured from an unquestionable source those for 1899 and 1900, and Father Vermeersch, whose sources of information like those of the authorities mentioned above, have, on this point, never been contested, claims to have ascertained the total realisations for 1904 and 1905. The

---

[1] The revelation of its existence was forced by a Parliamentary debate in the Belgian House in July, 1903.

figures for 1901–2–3 are unhappily still a mystery. A comparison of these figures with the estimates will be instructive :

Years.	Published estimates.		Realisations.		
1895	Frs. 1,250,000	Frs.	5,500,000	(Antwerp)	Wauters
1896	„ 1,200,000	„	6,000,000	„	„
1897	„ 3,500,000	„	8,500,000	„	„
1898	„ 6,700,000	„	9,000,000	„	Anton
1899	„ 10,200,000	„	19,130,000	„	Morel
1900	„ 10,500,000	„	14,991,300	„	„
1901	„ 17,425,000	„	—	—	—
1902	„ 15,452,000	„	—	—	—
1903	„ 16,440,000	„	—	—	—
1904	„ 16,440,000	„	27,057,510	Total	Vermeersch
1905	„ 16,500,000	„	24,061,590	„	„

Thus in the six years for which we possess information of the partial realisations of sales, and for the two years in which we possess information relating to the total realisation of sales, we find that the estimates are 48,949,400f. or just under £2,000,000 less than the receipts. The first £2,000,000 unaccounted for ! The misleading character of these revenue estimates does not stop there. The estimates include each year a given sum, which varies with the years, representing King Leopold's share in the profits of the "Companies" which run Part B of the Congo. These estimates are entered as "*produit du portefeuille,*" or proceeds from stock held, and a Congo official remarked to Consul Casement, with grim irony, that they would be more fittingly entitled "*produit du porte-fusil,*" or proceeds from the rifle. These estimates are invariably below the actual figure. For the two years 1904 and 1905 the estimates total 5,272,770f., whereas the proportion accruing to King Leopold, as holder of half the shares in three of these companies only, amounted to 9,003,914f., an excess or nearly £150,000 over the estimates.

As I have said the full amounts realised will never be ascertained probably, but the above figures are conclusive on one point. The revenues from Part A of the Congo territories—*Domaine Privé*—set aside to cover the expenses of running the enterprise have not been less than the expenditure as the published estimates would have us believe, but

The Beneficiaries

have largely exceeded the expenditure. There has been a substantial surplus in the last fifteen years which can be placed with the utmost moderation at £2,000,000, with the certainty of being far below the mark, and that surplus is nowhere accounted for.

We will now turn to Part B, the portion of the Congo made over by the King to financiers and friends who have floated "Companies" on the Belgian Stock Exchange—formed under Congo "law" in order to escape control of Belgian Company laws—and who dispose of the rubber they "collect," by the means we have noted, chiefly on the Antwerp market. These "Companies," or Trusts, are eight in number. The *A. B. I. R* (Lopori and Maringa), *Anversoise* (Mongalla), *Kasai* (Basin of the Kasai), *Commercial Congolais* (Wamba), *Grand Lacs* (Aruwimi), *Comité Spécial du Katanga* (Katanga), *Busira* (Busira), *Lomami* (Lomami). For all practical purposes we may leave out of account in considering the revenues derived from the rubber slave-trade up to the present time, the *Busira* and *Lomami* concessions, the *Grand Lacs*, or Aruwimi concession as it is usually but not quite accurately termed; the *Commercial Congolais* and the *Katanga*. The *Busira* and *Lomami* and *Commercial Congolais* are relatively small concerns; the "exploitation" of the rubber of the Aruwimi concession by the King's agents only began eighteen months ago, and the returns are not yet available. The Katanga concession has, for various reasons, been preserved hitherto from showing substantial profits; its future would seem to lie in its copper mines, which introduces a new element not ripe at present for examination. Both the Aruwimi and Katanga are sources of great potential wealth, and lie outside the scope of the present *exposé*. Up till now the *A.B.I.R.*, *Anversoise*, and *Kasai* have been the three great revenue producers among the "Companies," and to these I propose to confine myself.

The *A. B. I. R.* used to be known as the Anglo-Belgian India Rubber Company, in which Colonel North was at one time interested. Its career of "prosperity" began with its reconstitution in 1898 as a "Congo" Company, at which time, I believe, all British capital was withdrawn. Its

Red Rubber

nominal capital is £40,000, in 2000 shares of £20 each. King Leopold possesses 1000 of these shares. Its paid up capital is only £9,280. Its managing council is at present composed of M. A. Van den Nest, Senator; Count J. d'Oultremont, Grand Master of King Leopold's European Court; A. de Browne de Tiège, formerly Member of Parliament for Antwerp, a banker who some years ago lent money to the King[1]; M. Alexis Mols, Count Horace van der Burgh, and M. J. van Stappen. M. van Eetvelde, one of King Leopold's principal Congo Secretaries of State, and Baron Dhanis, an ex-Governor-General of the Congo, used to be on the Council ; and I believe they are now, but I am not sure.

The net profits of this concern in six years have amounted to 18,004,172f., and the dividends paid per share to 8,375f. Thus in six years this " Company " has made a net profit of £720,000 out of the rubber slave-trade on a paid-up capital of £9,280, and each share of a paid-up value of £4 6s. 6d. has received £335 ! The King's profits may be calculated on these figures.

But these profits do not stand alone. To stimulate interest among the Belgian public in the Congo enterprise, shares were split up into tenths, and they are still quoted in tenths on the Antwerp Stock Exchange. In this manner public speculation was excited, and those in the know have done well, for the shares rose prodigiously. Thus, in 1899, the Stock Exchange quotation for a full share was 17,950f.; in 1900, 25,250f.; in 1903, 15,800f. These extraordinary fluctuations are significant of much which goes on behind the scenes at the headquarters of the rubber slave-trade. In the three years given above the owner of 1000 full shares was either a millionaire or next door to it. Let the reader judge :

1000 shares paid-up value.		Stock exchange quotations.
Say £4,640	... 1899 ...	£718,000
,,	... 1900 ...	£1,010,000
,,	... 1903 ...	£632,000

---

[1] Which had to be paid back by the Belgian Parliament.

The Beneficiaries

Eight years of slaughter, endemic oppression, and exhaustion of the rubber-bearing vines have done their work. The output is falling rapidly, and the full share to-day is only worth £188. I say "worth"—I should have said quoted. It is not worth anything like that so far as its Congo expectations are concerned, but some of the blood-stained profits of former years have been invested in rubber plantations in the Malay States, and, doubtless, in other undertakings. The "property" of this "Company" on the Congo is virtually ruined, and precisely the same history is being repeated in the Kasai, to which we will now direct our attention.

Prior to 1902, the Kasai Basin was the only region of the vast Upper Congo left open to *trade*. This concession had been wrung out of the King by the opposition of the Belgian merchants established in the Upper Congo when the royal decrees (1891-2) interpreting the rights of "Sovereignty" into personal possession were promulgated. Fourteen Belgian and Dutch merchants *bought* rubber from the natives on fair terms, and did a brisk business. Then King Leopold stepped in, and forced these firms to amalgamate in a Trust. The natives became the property of the Trust, and the rubber in the forests also. The share capital is 1,005,000f. in 4,020 shares of 250f. per share, of which the King holds 2,010. The Administrators in Europe are appointed subject to the King's approval. The powers of this Administrative Council are controlled by a permanent Committee composed of four members, two of whom the King selects; the other two being appointed subject to the King's approval. The King appoints the Chairman of the Committee and he has the casting vote. The net profits of the concern have been as follows :

1902	...	...	Francs	1,465,279
1903	...	...	"	3,687,161
1904	...	...	"	5,597,449
1905	...	...	"	7,543,000

or in four years £731,680 on a capital—fully paid up, I believe—of £40,200. These shares are also dealt with in tenths. The value of the full share to-day is 15,500f.[1]

---

[1] Oct. 10th, 16,000f.

Red Rubber

The King's 2,010 shares are worth, therefore, at the present figure £1,244,200. The profits of the rubber slave-trade are not exactly negligeable! Twelve hundred tons of rubber on a total output of five thousand tons from the whole of the Congo were wrung from the Kasai natives last year. The state of things in this part of the Sovereign's property must beggar description. According to the best authorities the Kasai natives ten years ago were the finest races on the Congo, celebrated for "moral and physical beauty." They are now in process of being extirpated and dragged down to the level of the unhappy Mongos, Budjas, A-Babuas and other tribes inhabiting the rubber zone.

The history of the third great Trust, that of the Mongalla is more startling than its profits, which, however, are not to be despised. The European board consists of M. A. de Browne de Tiège (whom, as we have seen, is on the A.B.I.R. Board), M. C. de Browne de Tiège, M. Bunge (the King's broker) and Baron Goffinet, an "Intendant of the King's Civil List," otherwise stated one of the keepers of the Privy Purse—quite a happy family party. The capital is 1,700,000f., divided into 3,400 shares of 500f. each, of which the King holds 1,700. Moreover the King levies 15 per cent. on the Company's rubber profits when a fixed percentage of profit has been reached. The net profits of the three fat years 1898, 1899, and 1903 amounted to £360,000. Profit taking in 1900, 1901 and 1902 was sadly interfered with by the Budjas, a fierce tribe which declined to be enslaved. Now the profits are steadily rising again, the King having "taken over" the business; which means in practical politics that the natives are being kept "at work" wholly by the King's troops commanded by officers, instead of by the less efficient irregulars raised by the Trust and commanded by men of the Caudron type. It seems that the Budjas are now "working well," and the value of a full share (the shares are also quoted in tenths) is now £280. Seventeen hundred shares of a nominal value of £20 = £34,400 ; seventeen hundred shares at £280 = £476,000, Q.E.D. Shortly after the notorious Major Lothaire strung up Mr. Stokes to the nearest available tree, after a trial which Lord Fitzmaurice has recently called

The Beneficiaries

" one of the most disgraceful judicial farces which ever
sullied the annals of what purported to be a Court of
Justice," King Leopold appointed him to the post of
Managing Director of this concern in Africa, and it is said
that His Majesty had very weighty reasons for offering this
most energetic official a lucrative berth—which that berth
certainly proved itself to be.

* * * * * *

We now come to Part C of the Congo territory—
Domaine de la Couronne, whose revenues the absentee landlord
has appropriated to his own exclusive manipulation. The
world is not even favoured with estimates of these revenues.
Sown in blood,[1] they are harvested in secret. We owe to
Professor Cattier the first and the only disclosures of their
amount and the disposal of them. All we knew prior to
the appearance of his revelations this year were the names
of the three gentlemen appointed by the King to manage
them, viz. : Baron Goffinet, already holding a distinguished
position—as we have seen—in the Congo enterprise, Baron
Raoul Snoy, one of the King's *aides-de-camp*, and M.
Droogmans, secretary for the management of the *Domaine
Privé* or A revenues—again a harmonious family party.
With great elaboration, by carefully tabulated statistics, by
a system of double-check worked out in detail Professor
Cattier has been able to estimate that the net profits pro-
cured from this private preserve have amounted in the last
decade to a strict minimum of £2,854,000 or nearly
£300,000 per annum. In the course of the debate in the
Belgian Chamber last March, M. de Smet de Naeyer, the
Premier (of whom more anon) and M. de Favereau, the
Foreign Minister, upon both of whom the Congo autocrat
can rely under any circumstances, endeavoured to dispute
Professor Cattier's figures. But the attempt broke down
hopelessly. M. de Favereau described the estimates as " very
much exaggerated " but when pressed to give the actual

---

[1] *Vide* Mr. Joseph Clark's and Mr. A. E. Scrivener's evidence,
Section III. See also the terrible accounts gathered by Consul
Casement from refugees who had escaped from this territory.
(White Book, Africa, No. 1, 1904).

figure, replied, amid laughter, " I do not know what it is." [1]
M. de Smet de Naeyer was not much happier. Basing
himself upon data purporting to fix the total rubber-producing area of the Congo, and deducting therefrom the area of
the *Domaine de la Couronne*, he declared that the King's profits
had been nearer £720,000 than £2,000,000. Asked if he
"took the responsibility for this figure," M. de Smet de
Naeyer answered that he was " not called upon to establish
before the House the revenues of the *Domaine de la Couronne*,"
but was merely disposing of Professor Cattier's "errors." [2]
Unfortunately for the speaker, he was shown at a subsequent
stage in the debate to have himself been guilty of a
prodigious error, by including in the rubber-producing area
of the Congo—as quoted by him to the House—the area
covered by all the waterways of the immense fluvial system
of the country, plus the area where rubber is known to
exist but where it has not yet been "exploited "! Hence
Professor Cattier's estimates remain unshaken. He might
easily have been confounded, by the King furnishing the
Prime Minister of Belgium with the real figure, if that figure
had been lower than the Professor's estimates. That the Prime
Minister was not so furnished is pretty conclusive evidence
that the real figure is higher than Professor Cattier's estimates.

But this terrible critic of the absentee African landlord
did not end there. He succeeded in obtaining some
remarkable information as to the disposal of these revenues.
He found that they were utilised, *inter alia*, in the creation of
a Press Bureau, the subsidising of journalists, newspapers, and
jurists—for the drawing up of doctrinal theses, whereby the
King has sought to invest with legality the appropriation of
800,000 square miles of African territory to himself; the
construction of a "colonial school" at Tervueren ; the
construction of a triumphal arch in Brussels, the cost of
which the Belgian Parliament had declined to sanction
from the national funds ; improvements on a colossal scale
of the royal residence at Laeken ; last, but not least, the
purchase of real estate. It was in dealing with the latter
item that Professor Cattier was specially instructive. He

---

[1] Official shorthand report, Feb.-March, 1906.   [2] Ibid.

The Beneficiaries

searched through the register of mortgages for two of the wards or districts of Belgium (that of Brussels and that or Ostend) and he found that the King had purchased in the name of the *Domaine de la Couronne* (as purchaser) real estate to the amount—as entered on the bills of sale—ot £731,560. Eighteen pages of Professor Cattier's volume are devoted to a detailed enumeration of the 115 transactions, officially recorded in these two wards alone. Land, houses, gardens, hotels, woods, building ground, stables, etc., are mentioned in these astonishing purchases, which, as Mr. Harold Spender says,[1] look "as if King Leopold aimed at using the proceeds of the Congo for turning Belgium into his private estate." I do not know whether Belgian legislation includes what might correspond to our statutes of mortmain, but there would seem to be need of something of the kind.

The genius of Leopold Africanus has imagined yet another method of acquiring further sums from his African property, *e.g.*, by means of loans. The nominal liabilities of the "Congo State" are considerable. They are as follows :

1888 "Public debt"	.	.	Frs. 150,000,000
1890 and 1895 debt contracted with Belgium	.	.	„ 31,804,405
1896 Loan	. . .	.	„ 1,500,000
1898 „	. . .	.	„ 12,500,000
1901 „	. . .	.	„ 50,000,000
1904 „	. . .	.	„ 30,000,000

Or a total nominal indebtedness in round figures of £11,000,000!

The 1,500,000 100-franc bonds of the 1888 loan are redeemable in ninety-nine years by drawings on the lottery system. The guaranteed fund being sufficient to provide for interest and sinking fund, no interest is paid on the issues. According to M. de Smet de Naeyer 900,000 of these bonds have been issued. According to Professor Cattier the issue of the first 100,000 bonds was "authorised" in February, 1888, and the subscription list was

---

[1] *Contemporary Review*, July, 1906.

Red Rubber

opened on March 7 of the same year at the price of
83f. per bond : a further issue of 800,000 bonds was
"authorised by the decree of November 3, 1902." He
adds that this issue was partly converted in 1903. If
M. de Smet de Naeyer's figure is accurate—and his statements as we have seen must be received with caution—
only 200,000 bonds out of the last authorised issue have
been converted. A large number of bonds have been
placed in France, and M. Lucien Coquet, in an able treatise,
declares that in 1903 the number of bonds negotiable on
the French market was 796,875.[1] Should this be true it
means that France holds four-fifths of the total issue
up-to-date, an interesting circumstance deserving of note.

King Leopold pays no interest to Belgium on the money
borrowed from her in 1890 and 1895.

The loans of 1896, 1898, and 1901 bear interest at
4 per cent., and the loan of 1904 at 3 per cent. The
bonds created under the 1901 loan are reimbursable in
ninety years. The bonds issued under the 1904 loan,
known as the " 3 per cent. Congo," bear interest as
from March 1 of that year. A portion of this stock was
placed at par, the balance at a discount of no less than
28 per cent.

In addition to the nominal liabilities mentioned above,
an indirect debt was incurred in 1901, consisting of a
guarantee of interest of 4 per cent. on a sum of
25,000,000f. raised by the *Grand Lacs* Trust.

In his recent manifesto, King Leopold expresses his
intention of raising a further loan of 100,000,000f.—
four million sterling.

What has King Leopold actually received from these
loans ?

It is impossible to say with certainty. Professor Cattier,
after an elaborate analysis—based upon the sums set aside in
the annual Congo estimates for interest on loans—reckons
the figure at £3,200,000, exclusive of the 1888 loan. The
yield from the 1888 loan he reckons at £2,000,000 : total

---

[1] Lucien Coquet, "Fragments d'une étude sur les secrets
d'Etat." Paris, 1903.

148

The Beneficiaries

£5,200,000. A long and heated discussion took place in the Belgian Chamber over these figures last March. The upshot of it was that an actual yield of a little over £3,000,000 was admitted by M. de Smet de Naeyer, who gave no *proof*—as various speakers pointed out—that the larger sum estimated by Professor Cattier did not approximate more closely to the truth.

* * * * * *

And now let us sum up this astonishing series of facts.

King Leopold starts upon his Congo career by declaring that he has taken in hand a philanthropic enterprise. Stanley came over to this country as his mouth-piece, and —doubtless quite sincerely at the time—chided his audience for a latent scepticism, or lack of "sentiment." They could not, he told them " appreciate rightly, *because there are no dividends attached to it*, this restless, ardent, vivifying and expansive sentiment which seeks to extend civilising influence among the dark places of sad-browed Africa."

For several years the King sinks £40,000 *per annum* in the Congo, which he is gradually taking steps to turn into his private possession with everything animal, vegetable, and mineral within it included.

He publishes annual statements which profess to be estimates of the *total* revenues acquired by this philanthropic enterprise, and he invites the world to note that during the last fifteen years, notwithstanding his royal liberality, the enterprise shows a loss of £1,085,000.

Upon examination those estimates are found to have been below the receipts by something like £3,000,000, so that an alleged loss is converted into a profit of nearly £2,000,000 nowhere accounted for.

It transpires, moreover, that the King is the holder of shares in rubber " Companies," which he has caused to be formed and floated in Brussels and on the Congo, and which he controls through his creatures, and that the stock-exchange value of his holdings to-day is £2,000,000.

It transpires further that—after concealing the fact for eight years—the King has set aside a portion of the Congo

Red Rubber

four times the size of England, Scotland, and Wales, for himself exclusively, and that the net revenues he has derived therefrom in ten years amount to £2,854,000.

Thus we find that the King's philanthropic enterprise has in the last fifteen years produced a net profit of just under £5,000,000 instead of a deficit of £1,085,000, and that the close of these fifteen years finds the King in possession of shares in three rubber "Companies" of a total stock-exchange value of £2,000,000, apart altogether from the enormous potential value of his holding in two other Congo "Companies"—the Katanga (and its subsidiaries) and the *Grand Lacs* or Aruwimi. Holder of these shares, in two cases for eight years, in one case for four years, he has been in a position to reap all the profits from speculation thus afforded, and with the greater facility since the large proportion of shares held by him, carried with it control of the market.

The picture is completed by the revelation that *to meet an alleged published deficit of* £1,085,000, he has contracted nominal debts to the amount of £11,000,000 from which he has, admittedly, received £3,000,000 !

The whole of these vast sums are the proceeds of the rubber slave-trade of the Congo, raised directly or indirectly from the unspeakable oppression, misery, and partial extermination of the native of Central Africa.

Crime so awful, scandal of such magnitude, tragedy so immeasurable—the world surely has never seen their like in combination.

*　　*　　*　　*　　*　　*

The question with which this section is headed is now answered, and the facts herein tabulated can only be disproved in one way, viz. : by the production of audited balance sheets of the Congo revenues, covering the last fifteen years. And these will not be forthcoming.

King Leopold is the main beneficiary of the rubber slave-trade : a long way behind him, the chosen few whom choice or temporary necessity have caused to be selected as participants in the royal spoil. As a Belgian writer puts it: "The slave-trade has been re-established for the benefit of

The Beneficiaries

King Leopold and twenty rich families in Belgium." It bodes little what the sovereign of the Congo has done with this ill-gotten wealth. If he had spent it all, and all the additional wealth it has enabled him to amass in other fields, in charitable institutions, the crime, the scandal, and the tragedy would remain. True to his *rôle* King Leopold now seeks to pose as the celestially appointed agent to stem the ravages of malaria and sleeping-sickness. He has given £1,000 to Sir Alfred Jones—his Liverpool Consul and the ocean-carrier of his rubber—for the Liverpool School of Tropical Medicine (an admirable institution of which Sir Alfred Jones is the president), and in his recent manifesto offers to spend £12,000 towards "fighting" the sleeping sickness. The mere idea of a grant of £12,000 out of as many millions wrung from the Congo natives, fills this royal Pecksniff with such emotion at his own goodness that he declares :—

"If God gives me that satisfaction (victory over sleeping sickness) I shall be able to present myself before His judgment-seat with the credit of having performed one of the finest acts of the century, and a legion of rescued beings will call down upon me His grace." [1]

Prodigious! One feels inclined to suggest a special form of prayer for the use of the royal benefactor somewhat after this wise :—

"Oh! Almighty God, from my ill-gotten millions I devote unto Thee the colossal sum of twelve thousand pounds, to save Thy people in Africa from a disease which my policy towards them, by increasing their impoverishment and misery,[2] by destroying their confidence,[2] by robbing them of their staple food supplies,[2] by plunging them in wretchedness and despair,[2] has largely increased.[2] Stained as my policy is, with crimes innumerable, Thou wilt appreciate the extent of this, my pecuniary sacrifice. At the touch of my royal robe, whole tribes have disappeared as though struck down with a mysterious pestilence. The progress of my triumphal march through the Equatorial forest is marked by the bleached bones of men and women. But all good deeds have their painful sides, and what is the evil wrought, besides

---

[1] Royal manifesto, June, 1906.
[2] Evidence before Commission of Inquiry.

these twelve thousand golden pieces which I offer upon this my sacrificial altar, for the salvation of those of my black subjects whose eyelids (unhappily for them) are not yet closed in sleep eternal?"

It bodes little whether the bulk of this money has been, and is being expended on what the King considers the interests of Belgium—we shall see in the next section the peculiar way in which those interests are regarded by him. Obviously he cannot spend it all on himself, or his friends of either sex. The improvements at the Laeken Palace are to cost, when completed, £1,200,000. The triumphal arch erected in Brussels, and which the nation did not require, cost £200,000. Plans have recently been submitted to His Majesty for the erection of an enormous statue of himself mounted on a charger to be erected in Brussels in 1910 at a cost of £150,000. The investigations into the value of real estate he has purchased in Belgium have only begun. Professor Cattier has proved purchases totalling £731,560. Monsieur Vandervelde was able to inform the Belgian Chamber last March that Professor Cattier's disclosures by no means exhaust the list; that more real estate has been bought by the "Domaine de la Couronne" in the provinces of Louvain, Namur, and Luxemburg.[1] The same speaker alleged that other properties had been purchased by the King in the name of Baron Goffinet (with whom the reader will be familiar).[1] It is, of course, well known that the King owns large properties on the Mediterranean, notably at Cape Ferrat, where a magnificent residence and grounds are occupied by "Madame la baronne Vaughan." The French Government declined to recognise the "Domaine de la Couronne" as a valid purchaser, and the property was acquired in the name of the King's medical adviser.[2] M. Vandervelde estimates the purchase price of the properties at Cape Ferrat, and in Brussels under the name of Baron Goffinet at £680,000; and he is exceptionally well informed. It is, of course, equally well known that the King has invested large sums in Chinese railways, and in Persia, and there are rumours that his agents are

---

[1] Official Parliamentary Report.   [2] Ibid.

The Beneficiaries

conducting negotiations in San Domingo and Bolivia. He is reported to have invested £600,000 in Suez Canal stock.[1] Very large sums have certainly been expended in the campaign of mendacity organised throughout the world by his Press Bureau, especially in France, the United States, Italy, and Germany. A great deal of information has come into my hands on this subject, but not in a form which renders publicity always possible, or internationally desirable. There is not a well-informed Frenchman on Colonial affairs but knows that the present admittedly deplorable state of affairs in the African territory of France bordering King Leopold's preserve, is the outcome primarily of Leopoldian intrigue with a golden lining. The men who in France are struggling against the innoculation of French Colonial ideas by the Leopoldian virus—Anatole France, Francis de Préssensé, Paul Viollet, Gustave Rouanet, Pierre Mille, Félicien Challaye, and others—are fighting not only for the fair fame of their country, but—as we are fighting here— for the preservation of the native races of Central Africa, for the salvation of the African tropics from the destructive blight of Leopoldian precept and example. That great man, de Brazza, seeing with his own eyes the result of imitating Leopoldian methods in the French Congo, whither he had been sent on a mission of investigation by his Government, had determined to consecrate the rest of his life to opening the eyes of the French people, and fighting the modern slave-trade. Death has robbed us of him. But his Memoirs remain. May Madame de Brazza be inspired to give them to the world.

---

[1] *Le Patriote* (Royalist and Catholic), Brussels, August, 1905, in an interview " with an eminent authority of the first rank."

SECTION V

THE DUTY

I

THOU !

DID King Leopold know that the concomitants to the enormous revenues he has been drawing from the labour of the Congo races were the misery, degradation, enslavement and partial extermination of those peoples ?

*   *   *   *   *   *

Does the question require an answer, other than the answer these pages supply ?

Remember that power has been and is vested in him alone ; that that power is absolute, all controlling and directing ; that his Congo staff in Brussels is not composed of responsible officials, but of men whom he himself has selected and keeps upon it, revocable at his will and pleasure, answerable to him alone, paid out of his African revenues, men to whom no initiative is allowed, who are there to do his bidding, whose position is wholly dependent upon a slavish submission to his commands.

Remember that these men—if responsibility be shifted from the royal shoulders on to theirs—stand condemned on the face of the Report of his own Commission, stand condemned at the bar of civilisation, of having directed for fifteen years, from their offices in Brussels, a vast system of criminal oppression the like of which the world has never seen.

Remember that if the royal master was ignorant of their misdeeds, they have betrayed and disgraced him before the universe, they have bespattered the royal robe with blood, they have branded the royal name with infamy, they have been wicked servants; and their offence is the greater since he has profited from it, largely profited, profited beyond the dreams of avarice.

Remember that he has retained them in office, and that a Minister of Great Britain to the European country over which he rules as constitutional monarch, has still to conduct diplomatic negotiations through *them*, on behalf of the Government of his Britannic Majesty!

Remember that his Congo staff in Africa does but apply and carry out the instructions it receives from Brussels, and that the Governor-General is his "mandatory."

Remember that fourteen years ago he, by secret decree [1] —the contents of which were unknown until years later— gave to that staff a command which was to regulate their whole conduct, to be the motive force directing them, their paramount duty and their first consideration; and that command was *to raise revenue.*

Remember that for eleven years out of those fourteen the natives were "by force" [2] compelled to provide this revenue, illegally,[2] with no limitation as to quantity or time, and that members of his staff received in various forms commission proportionate to the revenue they secured.[2]

Remember that in the eleventh year, when revelations increased and multiplied every day, this raising of revenue "by force" was for the first time legalised, but limited by law in such a way as to provide that no native should be called upon to labour for the royal majesty in Brussels at the utmost more than forty hours per month or sixty days per annum.[2]

Remember that three months after the promulgation or this legal decision—which had then become the law of the country—the King's "mandatory" in Africa issued a private circular to the local staff to the effect that the revenues, under this new law—*which restricted to a fixed duration of time demands that for the eleven preceding years had been unrestricted and unlimited*—should not only be maintained at their previous figure, but should show "constant

---

[1] December 5, 1891.
[2] Commission of Inquiry's Report.

progression"[1] : and that one year after the new law had come into operation (November–December, 1904) the natives were being requisitioned " by force " to the raising of revenue for a minimum of three hundred days in the year.[2]

Remember that from this supreme "illegality " sprang acts all of them equally illegal according to the laws of the country, propounded for the ostensible purpose of protecting the native against outrage, which the supreme "illegality" rendered habitual and inevitable ; such as armed expeditions illegally sent against native communities, unwilling or unable to supply revenue in quantities considered requisite by the local members of the royal staff, who received a commission on that revenue ; the seizure of men and women and their illegal retention in hostage-houses, and so on.

Remember that all this while if *data* on the abominations committed under this illegal system for raising revenue in accordance with the King's command were accumulating in the mission stations, they were also accumulating in the official records and in the Public Prosecutor's office, which is supervised by the King's "mandatory" ; and that the King's Commissioners have declared that the material for the affirmations their Report contains, and for the conclusions at which they arrived, was supplied not so much from the evidence placed before them by European and native witnesses as from the examination of these official records.[3]

Remember that no members of the King's Executive staff in Africa have been prosecuted or even dismissed the royal service, but on the contrary have been honoured, promoted, and remunerated.

    *   *   *   *   *   *

Let those who from motives unquestionably good in the eyes of the men who hold them, motives made up of

---

[1] Commission of Inquiry's Report.
[2] Ibid. These demands continued as soon as the back of the Commission was turned, and they continue to this day.
[3] Ibid.

Red Rubber

traditions and a general trend of ideas that have much to recommend them in ordinary cases, seek some loophole of escape from a grim logic which will not be gainsaid, and find it in "Sinning Concessionnaire Companies"; let them remember who these "concessionnaires" are, and what these "Companies" are! Farmers of a portion of the royal revenues; organisations created and operating under the King's African code of laws, subjected to no control from the machinery of a European judicature.

Let them remember that the men on the Councils of the headquarters of these concerns are the King's Congo bodyguard; that all these years they have acted in the closest partnership with him—officers of his Privy Purse, functionaries at his European Court, bankers ever obsequious to the royal call!

Let them remember that these men still bask in the royal smile, these "Companies" still operate, the King's steamers still convey to their agents in Africa the rifle and cap-gun, the cases of cartridges, caps and loads, by which means they "stimulate" for themselves and for the King the rubber output!

Like the Brussels Executive Staff, like the Congo Executive Staff; the so-called "*concessionnaires*," the titled partners in guilt, the financial vampires in co-equal infamy, the beneficiaries from uniformity in outrage, remain.

The handwriting is on the wall! It blazes forth in letters of fire! They will burn through the ages unquenchable, ineffaceable, a transcendental testimony to the possibilities of individual crime, a supreme warning to mankind, and in the dim hereafter those who read them with happier hearts and in happier times will recollect that their message it was which pronounced the final judgment upon autocratic rule in the world of men.

II

"REFORM"

"My rights on the Congo are indivisible . . . none possess any right of intervention." Such is King Leopold's answer to the protest of civilisation. The tenure of he who makes that answer is so precarious that he has thought well to accompany such declarations with a series of decrees addressed to his Brussels staff, elaborating a number of "reforms."

Those "reforms" are left to the Congo staff to execute after having been drawn up by the Brussels staff!

The future destinies of the Congo natives are committed to the same hands which have dealt so gently with them in the past!

"Reforms," the need for which the Brussels staff has always rejected because it always denied the existence of factors requiring that attention which the Commission or Inquiry urgently called for, are conceded, in theory, just as they were conceded, in theory, ten years ago by the creation of the "Commission for the Protection of the Natives" and the "perfecting" of the "Organisation of Justice."

And observe in what manner they are issued to a wondering world. "We—that is, the most obedient servants of His Majesty's Brussels staff—have the honour to submit for the approval of your Majesty the legislative and administrative measures which appear to us of a nature *to continue the realisation of the programme which the King-Sovereign has been pursuing for more than a quarter of a century in Central Africa, at the price of his constant efforts and personal sacrifice.*" How true, indeed! For the items in the "programme" of this Leopoldian civilisation remain not only unaltered, but accentuated, re-affirmed in tones unmistakable, breathing an arrogance born of long immunity in wrongdoing.

The interpretation of "Sovereignty" to mean personal possession ; of an international trusteeship converted into private property ; of African production for the pursuance of alien aims ; of power absolute, unchecked, unfettered, uncontrolled, "indivisible," setting itself beyond and above the law of nations—all this is emphasised in the Royal Manifesto.

The "personal sacrifice" is exemplified by a tightening of the grip upon the revenues from the *Domaine de la Couronne* and *Domaine Privé*, while modesty still demands that the extent of the "sacrifice" should be withheld—in other words, that the amount of those revenues should still be wrapped in mystery as unfathomable as the regenerator of Africa can make it! Any outside interference in such matters "partakes of the character of positive usurpation."[1]

The realisation of the programme will be fulfilled "with the most immutable patriotism," and "in perfect harmony with my immutable will."[2]

That form does atonement take!

*   *   *   *   *   *

After this is it necessary to exame those "reforms"?

The produce of the soil of Central Africa still belongs to the King ; hence, too, the labour of the African without which the former is unobtainable. But the native will only be taxed "in strict conformity with legality"!

The royal profits derived from pillage, perennial outrage, and endemic oppression have been stupendous, but insufficient, as we have seen,[3] to provide for the feeding of native witnesses, whose attendance is required at Boma, the chief directing centre of the King's African estate. So, too, more officers will be drafted into the King's African army to secure the "effective control" of the troops, but only

---

[1] Royal Manifesto, June, 1906.   [2] Ibid.
[3] *Vide* Section IV., part iii.

" when the revenue permits of it " ! and *three* " Inspectors " shall be specially appointed to ensure a just relationship between European and natives in a country 800,000 square miles in extent as a preliminary to securing "a more complete administrative and judicial organisation " which, alas ! is " only possible through an increase in the revenue of the State " !

" The law "—we had been told of old time—" protects the freedom of the native by *forbidding any interference with the freedom of* business transactions," [1] and we are *now* informed that this principle remains unimpaired. Who could have doubted it, since the only articles on the Congo which can give rise to " business transactions " are the private property of the absentee landlord in Europe ! Have we not been told also that " the State has been at much pains to protect the natives from being robbed." [2]

The native is only required to work " forty hours per month " for the absentee landlord and his partners. Let the reader peruse once more the preceding chapter. . . . In the last seven years King Leopold's African estate has produced eleven million pounds sterling of india-rubber by claiming the labour of the African natives from the rising of the sun to the setting thereof, and enforcing that claim *vi et armis*, and the King's " mandatory " has declared that the amount must be increased under a law which demands of the native not every day in every year, but only sixty days. If this law were applied the revenues would decrease by four-fifths, and I am afraid that not only would the "effective control " of the King's African army, to say nothing of the " more complete administrative and judicial organisation " be delayed *ad infinitum*, but the native witnesses in criminal cases would need to go wholly unfed, and—still more terrible to contemplate—the next cheque for the Liverpool School of Tropical Medicine might conceivably become overdue, while the chances of fruitful speculation in rubber shares on the Antwerp *Bourse* would be inconveniently curtailed. " Personal sacrifice " would clearly be too onerous a moral asset on such terms.

---

[1] Official Bulletin.   [2] Ibid.

III

THE POSITION OF BELGIUM

"We are, therefore, armed. It is not the power to act, but the will to act, which the Government lacks, and I must add that I do not expect much from it, because the characteristic of its policy during the last few years has been complete acquiescence in everything which the sovereign of the Congo State has done."
—N. VANDERVELDE, 1906.[1]

NOT reform but revolution. Not the apothecary but the surgeon. Not poulticing but removal.

Can the European people over whom King Leopold—a foreigner to them—rules as constitutional monarch and whom he in his heart despises—can *they* apply the remedy ? Can they tear the races of Central Africa from that relentless grasp ? Are they able to do it ? Were they able to do it, could they shoulder the burden of introducing justice and good government where for fifteen long years massacre and pillage have gone hand in hand—a burden heavy, ungrateful, dangerous for so small a people—the more dangerous since their mental outlook on colonial enterprise has been greatly poisoned and corroded by the fœtid example placed before them ?

Between England and Belgium cling historical ties which make for the preservation of Belgium. The King of the Belgians is a bitter and malignant enemy of England. He has become so because England has supplied the pens and the voices which have exposed his African undertaking.

---

[1] Official shorthand report of the Belgian Parliamentary Debates, February–March, 1906.

The Position of Belgium

But in England, if there is no particular admiration for, there is no hostility to, the Belgian people.¹ Almost everywhere among us it is recognised that they have been misled as to sentiment, duped as to motives, misinformed as to facts, irresponsible as to action, foully betrayed by carefully combined co-operation in intrigue. Hence it is that a very general feeling prevails in this country in official circles and outside them that annexation by Belgium would constitute a solution, most to be desired on varying grounds, of the Congo outrage.

This hope has been frequently expressed. Let us, then, examine the possibilities. But in God's name let our examination rest upon and start from the real issue at stake—the salvation of the Congo races from the rubber slave-trade. Do not let us be decoyed by what may prove a mirage, capitulate before an idea merely because it appears attractive. A hideous mistake was committed twenty-two years ago. It must not be repeated. The Congo natives have paid too heavy a price to international thoughtlessness to be again sacrificed. Moreover, if we could suppose Belgium running the Congo on Leopoldian lines, such a condition of things would become a grave danger to the cause of international peace.

What is the position of Belgium with regard to the Congo to-day? It is an extraordinary position, and in many respects a most humiliating one. Belgium has no legal rights whatsoever over the King's enterprise, which, so far as she is concerned, is "a foreign State" outside the control or supervision of the Belgian Parliament and people.²

---

¹ They are active, industrious, very hard-working. The conduct of the brave handful who, at considerable personal sacrifice in at least one case I know, have endeavoured to save their country from moral complicity in the rubber slave-trade is absolutely beyond praise. Praise, indeed, in this case, would almost savour of impertinence.

² This has been repeatedly stated in Parliament by members of the present Belgian Cabinet. Again, in the last Congo debates (February, 1906), the Belgian Foreign Minister, attacking M. Vandervelde's interpellation, said, "He knows that the two Governments are distinct, and that we cannot be rendered responsible for acts in which we have not participated."

Red Rubber

Belgium cannot even insist upon information being tendered to her as to the financial and general management·of that enterprise by the King's Brussels staff, although Belgium has loaned over one million sterling to King Leopold as African sovereign, on which she receives no interest, and although she lends King Leopold the officers of her army to assist him in maintaining the rubber slave-trade, and her diplomatists and consuls to defend it. This state of affairs has been brought about by the subservience to the royal will of M. de Smet de Naeyer, the Belgian Premier, who in all matters relating to the Congo has placed the interests of King Leopold first, and the interests of Belgium a long way afterwards. This his lengthened tenure of office—due to the break up of the old Liberal party, the fear of Socialist legislation among the middle classes, and the preponderance of the voting power of those classes at the polls owing to the existing elective system, and the undoubted increase in the country's prosperity—has enabled M. de Smet de Naeyer to do with impunity. He has been in power twenty-three years, covering the whole period of the rise and enforcement of the rubber slave-trade. M. de Smet de Naeyer's predecessors were, to some extent at any rate, independent of the King's influence, but his docility has been remarkable, and as a reward he has been ennobled—a privilege never granted to his forerunners, although men of far greater personality and mental calibre. Believed to be above reproach in his private life, politically he is the King's creature, and the members of his Cabinet are merely figureheads. It is a puppet government of which the strings are pulled by the King who, through the veil of a constitutional monarchy, exercises with increasing force a despotic will, riding rough-shod over constitutional foundations. Never was the monarch's trend of mind in this regard shown more clearly than in his recent Manifesto, in which he lays down the law in matters affecting the interests of Belgium as though no constitutional formulæ and limitations existed.

The events which have led up to the position in which Belgium finds herself in regard to the Congo may be briefly summarised. After he had obtained the separate and collective recognition of his African enterprise from

The Position of Belgium

the United States of America and the European Powers, King Leopold applied for the sanction of the Belgian Chambers to his assuming the title of "Sovereign of the Congo State." This "fusion of the two Crowns," as it is called, was secured, not without opposition, by that Belgian statesman whose high reputation extends beyond the boundaries of his country, M. Beernaert. It will be borne in mind that in those days the King proclaimed (as he still proclaims *mirabile dictu*) that he was working solely in the interests of Belgium. In a letter to M. Beernaert, dated August 5, 1889, the King communicated to that statesman a will bequeathing to Belgium after his death all his "sovereign rights" over the Congo "*as they are recognised* by the Declarations, Conventions, and Treaties concluded since 1884, between the foreign Powers on the one side, the International Association of the Congo and the Independent State of the Congo on the other."

The words italicised should be carefully retained. The King's "sovereign rights" were indeed recognised, but the interpretation which the King has since placed upon those "sovereign rights" has *not* been recognised. It has been repudiated emphatically by the British Government, and, were the same interpretation adopted by his possible successor, that repudiation with all that it involves would hold good.

The King intimated in the above letter that, if before his death "it should be agreeable to the country (*i.e.*, Belgium) to establish closer links with the Congo, *I should not hesitate to place them at its disposal. I should be happy to see it* ["*our African*" *work*] *during my lifetime in the full enjoyment of their possession.*"

This "free gift" of the Congo to Belgium by a patriotic monarch was accepted by the Belgian Chambers in July, 1890, on the following terms. Belgium was to have the right to annex the Congo at any time within the ensuring ten years. She was to advance £1,000,000 sterling to the King's enterprise, paying £200,000 down and £80,000 *per annum* during the specified period. No interest was to be demanded from the King, but if at the expiration of the agreement, Belgium refused definitely to annex, then the loan would bear interest at $3\frac{1}{2}$ per cent. No further financial liabilities were to be incurred by the King without the assent of the Belgian Chambers, a most reasonable proviso, since Belgium from that date onwards stood in the light of prospective heir, and one which a monarch working in the interests of Belgium was bound to observe, apart from his plighted word.

This "free gift" then was secured by Belgium at a first cost of £1,000,000 (plus interest) to the Belgian taxpayer.

In 1898 the Count de Merode Westerloo brought forward an annexation project. The King worked against it secretly, and the Socialists opposed it with the greatest violence, especially when it transpired in the course of the debate that the King had broken his word, had borrowed £250,000 from M. de Browne de Tiège, that the time-limit was about to expire, and that with its expiration this astute banker, would come into possession for ever of a slice of territory—according to the terms of his private bargain with the King—on the Congo five times the size of Belgium. The patriotism of King Leopold was equal already, it will be observed, to the alienation of a substantial portion of the "patrimony" of his prospective heir! The annexation project was withdrawn, and the Chambers voted the money required to keep out M. de Browne de Tiège.[1]

Thus this "free gift" was secured at a second cost of £250,000 : total cost up to 1895 £1,250,000 (plus interest) to the Belgian tax-payer.

When the time limit approached for the expiration of the agreement of 1890, *i.e.*, in 1901, M. Beernaert drafted and presented an annexation bill. The Government appeared at first to acquiesce. The Socialists opposed, but the Liberal leaders were in favour, and M. Beernaert's bill was assured of a large majority. Then came the King's dramatic intervention. The infamous decrees of 1891–2 which had converted the "Congo State" into a piratical undertaking and drenched the Congo territories with blood, had also resulted in the acquisition of enormous revenues, and many more were in store—future prospects

---

[1] Who came in by another door! (*Vide* Section IV.)

were brilliant. The King was no longer eager to place the Congo in the hands of the Belgian people, no longer anxious to give them the "full enjoyment" of his patriotic schemes. He addressed a letter to M. Woeste, one of the leaders of the clerical majority and as devoted a henchman as M. de Smet de Naeyer, who communicated it to an astonished House. It was blunt, autocratic, to the point. If annexation were voted then "that is to say before the time has come *when annexation can give to Belgium all the benefits which I wish to assure her,*" the Sovereign would refuse to administer the Congo during the inevitable *interregnum.* In other words he would withdraw the whole machinery of "government"! The annexationists were non-plussed. The Cabinet went over to the King. No law existed for the governing of "Colonial possessions." The absolutism of the King's act was glossed over by the Government depositing a projected law for the above purpose. The Belgian Chambers were powerless. The time limit expired. With it even the shadowy control formerly exercised by Belgium over the King's African enterprise expired also, and the latter became completely independent. The Chambers had to bow to the inevitable, but not without many a speech of indignant and weighty protest. The Liberal leaders declared that their acquiescence was the acquiescence of "resignation" . . . "a solution which, in our view, is essentially provisional." M. de Lantsheere, a prominent member of the Clerical majority exclaimed : " The new position which has been created for us and which totally excludes Belgium from any intervention in Congo affairs, is going to place us in an untenable situation—to undergo all liabilities, without our having the least power, or the least liberty of action. No one in the world has ever consented to accept a responsibility which excludes the right of action, and liberty. From the Belgian point of view it will be liability for the acts of others : from the foreign point of view it will remain our liability." But the King got his own way, thanks to M. de Smet de Naeyer, who has pigeon-holed his projected law for the government of the "Colonial Possessions of Belgium" ever since, although "urgency" was claimed for it at the time, and the situation to-day is that which it has been since 1901, that which M. Beernaert described it to be in the debate of last March : "We can no longer obtain accounts or information of any kind, and, notwithstanding our triple position of presumptive heirs, furnishers of men and money, and creditors, we are, from the judicial point of view, in exactly the same situation towards the Congo as the other States represented at the Conference of Berlin," which declaration M. de Smet de Naeyer endorsed by the words, "that is quite accurate." "When we discuss Congo affairs here"—remarked Mr. Hymans, one of the foremost leaders of the Liberal Party, in the course of the aforesaid debate, "the Government declares itself incompetent to reply, and immediately afterwards we see the same Minister, who has sheltered himself behind this *non possumus*, speak and explain himself not as a Minister of the Belgian Government, but as an advocate of the Congo State. I do not understand how the head of a Government does not realise how abnormal and shocking such a situation is."

In the course of the March, 1906, debate, to which I have referred, the Belgian Chamber passed a resolution in favour of proceeding without delay to the projected law on the administration of the Colonial Possessions of Belgium. The Chamber meets in November. Meanwhile King Leopold, frightened for his revenues, has again flung out an *ultimatum*, fitting pendant to that of 1901. In his Manifesto he roundly declares that if Belgium ever annexes the Congo she must "respect all engagements" which he may have made with third parties! She must inherit the "obligations to diminish in no manner the integral revenues" of the *Domaine Privé* and *Domaine de la Couronne!* As for the *Domaine de la Couronne* its revenues are for ever inalienable! In other words, Belgium must bind herself to maintain unimpaired the atrocious system of pillage and grinding oppression under which these revenues are acquired, and which would disappear with the disappearance of that system. Her control must be for ever excluded from the *Domaine de la Couronne*, e.g., from a portion of the Congo ten times the size of Belgium. She must take over all the debts which the King has contracted, and respect the existing rubber "Companies" whose "administrators" are co-partners with the King. The King is good enough to add that in accordance with his "immutable patriotism" he will allow Belgium to annex when he considers she is in a position to reap the fullest advantages from the Congo "patrimony," but that if the members of his Brussels staff —to whom the Manifesto is addressed—are respectfully asked when that happy moment is likely to arrive, they will reply that the patrotic monarch has "nothing to say at present"!

What aspect does the "free gift" of 1889 take on in 1906 ?

A. A "free gift" which the royal giver withholds *aa infinitum.*

B. A "free gift" for which he has obtained £1,250,000 out of the Belgian taxpayer free of interest.

C. A "free gift" which he has saddled with nominal liabilities—*ex* the above—of £9,700,000, and with positive liabilities the amount of which he carefully conceals from his prospective heirs.

D. A "free gift," the potential value of which is decreasing every year with the blood-stained revenues he and his associates are drawing from it.

E. A "free gift" for which he has acquired from Belgium the services of her officers, diplomatists, and consuls, sheltered the infamies of his African rule in the folds of the Belgian flag, and in the name of "patriotism" sullied her fair fame throughcut the world.

Is there on record a similar instance ot a trusting, ill-informed nation being swindled so outrageously and treated so contemptuously, by a foreign monarch presiding over its destinies ?

The Congo enterprise has certainly created in Belgium a taste for foreign commercial expansion, and has given an impetus to Belgian industry abroad. That is undeniable. But at what a price ! So far as the Congo is concerned, Belgium as a nation derives little or no benefit from it. There is no *trade* with the natives. The produce of the country is extracted by force. Hence the exports from Belgium to the Congo are insignificant. On the other hand the pernicious ideals of colonial "policy" introduced

Red Rubber

by the King have worked moral havoc among a section at least of the well-to-do *bourgeois* classes of the country. The army has become impregnated with a detestable virus. The old slave-trade spirit has everywhere made inroads. The Nemesis is certain, is, indeed, approaching with strides more rapid than most persons suppose.

There are several other points of view to be considered, both Belgian and non-Belgian. What are the principal features of M. de Smet de Naeyer's projected law? They are such that if annexation took place on those lines, nothing would be changed except that a "Colonial Minister" would replace a "Secretary," and that "Colonial Minister" might very possibly be M. de Smet de Naeyer himself, to whom it is said King Leopold has offered the appointment under certain contingencies. The man who has declared as the pivotal basis and justification of an African undertaking that "the native is entitled to nothing,"[1] would be a worthy successor to Messrs. de Cuvelier, Liebrechts, and Droogmans.[2] M. de Smet de Naeyer's projected law retains " the whole civil, judicial, financial, military, and administrative organisation" created by the King. The King remains invested with the sole executive power. The finances are, as before, controlled by him absolutely. He drafts the "budgets" and registers the laws. The members of the Judiciary are, as before, subject to the Executive will, and revocable *ad nutum*. The "Minister" would have a seat in Parliament, and could only be interrogated once a year, when he presented his annual report; he would be, in effect, quite outside Cabinet or Parliamentary control, subject only to the King. "It is easy to describe the dominating idea which presided over the elaboration of this project ; to retain in the hands of the Sovereign all colonial affairs, withhold the latter as far as possible from Parliamentary interference, establish the financial independence of the colony ; these, without a doubt, are the objects which its authors have had

[1] Official shorthand report of Belgian Parliamentary Debates, July, 1903, and February-March, 1906.
[2] The principal Secretaries of the King's Congo Staff in Brussels.

The Position of Belgium

in view."[1] In other words, Belgium would in appearance become responsible; in reality she would, once more, be wax in the King's hands. It is, I think, inconceivable that annexation on this basis could be driven through the Belgium Chamber, especially in view of the revelations of the Commission of Inquiry and of the contents of the recent Manifesto, which seeks to bind down the Belgians to conditions which no people with an ounce of dignity could agree to. But assuming the incredible to happen, a solution such as this could not be accepted by public opinion outside of Belgium. In truth it would be no solution, but an aggravation of existing evils, at least from the international point of view.

Then there is another point, and a very pertinent one. Annexation of the Congo by Belgium on the Smet-de-Naeyer-royal-Manifesto basis I look upon, as I have said, as utterly impossible : and I do not think I shall be contradicted. But is a majority of the Belgian Chamber prepared to annex at all, even on national lines, which are not the King's lines ? Even at the price of a conflict with the King—a conflict which would necessarily be of a most determined and implacable character ? The liabilities, material and moral, are tremendous. Large sections of the country are economically exhausted. The decrease of the population is appalling. By a careful computation —but which, of course, can only be hypothetical—based upon accessible positive data relating to depopulation, an analysis of the whole evidence which has been accumulating since 1890, the ivory and rubber output, the quantities of staple food-supplies wrung from the people, the spread or disease, etc., I estimate that in the last fifteen years the population of the Congo has been decreasing at a *minimum* rate of 100,000 per annum, or say 1,500,000 in the past fifteen years. I am convinced that is the very lowest computation compatible with accuracy. Consul Casement considers it far too low. His opinion is that the last decade has witnessed a decline in the population by nearly three millions. Of the two opinions his is likely to be the

---

[1] H. Speyer, 1901. "Comment nous Gouvernerons le Congo."

173

Red Rubber

soundest, because he has seen with his own eyes the effects of the Leopoldian system upon communities which he knew in former years to be populous and thriving, and because he is a servant of the Crown with twenty years' African experience. It will take at least two, possibly three generations, for the country to recover from the havoc of the last fifteen years. If the Congo is to be *administered* not pirated ; if the produce of the soil—*e.g.*, the rubber and gum copal—is to be acquired in future by legitimate purchase instead of by pillage, then there will be an immense and immediate fall in the output, and, concurrently, in the so-called "public revenues." The native peoples in the exploited rubber zones are crushed, broken, sick unto death of the very name of rubber. "Rubber *is* death"—*botofi bo le iwa*—has become the motto of these races. With the withdrawal from the villages of the armed sentry, backed by overwhelming force behind him, with the cessation of hostage-taking and the hundred and one other concomitants of the Leopoldian system, an immense sigh of relief would arise from the Equatorial forest, and the natural reaction would set in. Commerce as a substitute for force would revive only by slow, very slow, degrees, and for many years to come, even if the huge army were cut down one-half, and strict economy exercised in other ways, Belgium could only hope to run her dependency at a heavy loss. The flow of gold from the Congo would be stopped, and the enterprises created from it and dependent upon its maintenance would collapse. Then, again, the burden of debts, with which this "free gift" has been thoughtfully loaded by the giver for the greater benefit of the prospective heir, is such that, with the certainty of lean years ahead under decent administration, any Belgian statesman worthy of the name would hesitate once, twice, and yet again before asking the country to assume it.

Thoughtful Belgians are reckoning all this up. They realise that the temporary "prosperity" of the Congo—that is to say what passes for prosperity, the gold in the shape of rubber rolling out of it—depends exclusively upon the system of oppression and tyranny to which the natives are subjected. They know that the public edifices which are being reared

174

The Position of Belgium

in Brussels as an advertisement for the King, out of Congo rubber and Congo loans, and which Belgium does not require, Belgium will have to pay for if she annexes : and pay through the nose for since they have been constructed regardless of economy. They know that with every year that passes the indebtedness of the King's enterprise increases, and with it the prospective liabilities of Belgium. They know that money has been borrowed at 28 per cent. discount, and that Belgium, if she annexes, will be mulcted to that extent with the bankers who have financed the King.

Such, then, is the position in which Belgium finds herself, thanks to the complicity of her Government with Leopold Africanus. The Clerical (or Conservative) party has blindly followed M. de Smet de Naeyer at the price of the abandonment by the King of his former agitation in favour of the personal military system of which he was once so strong an advocate.[1] It has given him *carte blanche* so far as the Congo is concerned, and only now is that Party beginning to realise the abyss which yawns beneath its feet and the country's.

On the one hand, annexation appears the only escape from the intolerable moral position which leaves Belgium besmirched by " the acts of others," as M. de Lantsheere predicted five years ago. But annexation on lines compatible with self-respect and common-sense is barred by the King, and short of a complete capitulation on his part, could be forced through only by a definite rupture between Sovereign and Parliament.

On the other hand, annexation even at the price of a rupture appears, the more closely it is looked at, as a highly questionable proceeding in the light of national interests.

The purchase system still exists in Belgium. Young men of the well-to-do class, and eligible for military service, can obtain substitutes by payment. This is very popular with the Catholic Party, to which a large portion of the well-to-do classes belong, and the King's campaign was looked npon with great disfavour by that Party. Before he dropped his agitation, the King made sure of securing Catholic support *urbi et orbi* for his Congo policy.

Repudiation, absolute and entire, would carry with it
of necessity the withdrawal of all Belgian officers from
the Congo army—following the example of Italy—and
the sundering of all diplomatic connections with the King's
African enterprise : and this, of course, would also spell
a definite rupture.

Amidst all this fog of doubt and uncertainty in which
the Belgian people find themselves enfolded, a question
is beginning to form itself on the lips of men :

"The 'fusion of the two crowns' was acquiesced in
by the nation. A nation can revoke the assent secured
under false pretences. Can the wearer of the Belgian
crown be allowed any longer to continue the holder of
the Congo Sovereignty ? " [1]

If King Leopold does not abate his pretensions that
question may well be answered by a negative which might
have results more far-reaching than the elevation, before
natural causes called for it, of Prince Albert to the throne
of Belgium.

---

[1] The "fusion of the two crowns" was merely a voluntary
act on the part of the Chamber. It is in no sense a statute
in the Constitution of Belgium. The assent can be revoked.
But the King can also revoke his will! He can leave the
Congo to the Sultan of Turkey, the Editor of *La Vérité sur le
Congo*, or Sir Alfred Jones if he likes, according to the lines of
his Manifesto.

SECTION OF VILLAGE

Burned by Raiders

IV

WHAT GREAT BRITAIN CAN DO

Extracts from speeches in the House of Commons and House of Lords :—

"It had always been the boast of this country, not only that our own native subjects were governed on principles of justice, but that ever since the days of Wilberforce, England had been the leader in all movements on behalf of the backward races of the earth. Here was an occasion when those responsible for our policy, basing themselves on a treaty publicly and solemnly made, might pursue those great traditions, and by taking the initiative in this matter might add to the annals of the good deeds of this country."—Mr. HERBERT SAMUEL (1903).

"It was obvious that there was a complete enslavement of the whole population. As the suppressors of slavery and the slave-trade we had always led Europe, and had the highest degree of responsibility under the engagement of the Powers at Berlin to watch over the execution of the Berlin Act for the protection of the natives."—Sir CHARLES DILKE (1903).

"The treaties made between the Congo State and ourselves had undoubtedly been over-ridden, and, therefore, he supposed the Under Secretary for Foreign Affairs would not deny their right to interfere. Then arose the question, was it expedient that they should do so ? His answer to that was in the affirmative."—Sir JOHN GORST (1903).

"He thought we could do something alone."—Mr. ALFRED EMMOTT (1903).

"He altogether denied that they could deal with the Congo State as if it were a State like France, Austria, Germany, or any other Power. The Congo Free State was an artificial creation."—Lord FITZMAURICE (1903).

"In face of the facts which are now officially admitted, he asked the House whether the time was not come when they

177

Red Rubber

should sweep away all the difficulties which stood in the way and force the Government to take stronger action than mere words in despatches, to deal with this horrible scandal."—Sir CHARLES DILKE (1904).

"He was driven to the conclusion, therefore, that the only remedy was for the public opinion of Europe, and particularly of this country, to bring into force the clause of the Convention under which the Free State was founded."—Mr. AUSTIN TAYLOR (1904).

"The Congo Free State lay absolutely at the mercy of this country or any other country which chose to say it would occupy the capital at Boma in the name of civilisation."—Lord FITZMAURICE (1904).

"There has never been a policy of which it might be said as truly as of this one that it was the policy not so much of His Majesty's Government as the policy of the House of Commons."—Lord PERCY (1904).

"He did not think any of the great European Powers, with the facts so clearly established as they now were, ought to be content, in view of their own honour in the matter, to sit still and do nothing."—Sir EDWARD GREY (1904).

"Our own position in Africa must be considered. The infamous treatment of the natives in the Congo Free State must affect the position of the natives throughout Africa. The knowledge of the injustice inflicted upon the natives in the Congo Free State was carried by those subterranern wires, which all natives employed, from one part of the continent to the other, and was bound to affect the condition of the natives under the British, German, and French flags."—Sir GILBERT PARKER (1906).

"We held a national responsibility. . . . The right of intervention seemed to him to be clear beyond dispute."—Sir CHARLES DILKE (1906).

"Apart altogether from treaty obligations, every State interested in any portion of the territory of the Congo comprised in the Convention had not only the right, but was under the obligation, from the point of view of self-interest, to consider how far the present system of misgovernment carried with it a serious menace to the reputation and even to the security of the European Governments."—Lord PERCY (1906).

"But I may add quite irrespective of any right we enjoy under the letter of these Acts, that we have a moral right to interfere, which comes to us in consequence of the false pretences— I cannot use a gentler word—under which the Congo State has acquired its privileged position in that part of Africa."—Lord LANSDOWNE (1906).

IN the last three chapters I have endeavoured to establish that from King Leopold no alteration in the existing state

of affairs on the Congo is to be looked for ; that to expect
"reform" from that quarter would be puerile ; that "reform"
can only come with a sweeping removal of the cause of the
evil by cauterising the evil at its roots.   If there was ever a
case where the old French adage *Il faut frapper à la tête*
applied ; surely this is one.

I have tried to show also how extremely difficult, not to
say virtually helpless—short of a complete rupture between
King and Parliament—is the position of Belgium, and how
foolish it would be to regard Belgian annexation as a certain
panacea within the pale of practical politics, or even as a necessarily certain panacea if it were within that pale.   Hostility
to a Belgian annexation of the Congo on the lines laid down
by the Berlin and Brussels Acts, there is none in this country.
But it is obvious that agreement to a Belgian annexation on
the lines laid down by the King is utterly impossible.   The
neutrality of Belgium is guaranteed by the Powers in the
interests of international peace.   The neutrality of a Belgian
Colony embracing the great heart of Africa and run like a
slave-farm through the medium of an ever-growing native
soldiery armed with weapons of precision, could be recognised by no Power with tropical dependencies contiguous to
its frontiers.   As it is, the policy of *laissez faire* adopted by
the signatory Powers of the Act of the West African
Conference of 1885 having possessions in Tropical Africa, in
permitting the evolution of an International Association for
the promotion of civilisation and commerce, from a "Congo
Free State," to a military despotism resting upon slavery
and rifles, is incredibly short-sighted.   To allow such a
condition of things to continue, with the substitution of the
Belgian for the Congo flag of King Leopold, would be
insensate.   Apart from all questions of humanity and
legitimate political interest in Africa, acquiescence would
imperil Belgian neutrality in Europe.   Of that no one who
understands this grave question can entertain the slightest
doubt.

But, after all, we have not to consider possibilities, but
actualities.   Discussion, passionate or otherwise, can be
renewed and yet again renewed in the Belgian Parliament ;
the projected law on the colonial possessions of Belgium,

Red Rubber

may give rise to endless debates. Compared with the existing facts, all this is academic. Existing facts they are which confront us ; which call out for immediate solution, drastic and thorough. The rubber slave-trade flourishes, unchecked, unimpaired, unaltered by all the talk and ink-spilling of the last four years. It has been exposed in all its horrors. But it is in being, its activity has been stimulated by a sense of precariousness in the future, its area of devastation increases, and with it the number of victims. That is the immediate consideration. All else is subsidiary.

* * * * * *

The year 1907 is a great anniversary, bringing with it a flood of recollections. The 26th of March, 1907, will be the centenary of the Royal Assent to the Bill passed in both Houses of Parliament abolishing the Over-Sea Slave-Trade.

From the ashes of an international conference, summoned in the name of Almighty God, has sprung a traffic in African misery more devilish than the old, more destructive, more permanently ruinous in its cumulative effects. A British Government (a Liberal Government) with many misgivings but with the best of intentions, by its active participation in that conference, and by its adhesion to the conclusions thereof, incurred a responsibility which cannot be set aside. To-day a British Government (a Liberal Government) is in power with an enormous majority, strong and respected abroad, and has been given a mandate by a democratic Parliament convinced and unanimous to deal with this new form of the African slave-trade, which the cupidity and the baneful ambitions of one man have reared in the heart of Africa. Behind a unanimous Parliament, stands a united Press. This Government, and its predecessor in office, have both alike addressed numerous protests to the author of the evil, publicly and privately; protests which have not merely been ignored in the sense of effecting improvement, but treated with contempt so marked as to be perilously akin to insult.

The evil continues.

What Great Britain Can Do

This Government and its predecessor in office have both alike held their hand when they could have struck hard and swift, and in strict conformity with the Treaty rights of Great Britain.

The evil continues.

Two years ago the predecessor of the present Government invited formally the co-operation of the other signatories to the West African Conference of 1885, to join with them in handling this evil ; but the invitation was not accepted.

The evil continues.

A few months ago the present Government reiterated informally that invitation.

The evil continues, and the author of the evil, in an insolent Manifesto addressed to his secretaries, and directed at Great Britain, has defied the British Government to carry out the mandate given to it by Parliament, placing himself above the reach of pledges and the law of nations.

And the great anniversary is upon us.

    *   *   *   *   *   *

We have put our hands to the plough. We cannot draw back. For the sake of our dignity as a great nation ; for the sake of our traditions as the emancipators of the races of Africa ; as an African power having legitimate interests to maintain, " we cannot wait for ever." [1]

But have we not waited long enough ? Surely the cup is full and overflowing ?

Internationally our position has seldom been stronger, nor the home popularity which would attend positive action more assured to our Government from every section or public opinion. So strong, indeed, do we consider ourselves to be that from this country, from its Foreign Minister, has come the first clear proposal for a reduction in the world's armaments ; from this country, from its Premier and leader in the Mother of Parliaments, has come a message of sympathy addressed to the youngest of Parlia-

---

[1] Sir E. Grey, July, 1906.

ments under circumstances which make of that message an historic pronouncement in favour of the liberties of men. Are we, then, not strong enough to rescue the races of Central Africa from enslavement and destruction at the hands of the man to whom we entrusted their destinies?

While we wait, they perish, and there is no reason why they should. No interests of a great misguided nation are concerned. No sentiments imbued in generations of thought have to be rooted up and educated out of existence. No cataclysm in world politics hangs in the balance. No onrush of religious fanaticism is to be apprehended. Action to stay the extirpation of these African peoples is attended by none of the perils bound up with the conflicting international claims and racial animosities, which make a satisfactory settlement of the Eastern question so difficult.

There is action we ourselves can take in virtue of Treaty rights, which in itself would almost of necessity give rise automatically to a renewed international conference. What is that action? Let us turn to the declarations exchanged and the convention passed with the representative of King Leopold in 1884. We recognised the flag of the International Association on specific grounds. What were they? That the Association had come into existence " for the purpose of promoting the civilisation and commerce of Africa, and for other humane and benevolent purposes." Twenty-two years later we find that King Leopold's enterprise consists, not in " promoting civilisation and commerce" but —as admirably defined by Lord Percy in the House of Commons—"in the accumulation of rubber at an infinite cost of human life and suffering," for " mercenary motives," to quote Lord Lansdowne. We have been grossly deceived, therefore, and in that deception practised upon us resides a *prima facie* case for declining any longer to regard King Leopold's African flag as the emblem of a civilised administration. An administration whose object is to accumulate rubber at an infinite cost to human life and suffering, as deliberately stated in the British House of Commons by the Under Secretary of State for Foreign Affairs, has no call upon our recognition in any case ; still less so when such an object

What Great Britain Can Do

is totally at variance with solemn pledges made to us in the past. The steamers which King Leopold employs under his African flag can be declined admittance to British territorial waters. At present they enter our ports, and at the most the Treasury would lose £1,000 *per annui* in the light dues and other port charges they pay. Not the most virulent lady hater of Mr. Asquith would attribute to him a desire to oppose the performance of a national duty for the sake of £1,000. The nominees King Leopold has appointed to represent exclusively his African interests in this country can be informed that we no longer recognise them ; in other words, the *exequator* can be withdrawn from the three or four "Congo Free State" Consuls who carry on their royal master's behests in England and in Scotland, and whose offices were until recently—when public attention was drawn to the fact—distributing centres for the scurrilous publications of the Press Bureau. It is a scandal that one of these "consuls" should be an Englishman and the President of a leading British Chamber of Commerce. Other measures are open to us. Those I have denoted are the mildest, and absolutely no impediment stands in the way of their realisation.[1] I pass to the Convention.

What are our rights under that Convention ? They are (1) that "until sufficient provision shall have been made for the administration of justice" on the Congo, "the sole and exclusive jurisdiction both civil and criminal over the persons and property of British subjects" shall be vested in British Consular Officers "in accordance with British law." (Article V.) This is called consular jurisdiction ; or the exercise of rights of extra-territoriality. They are (2) that British subjects are entitled at all times to "sojourn" and "establish themselves"; are entitled to enjoy the rights of "buying," "selling," "letting and hiring lands, buildings,

---

[1] If King Leopold attempted to retaliate we have merely to state that the Congo is an international highway not a private demesne; and that there are British subjects on the Congo, making the presence of British Consuls imperative for their protection. There are no Congolese subjects in Great Britain ' If King Leopold forced the issue, well . . . . !

mines and forests," "founding houses of commerce," "carrying on commerce under the British flag"; they are entitled to "protection," in "their persons," "property," "free exercise of religion," "navigation, commerce, and industry." (Article II.)

Very good. These pledges have not been kept. The need for British consular jurisdiction for the protection of our own subjects in King Leopold's estate is nowhere, and by no one disputed in this country. The present Government does not dispute it. The past Government did not dispute it. Speaking in office, Lord Percy said on June 9, 1904, "the only practicable suggestion which, I think, has been made this afternoon, is that this country should revive its claim to the exercise of extra-territorial jurisdiction in the Congo State." Sir Edward Grey, speaking in opposition on the same occasion, concurred : "He thought we might put the establishment of consuls (with consular jurisdiction) on the ground that if other Powers would not co-operate with us in this matter, in what we considered the general interests of humanity and civilisation, which were as much theirs as ours, we must at any rate see to the protection of our own subjects." Speaking in July last, Sir Edward Grey said : "The time must come when we shall have to consider whether . . . these rights should not be exercised." On the same occasion Lord Lansdowne said : "All I can say is that I hope, if these abuses continue, we shall claim our right to appoint consuls (with consular jurisdiction) in the Congo." At the very least one hundred public meetings—including two town's meetings, in Liverpool and Sheffield—held throughout England and Scotland in the last two years, have passed resolutions urging this step upon the Government. The marvel is that it was not taken years and years ago. British coloured subjects ill-treated, flogged, and shot ; an Englishman hung out of hand ; a British Consul so busy for two years inquiring into grave abuses perpetrated towards British coloured subjects in the very neighbourhood of the capital of the Congo itself, as to be unable to stir from the spot—and all this while a weapon lies rusting in our grasp ! And now King Leopold's anger is turned upon the British missionaries ; his so-called "administration of justice" is utilised to entrap and browbeat them; his object, to terrify them into silence; furious that they convinced his own Commission—they whom his Press Bureau and his Brussels staff have reviled with every opprobrious epithet—which placed on record that the natives had come to regard them as "the sole representatives of justice and equity" in the country; and still we hesitate. To leave these brave men—they are not all brave, perhaps, but many of them are, and to those who have spoken out, humanity owes a debt of gratitude—to leave them at the mercy of Congo "justice" is to acquiesce in their dragooning, is to show them that whatever the British public may think of their devotion in the cause of right, a British Government which to-morrow can ensure for them absolute security from molestation of any kind, looks askance upon their intolerable situation. Our duty towards these men is clear, and our duty towards the 2,000 coloured subjects of the Crown on the Congo is equally emphatic. They are entitled to claim protection; *Cives romanum sunt.* The case for consular jurisdiction for our own subjects is, on the face of it, overwhelming.

But consular jurisdiction has several other sides to it. Cases have occurred of British coloured subjects being employed as subordinate agents in charge of out-stations in the bush (rubber stations) and having committed, or allowed to be committed, in that capacity the brutalities which are inseparable from such work, and having been sentenced by the Congo Courts, whose severity towards such virtually helpless victims of the system is proportionate to the criminal laxity shown towards the real guilty parties, the European representatives of the King and his Trusts, whose instructions the former must needs obey. There is a tendency on the part of the Foreign Office to adopt a high, moral, wash-our-hands sort of attitude in regard to British coloured subjects thus involved. Several questions which I have caused to be put in the House relating to specific cases which came under my notice have been greeted as though there were something shocking and irregular in the slightest exhibition of concern in the fate of such unfortunates. It is an attitude with which I am wholly unable to agree. So

Red Rubber

long as the Congo judicial system is what it is (*vide* Section III.) so long will there be no thorough investigation into outrages perpetrated by or through the orders of persons directly or indirectly connected with the Executive, and so long will the Congo Courts fail to deal competently with cases of British coloured subjects who from time to time may find themselves mixed up in such outrages. Take, for example, the case of Silvanus Jones, a native of Lagos and a subordinate of the man Caudron (*vide* Section III.). If that case had been brought before a British court it would have yielded clear evidence of the moral complicity of the supreme Executive. That evidence is, indeed, afforded by the verdict of the court itself, but is purposely obscured by the refusal of the court to pronounce an opinion on the admissions showing Executive toleration for the deeds which the accused—acting under the direct orders of his immediate chief, Caudron, who himself acted in co-operation with the local sub-chief of police—is alleged to have committed. *The vital point is this, that no British Consular Court would have pronounced judgment upon Silvanus Jones without sifting to the bottom the responsibility for the acts sanctioned by him under the instructions of his European employer.* Now one of the most essential needs of the situation is the securing of positive documentary evidence in this regard, and British Consular jurisdiction would be an invaluable and unique means to this end in cases like that of Silvanus Jones. Consider, too, the personal aspect. A. The British Consul in the Congo reports that Jones "had no opportunity of engaging counsel" although he had enough money to do so if the option had been allowed him. B. He was sentenced to ten years' imprisonment for responsibility in the murder of one woman killed in the course of a raid upon a native village for shortage in rubber. C. Caudron, under whose orders he acted, was proved to have conducted raids which led to the positive murder of 200 people, of personally shooting a woman in the breast, of ordering a native chief to be shot in prison, etc., and only received five years' imprisonment.

The case of Cyrus Smith, of Freetown, is another in point. He had taken hostages—which, the reader will

What Great Britain Can Do

remember, the Governor-General himself has authorised and, indeed, recommended upon numerous occasions—for shortage in rubber, and the hostages, most of them women and children, had died of hunger. His defence was a simple one. He had nothing to give them to eat! Atrocious as this bald statement sounds, let the reader turn to the admissions made by the Commission of Inquiry (Sections III. and IV.) in connection with the food taxes, and bear in mind that such things as women dying in prison of starvation are all part and parcel of, inevitable incidents in, a vast system of criminal oppression to obtain revenues by armed force for private ends. The Court which tried him, and sentenced him, found that he too was acting with the toleration of the authorities in taking hostages. I repeat, then, that far from putting on a mantle of superior righteousness over these cases, it is the bounden duty of the British Government to provide the machinery requisite for plumbing them to their deepest depths.

So far we have considered Consular jurisdiction mainly in the light of the legitimate interests of British subjects, and to this I shall refer again in dealing with the missionary question. But as a means of coping with the paramount evil, the ill-treatment of the natives of the country, the efficacy of British Consular Courts can be doubted only by those who have not examined the subject. "I do not care in the least," said Lord Lansdowne last July, "whether there are British subjects to look after or not, but what I do feel is that the presence of half a dozen Englishmen will be worth more than a whole row of inspectors or officials belonging to the Administration of the Congo Free State." Precisely, but the contention can be amplified. A British Court of Justice once set up on the Congo with sole jurisdiction over British subjects, civil and criminal, would hamper at every turn the working of the system of injustice perpetrated towards the people of the land. The aborigines would be profoundly impressed by the knowledge, of which they would receive ocular demonstration, that the humblest Kru-boy, the veriest steamer hand or carpenter "boy" of slave-blood was certain of

187

Red Rubber

absolute justice in the teeth of the highest in the land, provided he were a British subject. They would compare the position of such men with their own miserable existence, a position incomparably more secure than that of the oldest and most venerable indigenous chief. They would realise what white justice at its best really was, and with that revelation would arise in their crushed spirits the glimmering of a new hope. The moral effect would react in a hundred ways against the present *régime*. The independence in wrong-doing, the right to work iniquity and fear no question would be struck at in its very roots, in the face of a tribunal whose sole duty it would be to find the truth and proclaim it. It is impossible to suppose the present machinery of the Congo Courts sitting side by side with a British Court without producing results from which, *inter alia*, the natives of the country would derive incalculable benefit. So much for the moral and material aspect of Consular jurisdiction on the Congo.

The moral effect in Europe of the establishment of British Consular jurisdiction on the Congo would be immense. It would show the world that the British people were determined to mark, by a step whose significance could not be mistaken, their abhorrence of King Leopold's methods, and their firm intention of passing from words to deeds. Our right to so act is unquestionable, and if any of the signatory Powers of the West African Conference were disposed to see in such a step a disquieting indication of exclusive British political interference in the affairs of the Congo, well, the remedy would lie with them. They could assent to our demand, made in the general interests of humanity, for an International Conference. Moreover, they could copy our policy, for several of them stipulated in 1884 for the same rights as ourselves.

Sir Edward Grey himself met that possible, but unlikely, difficulty in his usual straightforward manner two years ago. If the "susceptibilities" of other Powers should be aroused by such action, he said, "then by all means let them appoint consuls of their own," meaning, of course, as is clear from the text, consuls with consular jurisdiction.

188

What Great Britain Can Do

And for the rest we have, perhaps, consulted the "susceptibilities" of other Powers too much in refraining from
taking action which has been open to us, not as co-signa-
tories of the Act of the West African Conference, but
under our own treaty rights with King Leopold, rights
which can be contested by no Power or Powers. The
sooner we show other Powers that we are in earnest, the
sooner will talk give way to something more practical.
To obtain collective action—at which we aim—an individual lead is of paramount necessity.

What of our rights under Article II. of the Convention ?
Commercial rights entailing the freedom of purchase and
of sale, of buying and of leasing land, of every other thing
needful to the prosecution of legitimate trade ? I refer to
the general commercial position later on, contenting myself
at this stage with the remark that as commerce of any kind,
by any one, was swept from the vast Upper Congo in 1891,
so have our rights under that Article been cynically in-
fringed. What of the rights of British missions and
missionaries under Article II. ? How are they interpreted by King Leopold ? I do not know the exact
figures, but I think I shall be well within the mark in
stating that the British missionary societies have spent
some £300,000 on the Congo. From the purely secular
aspect this is a national interest which cannot be lightly
ignored by a British Government. The money thus
expended has come out of the pockets of the British
philanthropic public. It is entitled to consideration. Of
late King Leopold has quietly opposed the development and
extension of all religious propaganda on the Congo, Roman
Catholic and Protestant. It is true that he recently conferred special facilities upon an English Roman Catholic
organisation, granting it sites in close proximity with a
Protestant mission ; but this is an exception, and was due
to the expectation and the hope of affording an opportunity
for sectarian controversy, and to reap all the capital from
that which was possible ; to draw, as he has tried to do for
long enough, the red herring of religious squabbles across
the bloody trail of native persecution. The spokesmen of
the Belgian Roman Catholic Missions in Belgium, how-

Red Rubber

ever, are no less emphatic in their protests at the obstacles thrown in the way of Christian propaganda on the Congo than are the Protestant missionaries.[1] Towards the latter King Leopold's policy is one of open hostility. Round some of the mission stations he is making a waste. He refuses to sell new sites for extension of work. "We emphatically protest against the repeated refusal to sell sites for mission stations to our societies," says a protest and appeal signed by fifty-two evangelical missionaries of all nationalities—representing the totality of their brethren, perhaps some hundred and fifty in all—assembled in conference at Stanley Pool on January 16th of this year. He offers impossible sites for leases on impossible terms. In 1898 the Congo Balolo Mission desired to open up on the Juapa river. Permission was granted ; difficulties followed. The game of Jekyl and Hyde is time-honoured on the Congo. Finally the party of missionaries were turned off "by force." They were not permitted a glimpse into the interior of the *Domaine de la Couronne* through which the Juapa flows ! They were kept off the region where bloom the lilies of eternal peace, by a hedge of rifles and cap-guns.

"When it is remembered," wrote Dr. Guinness to Lord Lansdowne, on the 29th of November, 1905, in a letter recounting the grievances of his mission at the hands of the regenerator of Africa, "that the Juapa River, with its thirty-two tributaries, is comparable in importance to the Danube in Europe, it will be understood how serious, from a missionary standpoint, was the expulsion of the agents of the Congo Balolo Mission from the site of Bonyeka which they had selected. During the correspondence a map was kindly sent us with one site indicated where we were graciously permitted to settle, but this site corresponded accurately with an uninhabitable, low-lying, fever-stricken swamp."

Three years ago Morrison, the sturdy and eloquent missionary from Virginia, a man whom to know is to trust, after vainly appealing to King Leopold to redress the wrongs inflicted upon the wretched natives round Luebo,

---

[1] *Vide* Belgian Parliamentary debates, February–March, 1906.

came home and denounced the crimes there perpetrated to the world; then he went to Brussels and bearded King Leopold's principal secretary in his den—I beg pardon, his thickly-carpeted, heavy-curtained office, where reigns an air of mystery, where converse is the art of fence, where the visitor's chair is so placed that the light may fall upon its occupant's features while the inscrutable gentleman with the *pince-nez*, tall, slim, *très correcte*, and excessively subtle, reclines in discreet shadow. There, amongst other complaints, he protested against the withholding of mission sites. Here was an opportunity! A few days later all the subsidised organs rang with the news that Morrison had been pursuing "material interests," and, failing to secure them, had launched his accusations. He was an "infamous calumniator" like the rest.

When H. B. M. consul, Mr. Roger Casement, visited in the summer of 1903 the station of the Congo Balolo Mission at Bongandanga, in the A.B.I.R. territory, he found that the missionaries were being made unwilling and helpless accomplices in the illegal system—since condemned by the Commission of Inquiry, and persisted in—of forced levies of food-stuffs upon the natives by the officials of that concern. All free dealing in articles of food between missionaries and natives had been prohibited. You see, the missionaries were then writing home, denouncing the atrocities perpetrated in their neighbourhood, and this was the first form which their punishment took. Not even an egg could the missionaries buy from the natives; all their supplies they were compelled to purchase through the A.B.I.R., which procured them by the usual methods sacred to Congo custom! Consul Casement protested energetically to the Governor-General: "I have a right to request, and one that I would urge with most respectful insistence, that my fellow-countrymen residing in any part of the Congo State should not be forced, in order to have food for themselves and households, to share in measures which are repugnant to the most vulgar sentiments of civilised society."[1] Voluble assurances were given —— and broken; and for eighteen

---

[1] September 11, 1903.

months afterwards, until the repeated representations of the Congo Reform Association to the Foreign Office put a stop to the practice, the British missionaries were persecuted in all sorts of ways. Their food supplies were stopped altogether; the natives were forbidden to sell them anything on pain of instant punishment; natives were shot and imprisoned for contravening these instructions; their fowls were stolen; they were forbidden to cut wood without paying exorbitant fees; they were insulted and even threatened by the A.B.I.R. officials, one of whom became so violent that the British Consul (a thousand miles away insisted upon an armed guard being placed on their premises under an Italian officer. As recently as the beginning of this year a party of British missionaries itinerating in the Upper Lomako region received written communications couched in the most insolent terms (and in very bad French) from the local representative of the A.B.I.R., ordering them to clear out. Here are passages from these letters :—"The Company (*e.g.*, the A.B.I.R.) being *Domaine Privé*, you have no right to sojourn therein. . . . Your voyage to the Upper River cannot take place overland without the authorisation of the Director of the A.B.I.R. Company at Basankusu."[1] The latest form of persecution to which British missionaries are subject consists in that of prosecution for criminal libel for reporting evidence tendered before the Commission of Inquiry, in open court, which evidence, as I have explained further back, has been suppressed, because King Leopold is frightened that capital might be made out of it by the author of this volume![2] In reality, because he knows that that evidence, if produced, would stagger European public opinion. Mr. Stannard is the first victim of this ingenuity, and at the very time these farcical legal proceedings were in process, his nominal prosecutor, the chief of police of the district, was making use of the Press Bureau in Brussels to propagate throughout the world charges of incitement to rebellion, incendiarism and murder against the defendant and another

---

[1] On Sir E. Grey's demand, an "inquiry" has been opened.
[2] See p. 137.

missionary, Mr. Whiteside ! Moreover, a new law has been passed whereby any missionary who reports to a Government official, or to a judicial official, outrages committed or allowed to be committed by a white man, is liable to be tried for defamation and sentenced to five years' imprisonment ! As I write these lines, letters from the Congo inform me that native evangelists attached to British mission stations have been turned off the Bosombo River and forbidden to enter the region, where probably some devilry more pronounced than usual is taking place.

This sort of thing cannot be allowed to go on. The British Government is morally bound to insist that from this day forward the British Missionary Societies shall, in accordance with the terms of the Convention, extend their civilising labours where they like—aye, even in the heart of that inalienable holy of holies, the *Domaine de la Couronne*, —erect new stations at suitable sites (not pestiferous swamps), have perfect freedom of dealing with the natives, and generally benefit by the rights secured to the subjects of this country. British consular officers should be increased, and the slightest infraction of British rights should be at once reported, when the remedy is in our hands. I prefer, whenever possible, to quote the utterances of British statesmen when referring to what Britain can DO under certain contingencies, because a man who has led a campaign of denunciation and exposure is always liable to be called extreme. On this occasion I venture to quote Lord Fitzmaurice who, speaking in the House of Commons in 1904, said : " He would venture to remind the Congo Free State how easy it would be . . . for Europe, or, indeed, for any State that chose, to practically put an end to its existence by sending a few ships to the mouth of the Congo. . . . The Congo Free State lay absolutely at the mercy of this country, or any country, which chose to say that it would occupy the capital of Boma in the name of civilisation."

It would not be necessary to occupy Boma ! A single man-of-war stationed at the mouth of the Lower Congo with orders to prohibit the entry or departure of steamers, or craft of any kind, would be quite sufficient to bring

Red Rubber

King Leopold to his knees if not to his senses. The blood-stained rubber in the out-going vessels would be late for the Antwerp market, and the shares of the Trusts would collapse; and in six weeks King Leopold's officials at Boma would be howling for the supplies contained in the steamers due. Imagine the "superior" Congo official at the capital deprived of his tinned delicacies—even though of Chicago manufacture—sweet champagne, and vermouth! It is too horrible to contemplate.

Lord Fitzmaurice is perfectly accurate. King Leopold's African enterprise lies at the mercy of this country. He has broken every promise he made us under the Declarations and the Convention; instruments which concern us and us alone. To sum up :

We recognised a benevolent and civilising enterprise, not a piratical undertaking; and it is open to us to refuse steamers flying a piratical flag access to our waters, and to give the King's mischief-making Consuls in this country their *congé*.

We were given pledges that our subjects on the Congo would be assured of justice and protection. They receive neither, and we are entitled to establish consular jurisdiction.

We were given pledges that our merchants should be unhampered in the conduct of their business. The only elements in the country in which they could conduct commercial transactions have been appropriated by the King. Our missionaries were guaranteed unfettered liberty in the pursuit of their noble aims. They are interfered with, and now they are being persecuted for telling the truth. On both these grounds we are justified in taking drastic and immediate measures for the preservation of our incontestable rights. Heaven knows we have waited long and patiently, and put up with flouts and jeers which we should have brooked from no first or even third rate Power.

And what is our right has become our manifest duty in the general cause of civilisation and humanity.

* * * * * *

Having passed in review the various forms which British

action can take under our Treaty rights with King Leopold, let us examine successively the position Britain enjoys as a co-signatory with other Powers in the Act of the West African Conference of 1885 ; her situation in the world to-day ; the instrument which that Act provides in the event of the infringement of its clauses, and the considerations of weight which urge her to assume an energetic initiative.

I may be permitted, perhaps, at the outset to state with deliberate conviction which others can take at their own evaluation, but which has not been arrived at without consulting continental acquaintances whom I believe to be well informed, that a decisive step by this country under her own Treaty rights, on one or several of the lines indicated above, would in itself precipitate that renewed international conference which Lord Lansdowne formally invited in 1903. I have been repeatedly assured by men whose statements cannot be dismissed that the ill-success of the British Note of 1903 was due—apart from the circumstance that our prestige was not, perhaps, particularly high just then—to the belief rightly or wrongly entertained by Continental statesmen that the British Government was not in earnest in the matter, that it had obeyed a sudden and forcible mandate from an uninstructed House of Commons, and that its demonstration was of the platonic order. Students of the Congo question will remember that the attitude of the British Government subsequent to the issue of the Note was not precisely calculated to remove that impression. They will also recollect that the issue of the Note and the later communication of Consul Casement's report to the co-signatory Powers, led to a pilgrimage on the part of King Leopold to the European Courts and to the Elysée ; to a systematic and extraordinarily active campaign in three languages on the part of the Press Bureau, representing the agitation in England as confined to a small group of bitter and interested persons, the House of Commons as victimised by false information, and Consul Casement as an unreliable half-fanatic, half-adventurer ; and to the despatch of sundry " impartial investigators " to the Congo who traversed the consul's charges, described the missionaries as perjured liars, the state of affairs on the Congo as one of Elysian bliss, and the system erected by King Leopold a species of African St. Simonism, *et ainsi de suite*. That these concerted efforts, coupled with the impression mentioned, did at any rate affect Continental opinion is unquestionable.

The position which Britain holds as one of the signatories of the Act of the West African Conference is one of quite exceptional moral strength as compared with that of most of the other signatories, both as regards the historical part she played before and during the elaboration of the clauses of the Act, and in respect to her standing as a tropical African Power, and a great commercial Power, with thousands of miles of frontier running parallel to the " Congo Free State " in various directions. To a greater extent than is the case with any one of the other signatory Powers is it possible to affirm, that but for British acquiescence there would have been no " Congo Free State." The position of France, Germany, and Portugal alone, of the other signatory Powers, approaches in importance that of Great Britain. France, because of her long contiguous frontier, the fact that she holds a considerable proportion of the converted Congo stock (loan of 1888), and by the right of preference or pre-emption which King Leopold—without the consent, or recognition then, or since, of the other Powers—made over to her in the event of Belgium definitely declining to annex, and the " Congo Free State " coming, as it were, on the international market. Portugal, because of her contiguous frontier—which does not greatly affect the question, her frontiers being unoccupied, as is the case with France to a large extent. Germany, because of contiguous frontiers, the fact that she is a great commercial nation, and the circumstance that it was in reply to a German invitation and in the German capital that the West African Conference was held.

Few will dispute that the prestige of Great Britain in the councils of the world has seldom stood higher than it does at this moment. The ally of the Risen Sun in the Far East ; on terms of close political *entente* with France ; of sound friendship with Italy ; of historic friendship with

Portugal ; of friendship cemented by royal family ties with Spain, Denmark, and Norway—all three Powers (the latter with Sweden, of course) signatories to the Act ; of blood relationship with the United States, which, although they did not ratify the Act, sent representatives to it who played an active part in the discussion of the Protocols, did ratify the Brussels Act, and were the first to recognise the flag of the International Association—these connections give an aggregate of moral force to Britain which, if she but chooses to put her shoulder to the wheel and use the resources of her diplomacy to the utmost, ought to prove irresistible. The only cloud on the horizon is—or is supposed to be—Germany. But not only has " the first diplomatist in Europe" taken in hand the improvement of our relations with that Power, but there are indications in several quarters of a *rapprochement* which, *minus* a few fire-eaters, is desired by both peoples. Apart from this, the protests of the German Chambers of Commerce, of the German Colonial Society with its thirty thousand membership, and of other public bodies in Germany against King Leopold's African pretensions are on record, and if those protests have not been renewed of late, it is not because the situation which caused them to be uttered has become modified, but because the general political relationship between Germany and Great Britain has led to the suppression of all manifestations calculated to support British policy in any part of the habitable globe. But the policy of Germany in Tropical Africa is chiefly commercial ; she seeks, as we do, outlets for her commerce, and in that respect her true interests and ours in those regions are identical, now as they were in 1885.

It is only reasonable to assume, therefore, that by earnest representations to the co-signatory Powers—in hands so sound as those which hold the thread of our foreign affairs to-day—accompanied by a friendly notification of our intention to enforce strictly and without further delay our own Treaty rights, the British Government can bring about a conference of the Powers if it will.

It is, perhaps, less a matter of what we can do, than it is whether we should do it. The *cons* appear to be, first,

Red Rubber

that England may herself have been guilty of infringing
the letter of the Act of the West African Conference;
secondly, that as a nation our hands in Africa are not clean;
thirdly, that King Leopold, if we drive him too hard, may
succeed in embroiling us with some other Power. With
the last *con* is mixed up a great deal of excessively vague
talk about " pan-Germanism," secret treaties, Belgian
independence, fortification of Antwerp, and what not. It
seems to me that the third and last objection is unworthy
of consideration by a great nation, in the face of a clear
duty which brooks no denial; and discussion of its various
phases would lead us into an essay on contemporary European politics far removed from the objects of the present
volume. It is sufficient to remark that King Leopold
plays a splendid game of bluff, and that if he can bluff our
statesmen into believing that he holds all sorts of terrible
cards up his sleeve which he can remove therefrom and
brandish over their heads like a sword of Damocles, paraly-
sing their action at pleasure, he will certainly do so. But
it is ranking our statesmen rather low, and the idea will
be greeted with the most pronounced scepticism and in-
credulity by Englishmen of all parties. That King
Leopold is a dangerous man and a malignant enemy, we
know; that he is utterly unscrupulous and immoral alike
in his public as in his private life we know also; but in
Europe he is the constitutional monarch of a small neutral
State, not an autocrat ruling by force and violence. As
such his capacity for intrigue and evil has definite limitations, and in the interests of his dynasty he must needs
keep them within bounds.

So far as the first objection is concerned, two very
pertinent facts can be pointed out. The first is that the
few concessions given in British East Africa—which,
it is hardly necessary to say, are totally at variance
with King Leopold's system—were given while Lord
Lansdowne was in the Government, and that Lord Lansdowne is the author of the Note to the signatory Powers
suggesting a further conference. This does not look as
though we had done anything very dreadful which need
hamper our action on the Congo. The second fact is that

198

What Great Britain Can Do

Lord Percy, speaking in the House two years ago, declared that Great Britain was "perfectly willing" to submit the terms of those concessions to an international tribunal, with a view to ascertaining if they could in any way be regarded as infringing the Act of 1885.

The second objection has always struck me as lamentably weak. In the first place, the main purpose of the West African Conference of 1885 was to deal with the territories of the Congo Basin, and a renewed conference arising out of the violation of the clauses of the Act would obviously be confined to the same programme. Aside from this the argument would, as Mr. Bennett stated with such admirable force in the House last July, "If pressed to its conclusion stultify all human effort towards improvement." To contend, moreover, that any political errors or individual abuses which have occurred in Tropical African dependencies are in any sense of the word comparable with the system of pillage and destruction deliberately wrought on the Congo by King Leopold and his associates in the interest of private profit, is to exhibit a lack of proportion and absence of mental balance beyond the boundaries of reasonable discussion. The hands of *no* colonising Power are clean in the sense that no colonising Power has been free from political error, or political injustice, and that no colonising Power has been free from the presence of incompetent and vicious servants among its *personnel* in colonies or dependencies. Shameful things have been done in British, French, and German Africa—especially in time of war—and when those shameful things have come to light, public opinion has denounced them and insisted upon redress. But here is no question of the occasional back-slidings which have marked, and ever will mark—especially when passions are aroused locally—the relationship of the forward and backward races of mankind. Here is a policy cynically and ruthlessly elaborated and pursued by one man for his own personal ends, and for the enrichment of a handful of individuals at the cost of untold human suffering. Here is one man living in luxury in Europe, claiming before the world his right to regard the greater portion of Central Africa as his private property, the people inhabiting it as his serfs, the riches it contains as his own, and his power to utilise the labour of the people of the land for the acquisition of those riches, absolute and unquestioned! Here is raid, massacre, mutilation, torture, incendiarism, and destruction visited upon a people, not in a state of war at all; but merely as incidental features in the raising of " taxation "!

Since Pharaoh enslaved the Israelitish nation to minister to his ambitions, there has been no parallel to this! To acquiesce in such a monstrous emendation from a disordered brain, because the millennium has not yet dawned, would be tantamount to committing moral suicide. No; that second objection has only to be dissected in the light of common sense to be rejected. It is worthily inspired, but, if adopted, would lead Christianity to the abyss of self-destruction.

So much for the *cons*. What of the *pros?* Above and beyond them all is the great cry for Justice and Mercy which arises from the Congo forests. Can we be deaf to it, we who are of the race of Clarkson and of Wilberforce? Can we forget our glorious part in the emancipation of the negro race ? Can we forget that our forefathers in the teeth of Parliamentary opposition, class prejudice, mob violence, fought a system hoary with age, and sanctified by custom, and carried that fight to a glorious victory. Can we fail to see the finger of God pointing out to us the path we are called upon to tread in the extraordinary coincidence that the real awakening of the British conscience to the great Congo tragedy synchronises with the Centenary of the most noble act which our historical annals record ? Let us reject with indignant scorn the croaking of the pessimists who tell us that our people have deteriorated, and that they have forsworn the ideals of their forbears! Let us prove to them that they are wrong! Let us prove to them that the heart of the nation still beats soundly as of yore, by the performance of our plain and simple duty, by saving the races of Central Africa from the grip of the modern slavers!

Morally we would seek in vain to escape from our responsibilities. Materially Britain has legitimate considerations to invoke which impel her to action in the interests of her own people and in the interests of the communities which in Africa recognise her flag and enjoy her protection. In invoking them she deals a crushing and irrecoverable blow to the basis of legal shams on which the rubber slave-trade seeks at once to justify its existence, and hide its veritable character. We know that the subtlety of jurists is seldom at a loss. It can be utilised, and has been utilised again and again, in the defence of the indefensible. But before great principles interpreted by the instruments of fairness and plain, straightforward argument, it breaks down. The subtlety of the jurist has been called upon to justify the pillage of the Congo Basin and the enslavement of its inhabitants. On the untenable premise (*vide* Section IV.) that King Leopold's African enterprise constitutes a "State," jurists have evolved the theory that he is entitled to lay claim to the land, and the produce of the land—*e.g.*, its realisable wealth—which can be gathered only by the inhabitants of the land, and to delegate in part his ownership of that land and its produce to those upon whom it may please him to confer such powers—to you, or I, or any one. That, be it noted, is the legal or juridical defence of pillage and enslavement in Tropical Africa. Its audacity is truly prodigious. It can be met in argument by the simple enunciation of a principle which is, and ever must be, the cardinal feature of all legitimate European enterprise in the African tropics.

In those whose labour is alone available for the cultivation of the land and for the harvesting of its natural wealth, in those is ownership of the land and its products vested ; and with those—the people of the land—must the white man negotiate on terms of honest commercial dealing if he would acquire those products of which modern industrialism has need.

From this fundamental principle which regulates and directs relationship between the white man and the black in the African tropics (where the white man cannot cultivate the soil or harvest natural wealth), save in the Congo Basin since King Leopold's decrees came into force, there can be no derogation. To retreat a single inch in this regard is to leave the door wide open to the buccaneer, the pirate, and the slaver ; is to abandon the African tropics to the rapacity of unscrupulous speculators ; is to decree the enslavement of the African races by men who sit at home and pocket the dividends, leaving their foul work to be carried out by others.

This principle is termed TRADE.

Trade means barter, or exchange. Between individuals, as between communities, as between nations, it presupposes, and in practice necessitates, the possession on either side of commodities to sell with which to purchase. In the African tropics the commodities possessed by the inhabitants are the raw products of their plains and their forests, products which they alone can cultivate or gather. When transactions are localised in far inland regions—such as the Congo—involving heavy expenses on the part of the European purchaser of raw produce in conveying it to the nearest port of shipment, the only commodities which the African can offer in exchange for the white man's goods are rubber, ivory, and a few valuable resins, such as gum copal and gum arabic. These are the only articles the white man can purchase and make a profit on, for they are the only ones which will bear the cost of transport to Europe. Be it understood, therefore, that these commodities constitute the wealth actual and potential of the African, apart from and outside of his local wealth, which is represented by the extent of his household, domestic slaves (or more accurately, domestic servants), food plantations, fishing grounds, cattle (if the country is cattle rearing), poultry, and rude industries. Unlike the European in the actual stage of our evolution, the inhabitant of Tropical Africa is not, in his normal state, called upon to labour more than is necessary to supply himself and his family with food, shelter, weapons of war and the chase, baskets and nets for fishing, receptacles for culinary and domestic uses, and so forth. Moreover, living as he does under a communistic society where the chief is at once the head and the " father " of the clan, his wants if he falls sick, or when he gets infirm and unable to labour, are supplied by the clan. There are no workhouses in the African tropics, and save under the stress of drought, or famine due to failure in crops or other cause, there is no poverty. The labour, then, which the African may give to other purposes than those of sustaining life in conditions as comfortable as his needs and ambitions dictate, is not necessary to life.

Yet, throughout the African tropics wherever and whenever the white man has come with commodities to sell which the native has not possessed, and has become attracted by, the latter has voluntarily grafted upon himself extra labour in order to gather and reap commodities produced by his land which the white man required in exchange for what he brought. In this natural keenness of the African in the "great Black Belt" to trade, lies at once the key-note to Afro-European relationship in that Belt, and the explanation of the white man's presence therein. The Phœnicians were the first to recognise the commercial instincts of the West African native, and successive relays or white-skinned peoples have followed their lead. The West Central African trade has grown to great proportions, and with the advent of the iron horse is increasing every year. Its future is incalculable, and in time West Central African production will appreciably affect all the markets of the Western world. The "laziness and indifference" of the native to which King Leopold, who has robbed him of countless millions, testified publicly in Brussels last year, is exemplified by the millions of pounds sterling worth of palm oil, palm kernels, mahogany, rubber, gums, wax, piassava, groundnuts (and now raw cotton can be added to the list) which every year is brought to Europe in ocean steamers, products of the voluntary labour of the African in his own land, owner of the soil, owner of its fruits, cultivator in his own right, proprietor of his own mighty muscles! The value of all this produce *does* return to Africa ("for which it proves a source of prosperity"—*vide* Section I.) in European and American merchandise, and so the African gives employment to tens of thousands of European workmen and artisans, and provides thousands of European families with the wherewithal to obtain the necessaries of life, in the shape of wages arising from the labour of the African thousands of miles away. When the Labour Parties of England and the Continent have realised that between the labourer at home and the labourer in Africa there is practical community of interest as co-partners in the world's production, *constructive* assistance in the problems connected with the administration of Tropical African dependencies may be expected from them.

Now, on the Congo, since the Decrees of 1891, an altogether different conception prevails. There, as I have said, everything is abnormal. Sitting in his royal palace five thousand miles removed from his black subjects whom he has never seen, King Leopold has with a single stroke of the pen robbed the native of his entire wealth, actual and prospective, and calmly appropriated it himself. So colossal a theft has never been imagined by mortal man. The rubber which grows in the forest does not belong to the native. It belongs to King Leopold! And so with "dead" and "live" ivory, and so with the valuable resins, and so with everything! And observe how this works out, and must work out, in practice. I may write down, "The contents of the Bank of England belong to E. D. Morel." That would be foolishness, would it not? Equally foolish would it be for King Leopold to write down, "The wealth of Central Africa belongs to me"—if he stopped there. But the regenerator of the negro race is anything but foolish, and he did *not* stop there. Having appropriated on paper, he proceeded to acquire in deed. So he claimed the labour of the people to bring him their wealth which he has pirated. There is no need to purchase what belongs to you, by virtue of your royal will. So the abnormal replaces the normal. Armed force replaces trade. The revolution is accomplished, and the enslavement of the people, so long as that armed force can be maintained, is complete. It is marvellously simple.

* * * * * *

The one weak part of the British Note to the Powers in 1903 is the paragraph in which the suggestion is put forward that the question of "commercial freedom"—otherwise trade—as laid down in the Act of the West African Conference, should be separated from the question of the treatment of the natives, and referred to the Hague Court. But nothing is more patent than that the two questions are inextricably interwoven. They cannot be separated. They make one. If the right to trade in the produce or his country is taken from the native by a *prima facie* claim to possession of that produce, ill-treatment necessarily follows as night follows day, for such a claim is merely grotesque unless it be enforced, and it can only be enforced by compelling the native to collect that produce through the constant use of armed coercion, involving the inevitable perpetration of incessant outrage, wholesale and detail. To submit the effects of a given cause to one international tribunal and the cause itself to another is surely amazing illogicalness?

I maintain that it is the duty of the British Government, above all Governments, to uphold the principle of trade in the African tropics, in the legitimate interests of the people who have entrusted it with power. This is no question of Protection *versus* Free Trade, of irritation with other Powers because they put on differential tariffs against our goods, and we should prefer they did not. It is a question of trade itself, the pivotal element which unites all societies, the link which binds together in a practical sense the various branches of the human family. I can only attribute the peculiar horror which seems to strike some worthy persons at the mere mention of the word "trade" or "commerce" in connection with the Congo problem to ignorance of the essence of that problem, and to forgetfulness that the very existence of this country is dependent upon trade. Trade spells freedom for the inhabitant of the African tropics. Its suppression spells his enslavement by those who deny him the right to own the produce of his country, deprive him of his right to buy and to sell, strangle for ever his economic development, force him at the end of the lash and at the muzzle of the rifle to harvest what was once his wealth before they stole it from him, and lay it at the feet of the despoiler. Surely those who label themselves humanitarians, affect to look upon the African as a cross between a babe and a saint (he is neither), and boast of a superior moral sense, should consider this aspect of the matter, if their nerves are unwrought at what they deem the utilitarianism of the other? The plain fact of the matter is that to insist upon the principle of trade relationship between the Euro-

pean and the Negro in his own home as the basic principle
in that relationship is synonymous with declaring that the
Negro must be treated (not as a half-babe, half-saint, to be
petted and veneered with an outward culture altogether
foreign to his ideas, leaping over twelve centuries in a few
years) as a Man with the rights of a Man—not as a brute-
beast.

To great commercial nations like England, Germany,
and the United States the closing of the greater part of
Central Africa to trade is a blow dealt straight at the
legitimate interests of the British, German, and American
peoples by a monarch whose "sovereignty" over the Congo
was recognised by them principally on the ground—*vide*
Section I.—that his intentions were to facilitate in every
conceivable manner the development and extension of trade.
Stanley, speaking at Manchester in 1884 in favour of King
Leopold's enterprise, went into flights of rhapsody over the
potentialities of the Congo as a market for British manufactured cotton goods. Mr. Frelinghuysen, American
Secretary of State, in a letter to Mr. Tisdel, said, "Soon
these millions of people inhabiting the interior of Africa
will, under the inspiring influence of civilisation, become
purchasers of every kind of provision, manufactured goods,
agricultural implements, &c, and I see no reason why the
people of the United States should not come in for a large
share of the valuable trade which must soon be developed
in this region." Mr. Kasson, the American delegate at the
Conference, congratulated himself that "we secure (by the
action taken at Berlin) the abolition of all monopolies
private or co-operative." [1]

"Monopolies" have become one gigantic monopoly,
going far beyond a monopoly of trade, which signifies the
right of a certain party to be the exclusive purchaser of
produce in a given region ; involving claim to personal
possession of the very elements of trade, thus doing away
with the need of purchase altogether. An owner, let it be
repeated, is not called upon to *purchase* what belongs to
him !

---

[1] *North American Review,* February, 1886.

What Great Britain Can Do

"The importance of the rich prospective trade of the Congo valley has led to the general conviction that it should be open to all nations on equal terms," said President Arthur in his message of December, 1884.

It is not only closed to all nations, it is extirpated! "The fundamental idea of this programme is to facilitate the access of all commercial nations in the interior of Africa," declared Bismarck at the opening of the Congress. "Freedom of trade—remarked Lord Vivian at the Brussels Conference in 1890—was established in the interests not only of civilisation but of the native races of Africa."

Thus it will be seen that the representatives of the great commercial nations saw nothing to be ashamed of in consecrating aloud the principle of trade in the Congo basin. Why should Englishmen be afraid of upholding that principle to-day? Lest they be accused of "ulterior motives"? Where are the "ulterior motives"? They are not "ulterior," they are actual, legitimate, common-sense. They should be boldly proclaimed, insisted upon. The British merchant has the right of erecting factories and trading with the natives all over the Congo, even in the *Domaine de la Couronne*, for all its inalienability! That every square yard of the territory should be claimed by King Leopold and his financiers, and everything of economic value thereon, matters not one jot. The claim is preposterously impudent. British trade, with or without the medium of the British merchant, has the right to penetrate into every corner of the "Congo Free State." That King Leopold's principal secretary in Brussels should inform the British Government, in effect, that trade is impossible on the Congo because "there are no longer any unappropriated lands there" is mere insolence. That the same official should declare in reference to the British Note that it "confuses the utilisation of his property"—that is King Leopold's property, *e.g.*, 800,000 square miles in Central Africa—"by the owner"—that is King Leopold—"with trade"—that is the right of the natives to buy and to sell—and that "the native who collects on behalf of the owner"—King Leopold—"does not become the owner of what is so collected, and naturally

207

cannot dispose of it to a third party " [1] is, with the exception of King Leopold's Manifesto of 1906, the most cynical avowal of wholesale spoliation ever penned. What! The Power to which King Leopold came on bended knees twenty-two years ago begging for support, calmly informed to-day by the same Potentate that the British merchant, and that British trade are shut out from Central Africa, because it has pleased him by a stroke of the pen to substitute himself for the native as the owner of the commercial wealth of Central Africa, and that consequently the native has nothing to exchange for British goods! In very truth the proposition is laughable in its audacity. To use an historic phrase " Enough of this foolery." Aye, and more than enough, for it exercises itself not only at the expense of the legitimate interests of great nations, but at the price of African blood shed in torrents, and African misery unportrayable in words.

And, finally, there is another reason why Britain should decline any longer to recognise the pretensions of King Leopold. To every Power holding possessions in the neighbourhood of his " fine stations," and in proximity to the operations of his ivory and rubber-raiding officials, the seizure and collection by armed force of his revenues, is a positive danger and disturbance. The presence of a lawless, marauding soldiery ever increasing in numbers, and only held in nominal discipline by the conferring of full freedom to loot and rape is a menace. The erection of frontier-forts armed with heavy guns, a threat. The importation of enormous quantities of ball cartridges and ammunition to make rubber, à *la Congolaise*, which includes the provisioning of fighting clans with material of war to force rubber in the royal interest from their weaker neighbours, when the " regulars " are employed elsewhere, is a peril which it would be folly to ignore. Two great rebellions of native soldiery, which brought the " Congo Free State " almost toppling to the ground, have occurred in the last ten years. Even the fort at Shinkakassa just outside Boma, the capital, was seized a few years ago by the garrison exasperated with

---

[1] Memorandum, September 17, 1903.

the treatment of their women by King Leopold's officials, who, terrified out of their lives, ran hither and thither like scared rabbits, for all their gold-lace and impeccable ducks : Boma itself being saved from destruction only by the ignorance of the mutineers in the working of the time-fuse ; and from pillage, by the action of a brave British coloured subject of Lagos, who organised his compatriots from the British West African colonies (settled in various capacities at Boma) into patrols, which marched through the town, and who was destined later on to be hounded to a suicide's grave by the malignity of the men he had rescued.[1] Bands of these revolted soldiery have on several occasions invaded and committed havoc in the contiguous British possessions, and to this day hold parts of the Congo territory into which no official dare set foot. Any moment may bring forth another and graver revolt, and any day may see the rise of an intelligent native corporal with a brain above his fellows, some bastard Arab blood in his veins perhaps, who will make a bold bid for empire against the officials of the absentee landlord. And over all the land broods the shadow of a great crime, filling the breasts of the miserable people with an undying hatred of the accursed white man and all his ways. Given the slightest chance at combination, given a leader, given a favourable set of circumstances, and the smouldering embers will burst into a flame, and the conflagration might well spread until every official of the King with his throat cut had been flung into the river. It would be a just retribution, but what sort of task would confront the criminal apathy of Europe ! Sir Harry Johnston is not given to sensationalism, or rash predictions, but this is what he wrote in 1902—four years ago, before the charges against King Leopold's enterprise were thoroughly established—" if all the stories are true of the wickedness perpetrated in the Congo Free State since 1885 there will some day be such a rising against the white man

---

[1] Mr. H. A. Shanu, who held a store in Boma much patronised by the officials. Denounced in 1904 for the heinous crime of communicating with me, he was boycotted by official instructions, his business ruined, and himself reduced to despair. Shanu was a man of the highest integrity and honourable standing.

and such punishment inflicted on European interests in the
heart of Africa as will surpass any revolt that has ever yet
been made by the black and the yellow man against his
white brother and overlord." To watch with philosophic
eye this cauldron of native discontent and misery fed with
the ingredients of a civilised barbarism, go seething on, is
madness. Arguments drawn from the necessity of keeping
up the "prestige" of the white man in the African
tropics do not appeal to me very much, for the surest
foundation for the maintenance of such is justice, "even-
handed, tiger justice," as poor Mary Kingsley used to say,
but I often wonder that the White Powers can continue
their supine contemplation, while deeds are done in the
Congo Basin which brand with indelible infamy the white
race in the eyes of the black, deeds which in Lord
Fitzmaurice's words "make civilisation ashamed of its
name," deeds which cry to Heaven for vengeance, and for
which, some day, in the fulness of time, a fearful penalty
will be enacted.

* * * * * *

The Act of the West African Conference provides a
weapon which can be wielded against the "civilised
barbarism" introduced by King Leopold, with or without
the convocation of a renewed Conference of all the
Signatory Powers of that Act, a weapon which requires but
five of the Signatory Powers to make up their minds to use.
(Act 1) That weapon is the "Navigation Commission"
which has never been invoked, although the essential
clauses of the Act have been violated with impunity for
fifteen years. The question of navigation on the Congo
waterways is intimately bound up with the question of the
trading rights of European merchants and of the natives,
for it is obvious that freedom of navigation is a misnomer if
trade is non-existent ; consequently the general question of
maladministration, misrule and spoliation is also involved.
Indeed the idea entertained by the Plenipotentiaries of the
Powers at Berlin in providing for a Navigation Commission,
was clearly concerned with the protection of trade. Thus
M. de Kusserow, one of the German delegates at the

Conference, declared (Prot. 3 : sitting November 27, 1884), that in the view of his Government freedom of trade should not be left unsupervised (*sans contrôle*), and he added " The International Navigation Commission appears to it (the German Government) a competent instrument to be provisionally entrusted with this supervision." Moreover the Act itself as signed by all the Powers is explicit. Article 25 reads, " This provision of the present Act of Navigation shall remain in force in time of war. Consequently all nations, whether neutral or belligerent, shall be always free, for the *purposes of trade*, to navigate the Congo, its branches, affluents and mouths as well as the territorial waters fronting the embouchure of the river."

The powers enjoyed by this Commission as provided in the Act, would be as considerable as those enjoyed by the Danube River Commission. They would be virtually sovereign powers, in regard to everything affecting navigation, and who controls navigation in the Congo basin controls the arteries and veins of the " Congo Free State." It is " independent of the territorial authorities " (Art. 20). The Powers composing it " can have recourse " to their own ships of war. It can raise loans (Art. 23).

In short, the appointment of this Commission would be the stepping stone for that wider and closer international control of the Congo which, failing the possible but unlikely solution of Belgian annexation *on lines acceptable to public opinion*,[1] honour and safety alike demand shall no longer be delayed.

With these considerations I bring this chapter and with it this volume to a close. I have indicated the specific courses of action which are open to Great Britain under her own Treaty rights,—rights which no Power would dream of contesting, and I have given expression to a widely spread conviction that the adoption by Great Britain of one or more of the steps denoted would compel international interference. To these I may here add that Great Britain

---

[1] Let it be clearly understood that what I mean to convey is not the doubt that the Belgian people would *desire* to do the right thing, but the doubt of their being in a position to do it. *Vide* last chapter.

Red Rubber

would appear to be entitled (with or without the appointment of a Navigation Commission) to place a gun-boat on the Upper Congo, and that she ought to do it on behalf of her own subjects : and, I hasten to add, other Powers would seem to have precisely the same option in that respect. I have given reasons—and no one can deny that they are grave, legitimate, and weighty reasons—why Great Britain should drop the policy of vain expostulation pursued for ten years, and take energetic measures to abide by, and if necessary to enforce, her Treaty rights in her own justifiable interests ; and I have proved, I venture to think to the satisfaction of all reasonable persons, that in so acting Great Britain would be serving the general interests of humanity. With respect to the position of Great Britain as one of the signatory Powers of the Act of the West African Conference I have shown how preponderating is that position in regard to the corresponding position of most of the Signatory Powers ; how great is the prestige of Great Britain abroad at the present moment : how immensely important are the issues at stake : how duty and honour summon the British Government to a vigorous initiative. Finally, I have drawn attention to the very definite instrument which the Act of the Conference provides for the invocation of practical international control over the vast fluvial system of the Congo.

What remains to be said can be embodied in a couple of paragraphs.

Nothing impracticable, nothing unrealisable is being demanded on behalf of the Congo natives. No grandmotherly legislation, no sentimental claims are being urged in their interest. Only justice. They have been robbed of their property. We demand that their property shall be restored to them. They have been robbed of their liberty. We demand that their liberty shall be restored to them. They are bound in chains. We demand that those chains shall be rent asunder. For fifteen years they have been degraded, enslaved, exterminated. We demand that this shall stop, not fifteen years, or five years, or one year hence : but now.

The " Congo Free State " has long ceased to exist. It